The National Educational Association *and the* Black Teacher

The National Education Association

and the Black Teacher

*The Integration
of a Professional Organization*

by Michael John Schultz, Jr.

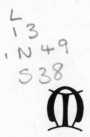

UNIVERSITY OF MIAMI PRESS
Coral Gables, Florida

Hz 11-15

To the Gateway Education Association:
The New Breed in Education

Contents

Foreword

This work by Dr. Michael Schultz is no mere chronicle of the superficial aspects of exciting events. It is a penetrating historical analysis of institutional travail under the stress of changing times and pressures and counterpressures.

At one time, and that only a few years ago, the National Education Association, in its surface posture at least, gave the impression of impenetrable lethargy and bureaucratic immobility. At that time one loyal critic within the organization spoke of the lack of strongly defined commitment to desegregation as "the moral dilemma of the NEA."

Beyond the surface posture, however, a great institutional power struggle was taking place. Since 1954, decisions were effected that produced drastic and effective resolutions of the central dilemma.

One major significance of this work is as a study of large institutional functioning; it is an enlightening historical commentary on the ways of bureaucracy. Bureaucracies are hard to move; what makes them so, what factors impede change, how they can be brought into movement,—these questions are within the implications of this study.

Schultz works profoundly to root his historical analysis in a sound report on the political science of the NEA, the ostensible and the actual decision-making process. It seems probable that his study would not have bitten so deeply below the surface had he neglected this hard job of conceptualization.

A large merit of this work will be apparent from the calm and sure tone of the text. But one who knows the researcher and his research quite closely must speak the warranty further. This is a history of deepest controversy, of events and decisions that tore at the foundations of institutional arrangements. The convictions, the emotions, and, indeed, the passions of variously minded men were involved. Schultz inquired rigorously into these. In his report, however, he chose wisely and responsibly to write well within his evidences. The drama and tension of the events are sufficient unto themselves. This historian thus keeps his generalizations central to his evidences; he does not push them to the peripheral, even though he might have supported them in the further reaches. The solid quality of the work is, therefore, not merely in style and appearance, but an intrinsic product of a deeply responsible methodology. Schultz juggles the semantics of racial designation according to sound criteria, yet with no delusion of being universally approved. His work is motivated by, among other things, a large respect and concern for black colleagues in the teaching profession. He would scarcely have undertaken the study otherwise. He has chosen, I think appropriately, to use the designation *Negro* when referring to times when this was the preferred manner of respectful address. He shifts to *black American* or *black teacher* somewhat in tune with the change in preference among those designated. He is aware of the sophistication of the semantic issue; he has tried to respond sensibly; he is by no means smugly confident that his choices are beyond dispute.

It was, this commentator happens to know, a very satisfying course of events that the author recorded. As a man profoundly concerned for equality, decency, and fair play, he had known dismay at one period in these events. He was well pleased to see the NEA move to a vigorous definition of position even while he studied it. Militancy became a key concept within this historical period. Schultz is himself most loyally a protagonist of teaching profession vigor. That the NEA moved to greater professional vigor in late years is a part of the record that this historian sets down. It was also a development satisfying to the historian who is a professional teacher in the most definite sense of the term.

I think it worked this way: Schultz wrote this history as a historian, letting the facts dictate the record; but had Schultz not been a sophisticated educator as well, he could scarcely have assessed the facts half as well nor grasped their implications so surely.

RYLAND W. CRARY

Acknowledgments

I consider this page the most important page in this book because I would never have been able to accomplish this project without the aid of my friends, colleagues, and family. I would like to express my gratitude to Mrs. Marion Straw and Mrs. Grace Gunderman for their invaluable assistance and suggestions during the development of the manuscript. I would like to acknowledge appreciation to Dr. George Fahey and Dr. Richard Seckinger for their helpful criticism. Particularly, I owe a great debt of gratitude to Dr. William H. E. Johnson and Dr. Ryland Crary. Dr. Johnson has been an advisor to me since I first met him at the University of Pittsburgh in 1961. To me, he is the epitome of the age-old maxim: a gentleman and a scholar. Dr. Crary, a great intellectual stimulus, has been responsible for widening my academic awareness. His probing questions increased the scope of this book. Finally, I would like to give special thanks to my children, Mickey, Bill, Jim, Madge, and John, and to my wife, Marie, for their patience, forbearance, understanding, and love.

Introduction

In 1954, the United States Supreme Court issued its historic decision, *Brown* v. *The Board of Education,* calling for the desegregation of the public schools. This edict, triggering a social revolution that has been constantly growing in momentum, has had a profound impact upon this country. Many people, black and white, hailed the decision as being long overdue, while others sought to hinder it or block it completely.

Resistance soon came. First, most Americans were puzzled. Then, they looked in shocked disbelief as fully-armed National Guardsmen escorted children to school in Little Rock, Arkansas. But the drama had just started to unfold. Negroes schooled in Henry David Thoreau's civil disobedience theories staged sit-ins, boycotts, and other forms of civil demonstrations that enjoyed some degree of success, thereby encouraging other people to similar action throughout the United States.

Violence occurred all too frequently, but inexorably the civil rights tide continued even though resistance stiffened. Confrontations between individual states and the federal government occurred. Some southern universities faced with Negro enrollees defied the federal government. Public school integration came more slowly and with even more difficulties. Some states became virtual islands left behind in the backwash of federal action.

The onslaught upon three centuries of inequality continued into the 1960s. In August 1963, over 200,000 civil rights workers and supporters marched in a peaceful demonstration to the Lincoln Memorial in Washington, D.C. A flurry of congressional activities, led by President Kennedy and President Johnson and prodded by the conscience of the Supreme Court, resulted in civil rights legislation unparalleled in our nation's history.

The United States has been, and still is, undergoing a great transformation that many people find difficult to accept. Traditions and beliefs die slowly. Institutions within our society change. Serious internal disputes caused by the Negro problem grip labor unions, churches, fraternities, and professional organizations. Each has to reconcile itself with the onrush of contemporary events. Much soul-searching has to be done.

In this circumstance the National Education Association has been similar to many professional societies. Many people looked to the NEA for direction, mindful that Robert Campbell, a Negro, was a charter member of the National Teachers Association, a forerunner to the NEA.[1] Others in this august assembly pointed with pride to the 1943 NEA Convention that ruled that all future conventions must be held in cities having integrated facilities.

Recently the NEA has been moving toward complete integration. Since 1963, the annual conventions have issued very strong resolutions on the subject. Merger plans with the American Teachers Association, comprising almost 70,000 black teachers, were begun in 1963 and consumated in 1966. By the end of 1966, all states had removed their racial membership restrictions.

The integration of the NEA has been a very trying and arduous procedure. The conflict did not destroy the association, but it has placed some great strains upon its organizational structure. Since 1954, the NEA has been under the spotlight of national attention regarding its posture toward the black teacher. Some people charged that the NEA was too slow, while others advocated the gradual approach. Perhaps out of necessity, the NEA moved to liberalize its integration stance and in accomplishing this, coalesced several factions, thus greatly increasing the broad-based teacher support of the Association.

The National Education Association *and the* *Black Teacher*

The Organizational Structure of the NEA 1

Prior to examining the integration process of the NEA, the reader must understand the Association's basic organizational structure so that he may determine who makes policy within the NEA and how implementation occurs. Emphasis is upon the Representative Assembly, the Board of Directors, and the Executive Committee because these are the three major divisions in the NEA. These units are analyzed in relationship to the power and authority granted to them by the Charter and the Bylaws. The interrelationships of each unit to the other units are studied in order to discover the theoretical and the practical ramifications of the Charter and the Bylaws.

The National Education Association is an independent national organization whose membership is open to all educators. Founded in Philadelphia, Pennsylvania, in 1857 as the National Teachers Association, it merged with the National Association of School Superintendents and the American Normal School Association in 1870 and became the National Educational Association. The Association received a charter from the United States Congress in 1907 and adopted as its official name the National Education Association.

The organizational structure of the NEA consists of four types of units: (a) commissions and councils; (b) committees; (c) departments and institutes; and (d) divisions. These encompass thirty-four departments and one institute, eighteen headquarters divisions, and twenty-five commissions and committees.[1] The Representative Assembly creates these units on the advice of the Board of Directors. The executive secretary appoints the chairmen of

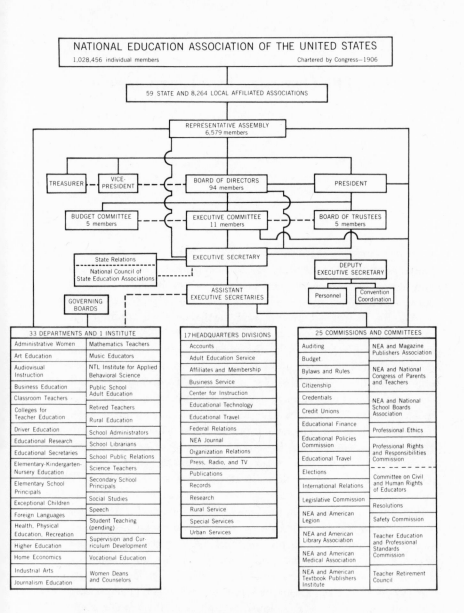

NATIONAL EDUCATION ASSOCIATION OF THE UNITED STATES

1,028,456 individual members Chartered by Congress—1906

59 STATE AND 8,264 LOCAL AFFILIATED ASSOCIATIONS

REPRESENTATIVE ASSEMBLY
6,579 members

| TREASURER | VICE-PRESIDENT | BOARD OF DIRECTORS 94 members | PRESIDENT |

| BUDGET COMMITTEE 5 members | EXECUTIVE COMMITTEE 11 members | BOARD OF TRUSTEES 5 members |

EXECUTIVE SECRETARY

State Relations
National Council of State Education Associations

GOVERNING BOARDS

ASSISTANT EXECUTIVE SECRETARIES

DEPUTY EXECUTIVE SECRETARY

Personnel | Convention Coordination

33 DEPARTMENTS AND 1 INSTITUTE

Administrative Women	Mathematics Teachers
Art Education	Music Educators
Audiovisual Instruction	NTL Institute for Applied Behavioral Science
Business Education	Public School Adult Education
Classroom Teachers	Retired Teachers
Colleges for Teacher Education	Rural Education
Driver Education	School Administrators
Educational Research	School Librarians
Educational Secretaries	School Public Relations
Elementary-Kindergarten-Nursery Education	Science Teachers
Elementary School Principals	Secondary School Principals
Exceptional Children	Social Studies
Foreign Languages	Speech
Health, Physical Education, Recreation	Student Teaching (pending)
Higher Education	Supervision and Curriculum Development
Home Economics	Vocational Education
Industrial Arts	Women Deans and Counselors
Journalism Education	

17 HEADQUARTERS DIVISIONS

- Accounts
- Adult Education Service
- Affiliates and Membership
- Business Service
- Center for Instruction
- Educational Technology
- Educational Travel
- Federal Relations
- NEA Journal
- Organization Relations
- Press, Radio, and TV
- Publications
- Records
- Research
- Rural Service
- Special Services
- Urban Services

25 COMMISSIONS AND COMMITTEES

Auditing	NEA and Magazine Publishers Association
Budget	
Bylaws and Rules	NEA and National Congress of Parents and Teachers
Citizenship	
Credentials	NEA and National School Boards Association
Credit Unions	
Educational Finance	
Educational Policies Commission	Professional Ethics
Educational Travel	Professional Rights and Responsibilities Commission
Elections	
International Relations	Committee on Civil and Human Rights of Educators
Legislative Commission	
NEA and American Legion	Resolutions
NEA and American Library Association	Safety Commission
NEA and American Medical Association	Teacher Education and Professional Standards Commission
NEA and American Textbook Publishers Institute	Teacher Retirement Council

Organization Chart 1967-1968*

*NEA Handbook, 1967–1968, p. 18

these units with the consent of the Executive Committee. These units work under the direct supervision and control of one of the six assistant executive secretaries who are also appointed by the executive secretary. The Executive Committee appoints the executive secretary, the chief administrative officer of the NEA. The chain of command continues upward to the Executive Committee, which has ten members. The Board of Directors represents each state, commonwealth, and District of Columbia affiliate. Ultimate authority rests with the Representative Assembly, the overall governing body of the NEA.

THE REPRESENTATIVE ASSEMBLY

The origin of the Representative Assembly has its roots set firmly in two distinct areas. The first area consists of the reform element of the NEA, which constantly is attempting to democratize the Association, thus resulting in more power for the teachers. In the second area, one must view the creation of the Assembly and the subsequent reorganization of the NEA as a means to establish a more definite link between the national organization and the state and local associations.

By the time that the NEA celebrated its fiftieth birthday, there were many critics who questioned the procedures and practices of the "old guard" relative to the operation of the NEA. The "old guard" consisted of college presidents and chief school administrators who formed the working nucleus of the NEA. Meetings followed a procedure that had evolved from the past.

The leaders adhered to a strict decorum.[2] For example, no one ever actively sought the presidency; to do so was considered a breach of ethics. The office sought the man. The nominations committee, after much deliberation, named a person to the position and this action was tantamount to election. In 1910 the nominating committee's decision was overturned by a rebel group using modern campaign techniques. This group supported Mrs. Ella Flagg Young for the presidency, and they passed out buttons and wrote letters urging members to elect her to the office. These techniques had never been employed on behalf of a presidential candidate and

caused much criticism. Miss Grace C. Strachen of New York replied to this criticism:

> There have been some objections to the tactics used by some of the
> women interested in Mrs. Young's election. I am very glad to have
> you know and all of you to see that there are some men who desire
> the election of Mrs. Young; but when one considers the objections as
> to the tactics one feels that they are very trifling. For instance I ask-
> ed someone what the objections were, and he said, "Well in the
> matter of these badges; never before has the candidate for the presi-
> dency had a personal badge passed around." This is the age of bad-
> ges. We whom I represent wear this red badge. I represent fourteen
> thousand women.[3]

In the first half century of the NEA's growth, the new people in
the organization had to be seen but not heard. They had to
serve rather lengthy periods of apprenticeship before ever having
a possibility of gaining access to the power center of the Association.[4] Consequently, many of the younger people within the
Association demanded change and insisted upon a greater voice in
the organization.

In addition to the internal conflicts apparent, another fact slowly began to emerge. As membership in the organization began to
increase in the first two decades of this century, the convention
machinery started to weaken under the strain. The annual meetings
of the NEA were conducted on a town meeting basis with all members who attended having the right to vote. Membership in the
NEA was small, and most members could not attend the meetings
because of the great distances involved; therefore, generally there
were more delegates present from the host city than from all the
other areas in the United States.[5] This represented a basic flaw in
the organizational structure of the convention. Many members
feared that local and regional delegates could, because of their
numerical preponderance, actually dictate their wishes to the
convention, thus changing radically many of the practices of the
association.

They had justification for their fears, since at the 1910 convention at Boston, Massachusetts, a contingent of teachers had come
with but one purpose in mind—to elect Mrs. Ella Flagg Young
president of the NEA.[6] The Committee on Nominations recom-

mended X. Z. Snyder of Colorado for president by a majority of twenty-eight to nineteen,[7] but when the committee gave its report to the convention, Miss Katherine D. Blake of New York proposed a minority report that would substitute Mrs. Young for Mr. Snyder.[8] A confrontation between the factions had occurred; but before the delegates had a chance to decide between the two reports, Grace C. Strachen of New York rose to give a floor speech in which she alluded to the tactics employed by Mrs. Young's supporters:

> Another objection is that some of the advocates of Mrs. Young began several weeks ago writing around the country with reference to Mrs. Young. Now it may be a matter of thanksgiving that they did not begin any earlier, because if they had, there would have been so many women from the city of New York that we would have had to go to the stadium for the election.[9]

After Miss Strachen's speech, the delegates closed debate and called for a vote between the two reports. The initial minority resolution won by a vote of 617 to 376.[10] Mrs. Young was substituted for Snyder and the delegates elected her unanimously.

The 1912 convention held at Chicago, Illinois, saw another attempt to speed the decision of the nominating committee. The committee selected E. T. Fairchild as candidate for president by a 34 to 12 decision, but Katherine Blake again proposed a minority motion to replace Fairchild with Grace C. Strachen of New York.[11] The success at Boston did not repeat itself at Chicago, for Miss Strachen had very formidable opposition from another group of teachers from Chicago led by Margaret Haley, who supported Fairchild. Miss Strachen and Miss Blake traded verbal broadsides with Margaret Haley in a floor fight that consumed over two hours of the business meeting.[12] Strachen, in a long floor speech, accused the Chicago delegation of power politics while denying charges made by Miss Haley that she attempted to influence the Chicago teachers by making a visit to the mayor of Chicago. The delegates defeated the minority report by a standing vote, but not until Strachen's backers had exhausted all of the parliamentary maneuvers available to conduct the election by secret ballot.[13]

The 1912 convention indicated that the town meeting device of

conducting the business meetings of the NEA was outmoded. Packing the convention was no longer uncommon. Strachen admitted
that over eighty teachers from New York went to the Boston convention in 1910 with the sole purpose of electing Mrs. Young as
president of the NEA.[14] After the 1912 convention at Chicago, the
Educational Review charged the Chicago teachers with packing
the convention. The magazine claimed that 712 Chicago teachers
attended the convention and that 669 of them were newly enrolled
members in the NEA.[15] O. T. Corson, president of the NEA in
1900, indicated in 1910 that the danger of packing the convention
had existed for the past twenty years and he did not foresee that
the situation would change under the present convention organization.[16] Writing prior to the 1912 convention, Charles Judd advocated a creation of some type of representative body to conduct the
business meetings since the present way was obsolete.[17] Most members by this time had come to the conclusion that some change
would have to occur or the 1912 experience could be an annual occurrence.

At the 1915 convention held at Oakland, California, a reorganization plan was proposed officially for the first time. William T. Owens of Illinois presented a reorganization resolution to
the delegates:

> Moved that the Association authorize the appointment of a special
> committee on organization to consist of nine active members, to
> consider and recommend at the next annual meeting such changes
> in the forms of organization in the Association as will make it more
> truly national in its extent of its membership, the scope of its delib-
> erations, and the provisions for the conduct of its business, and that
> the Executive Committee be authorized to pay, out of funds not
> otherwise appropriated, the necessary expenses for typewriting and
> postage incurred by the committee.[18]

After presenting the motion, Owens attempted to assuage the
fears of some of the members by pointing out that the resolution
would merely create a committee that would study organization
and present a report upon it at next year's business meeting. Then
if the members should desire reorganization, the amendment
would have to lie on the table until the 1917 convention because

of the provisions of the NEA Charter. He closed his presentation on a strong note by saying:

> Someone may ask about the general idea of the motion. It seems to me that the problem of organizing the Association so that there shall be something like an organic connection between the different state associations and the national Association be considered, and that we should have a method of doing business that will make the deliberations really the deliberations of a national body. This plan, or the thought of producing that result, hardly needs defense, in the view of the events of the past four or five years. I do not think I need to discuss this any further.[19]

The motion passed with no debate, and the NEA moved toward the creation of a delegate assembly.

At the 1917 convention held at Portland, Oregon, reorganization was an important topic on the agenda. Arthur H. Chamberlain, a member of the reorganization committee, proposed that the Association move itself closer to the state and local organizations. He proposed that Article 15 of the Bylaws be amended to bring reorganization about.[20]

The Committee of Reorganization of the NEA gave a report to the Council of Education and the Department of Superintendents at Atlantic City, New Jersey, in February 1918. They approved of the proposed changes and recommended approval of these amendments at the annual NEA meeting later in that year.[21]

The NEA met at Pittsburgh, Pennsylvania, and the climate for change that existed at Atlantic City was not too much in evidence. W. B. Owens, chairman of the committee, finally recommended that the action of the committee be deferred for one more year.[22]

The delegates met at Milwaukee, Wisconsin, the following year, and President George Strayer raised the hopes of the reorganization advocates by emphasizing, in his presidential address, the real need for reorganization "as was apparent in the minds of all of us at the Pittsburgh meeting."[23] He stressed the need for a closer rapport between the teachers and the administrators and suggested that the NEA might lead the way by creating closer ties to the state and the local associations. Strayer appealed for harmony and unity of the members, but it soon became evident that much unrest prevailed.

The officers of the NEA called for the business meeting on July

4, at nine in the morning. When Strayer called the meeting to order, sharp controversy immediately broke out as to the real reasons for the early hour of the meeting. The Milwaukee representative of the teachers claimed that many of his colleagues would be denied the right to vote on this issue because everyone knew that they were busy until eleven in the morning conducting a parade in the city park. Debate over the starting time continued until most of the teachers from the city arrived.[24]

Margaret Haley and S. Y. Gillan of Milwaukee represented the forces who opposed reorganization because they claimed that reorganization was contrary to the original charter granted to the NEA. The basic reason was that certain key cities, such as Chicago, would lose their power at the annual meetings if the town meeting type of organization were changed. Haley indicated that the *Chicago Tribune* sent out a distress signal to all the Chicago teachers concerning the Milwaukee meeting, and urged them to go to Milwaukee and support Margaret Haley because the Association was in great danger.[25]

Both sides fought hard, and at times the debate became quite bitter; things soon reached an impasse. Neither side could muster the votes to win, nor could it totally defeat the opposition plan. Howard R. Driggs got the convention off dead center by proposing "that all changes in the Bylaws lie over for one year."[26] The delegates accepted this motion without much debate.

Ironically, the anti-reorganization forces won the battle but lost the war because their technique of packing the annual meetings was now adopted by the reorganization forces. The 1920 convention was held in Salt Lake City, Utah, where feeling ran high for reorganization. *School Review* said, "The people who went to Salt Lake went there because they were intent upon business"[27] [reorganization]. The Executive Committee had already laid the groundwork for the Salt Lake City meeting by securing from Congress in May 1920, authorization to change the Charter, creating a Representative Assembly. Margaret Haley again led the forces opposed to reorganization, but the packed convention ignored her.[28]

With the enactment of reorganization of the NEA, it became a more national organization. Reorganization created a Representative Assembly authorized to conduct the business meetings of the

NEA. It called for affiliation of the state and local associations with the national Association and set up a procedure of selecting state and local delegates to the Representative Assembly. All members of the NEA could attend the conventions, but only the authorized delegates to the Representative Assembly had the right to vote at the meetings.[29] The *Educational Review* hailed the reorganization as a "triumph of democracy," and indicated that reorganization would usher in a new era for the NEA, bringing into the membership a majority of the teachers of the country.[30]

Reorganization was an immediate success.[31] At the 1921 convention, delegates from forty-four states and 540 local affiliated associations attended. This marked the beginning of a very rapid period of growth for the NEA. Table 1 shows that NEA membership nearly tripled from 1920 to 1930, doubled its growth from 1940 to 1950, and finally in 1966, membership numbered over a million people. Wesley attributed much of this growth to the creation of the Representative Assembly because the Assembly was "incontrovertible proof that teachers could actually control the policies of their association."[32]

Table 1
Membership in the NEA*

Year	Total	Year	Total
1857	43	1920	52,850
1870	170	1930	172,950
1880	354	1940	203,429
1890	5,474	1950	453,797
1900	2,332	1960	713,994
1910	6,909	1968	1,081,660

*NEA Handbook, 1968, p. 398.

Presently the Representative Assembly has over 7,000 members who are selected by state and local affiliates of the NEA. Each affiliated local organization is allowed one delegate and one alternate per 100 members up to 500 members. After that, each unit is allowed one delegate and one alternate for each additional 500 members.[33]

The Representative Assembly meets annually during the last week following the last Sunday in June. According to NEA Bylaws:

> The Representative Assembly shall be the legislative and policy forming body of the Association. It shall have the power to elect the officials of the Association, adopt the annual budget, act on annual reports, approve resolutions and platforms, and following the consideration and advice of the Board of Directors, may create or discontinue committees, commissions, councils or departments, and shall adopt the procedure to be followed in the disqualifying, censuring, and reinstating an affiliate. The Representative Assembly shall be the final judge in the qualification of the delegates, and of the requirements for the determining of the eligibility for the affiliation with the organization. It shall have the power to approve the amendments to or the revisions of the Bylaws as approved by Article XV of these Bylaws, and shall adopt the Rules Governing the Annual Meeting. It shall conduct any other business of the Association and shall be the final authority in all matters not otherwise specified in these Bylaws.

The culmination of the policy-making process of the Representative Assembly is the formation of the official Platform and Resolutions of the NEA:

> The Platform states the principles, policies, and the goals which guide the Association. The Resolutions supplement the Platform in two ways: by directing the officers and the staff of the Association to undertake specified action and by stating the official position of the Association in matters—educational in nature and national in scope—which are of current importance to the profession of education. The Platform and the Resolutions together govern the officers and the Association and guide the members in professional activities.

Integral Committees within the Representative Assembly

Since the number of delegates to the Representative Assembly at the 1968 convention totaled over 7,000, certain key committees within the Assembly must construct the groundwork for an efficiently functioning convention. The Committee on Audit, Committee on Budget, Committee on Credentials, Committee on Elections, Committee on Bylaws and Rules, and Committee on Resolutions share this responsibility.

Committee on Audit. The president of the NEA appoints three people to the Committee on Audit prior to the convention. The committee examines the report of the independent auditors and evaluates this report. Then the committee presents its findings to the Representative Assembly during the convention.[34]

Committee on Budget. The Board of Directors selects the Committee on Budget whose main purpose is to examine the programs of the NEA, identify priorities, and recommend a budget to the Board of Directors who, in turn, present the budget to the Representative Assembly for final approval.[35]

Committee on Credentials. The Committee on Credentials has five members appointed by the president for rotating terms of five years. The committee does its work concurrently with the annual meeting of the Assembly.[36] According to the Standing Rules of the NEA, the duties of the Committee on Credentials are:

> The committee shall be responsible for the supervision of the accreditation of the delegates and the alternates at the meeting of the Representative Assembly and for the seating of the delegates. The decision of the committee shall be final unless overruled by the Representative Assembly. The chairman of the Committee on Credentials shall give a preliminary report at the first session of the Representative Assembly and a final report when registration is complete.[37]

Committee on Elections. The Committee on Elections includes twenty-five members appointed by the president of the NEA prior to the annual convention. The committee prepares ballots, supervises all aspects of the elections, and counts the ballots.[38]

Committee on Bylaws and Rules. This committee consists of six members appointed by the president of the NEA for staggered terms of five years each. The committee examines, judges, and expedites all amendments to the Bylaws and the Standing Rules of the NEA. The committee members serve as advisors and consultants to the officers and the Association concerning the proposed amendments to the Bylaws and the Standing Rules.[39]

Committee on Resolutions. The most important committee within the framework of the Representative Assembly is the Committee on Resolutions. The committee recommends to the Assembly platform proposals that "state the principles, policies, and goals of the Association; and Resolutions which direct action or state the positions of the Association on matters of current importance."[40] This committee consists of a five-man Editing Committee appointed by the

NEA president for five-year terms on a rotating basis.[41] The committee also includes additional members equal to the number of members of the Board of Directors from each state, commonwealth, or District of Columbia. The duties of this committee are:

> The Resolutions Committee shall prepare and present to the Representative Assembly proposed resolutions for adoption. They shall be printed and made available to the delegates at least one day before action is scheduled thereon by the Representative Assembly. The form and text of each resolution shall be approved by a majority vote of the resolutions committee before presentation to the Representative Assembly, provided, however, that a minority report may be presented to the Representative Assembly by any member of the committee. The chairman of the resolutions committee shall present the report of the committee, together with any minority report, to the Representative Assembly for consideration at the time and place designated by the official program.[42]

The Executive Officers of the NEA

The executive officers of the NEA are the president, vice-president, immediate past president, treasurer, and the executive secretary. The Representative Assembly elects all but the executive secretary. The president and the vice-president have terms of one year, and the latter automatically assumes the presidency upon the completion of his term as vice-president. The president, vice-president, and the immediate past president serve on the Executive Committee for a total of three years. The president is chairman of the Executive Commitee and of the Board of Directors of the NEA.

The vice-president and the immediate past president also serve on the Board of Directors. The president has some powers of appointment; he does appoint chairmen and committee members except when otherwise provided by the Bylaws and Standing Rules.[43]

The treasurer is responsible "for the safe keeping of and the accounting of the general funds of the Association."[44] He makes annual reports to the Representative Assembly and to the Board of Directors and is a member of the Executive Committee. The treasurer is an ex officio member of the budget committee and has voting rights.[45]

The executive secretary is the chief administrative official of the Association.[46] The Executive Committee appoints him for a term of four years at a present salary of $50,000 annually. He has two principal functions:

> To provide leadership in interpretation of education and the profession to the members and the general public; and to provide administrative leadership in the general supervision and management of the Association. He identifies significant issues of education and the problems of the profession, interpretating them to the membership, governing bodies, and staff so that the Association's action program may make major contributions to the field of public education. He develops an administrative structure through which the staff are organized, coordinated, and integrated to accomplish the Association's objectives and long-range goals.[47]

The powers and duties of the executive secretary as stated by the Bylaws are as follows:

> The executive secretary shall supervise and coordinate the administrative, financial, and professional activities of the Association, and shall direct the employed staff in accordance with the policies and procedures authorized by the Representative Assembly, the Board of Directors, the Executive Committee, and the Board of Trustees. He shall be secretary to the Representative Assembly, the Board of Directors, and the Executive Committee. He shall keep a record of the stated meetings of the Association; notify officers and members of committees, commissions, and council of their election or appointment; provide assistance to committees, commissions, and council in connection with their activities; render such reports as may be required by Representative Assembly, or by the officers and executive bodies of the Association; to be the keeper of the official seal of the Association.[48]

The executive secretary has great powers of appointment, and is in effect employer of over 1,300 NEA staff members. He appoints staff members to the divisions, committees, and commissions and selects chairmen to these units with the approval of the Executive Commitee.[49]

Since the NEA created the position of executive secretary in 1893, only six people have held this position. Irwin Shepard served from 1893 to 1912; Durand W. Springer served from 1913 to 1917; James W. Crabtree served from 1918 to 1934; Willard E. Givens served from 1935 to 1952; and William G. Carr served from 1953 to 1967. Sam M. Lambert presently holds this position.[50]

During this same period in American history there have been thirteen presidents of the United States.

The Representative Assembly Today

The Representative Assembly is a jealous guardian of the rights and interests of the teacher in the NEA, and forces similar to those that led to the creation of the Representative Assembly in the early part of this century still function. Also the many critics of the Association today are not reluctant to point out the flaws of the Association in general and specific weaknesses of the Assembly.

The Assembly meets annually and makes policy for the entire Association. This is a Herculean task. The United States Congress has but 535 members and cannot complete its work in any given year. The House of Delegates of the American Bar Association has less than 200 members;[51] but yet, the delegates of the Representative Assembly soundly defeated the most recent attempt to limit the size of the Assembly to 5,000 members.[52] The size of the Representative Assembly has long been a concern both to friends and critics of the NEA. Erwin Selle, in 1932, expressed the concern about the Assembly reaching total membership of 2,000.[53] Twenty-four years later, Myron Lieberman said, "It appears to be too large to function effectively as a delegate body."[54] Regardless of this criticism, the number of delegates has increased by over 2,000 in the past thirteen years.

Another factor that mitigates against the Assembly as a totally effective legislative body is the number of delegates who attend the annual convention for the first time. Lyle W. Ashby, Deputy Executive Secretary, estimated that it was possible that as many as sixty percent of the delegates to the 1967 convention attended the convention for first time as authorized delegates.[55] Edgar Wesley asserted, "An assembly composed of changing personnel is naturally less effective than one which consists of experienced delegates."[56] Henry Stoudt, a member of the NEA Board of Directors from Pennsylvania, questioned how:

Representatives attending a meeting for the first time can render earth-shaking, policy-making decisions without benefit of study that has been devoted to a particular subject by those who are paid for it or by those who voluntarily give of their services anywhere from twelve to thirty days per year trying to learn the background for certain issues.[57]

Still another factor that clouds the power demarcation of the Assembly and the other units of the NEA is the position of the president of the NEA. The Assembly elects the president of the NEA, but *Newsweek* called this position merely a figurehead.[58] There is sound basis for this argument. Article III of the NEA By-laws lists the officers of the NEA as the president, vice-president, immediate past president, treasurer, and the executive secretary; however, the *NEA Handbook* states that "the chief administrative officer of the Association is the executive secretary."[59] The executive secretary is elected to a term of four years, can succeed himself, has great powers of appointment, and receives a salary of $50,000 a year; whereas, the president of the NEA has a term of one year, cannot succeed himself, has few significant powers of appointment, and receives a salary of $21,000 a year.[60]

When examining the list of NEA presidents who served prior to 1920, one finds some of the great names of American educational history: William T. Harris, Ely T. Tappan, Nicholas Murray Butler, Charles W. Eliot, David Starr Jordan, and George S. Strayer. These men served prior to the creation of the Representative Assembly in 1920. After 1917, the custom of electing a man and a woman as president in alternate years began and has continued.[61] Since that time, notables in American education seem to have shunned the presidency of the NEA. One can assume that while the creation of the Representative Assembly has had very positive democratizing aspects upon the growth of the NEA, the office of the presidency has diminished in stature.

That weaknesses exist in the Representative Assembly cannot be denied, but one must recognize, however, that most active members of the Association are aware of flaws. The recognition of these drawbacks of the Assembly causes further internal stresses as the Assembly constantly has been atempting to define its policy-making position within the Association. The internal stresses have been evident in the Representative Assembly for the past few decades.

The membership attempted for years to eliminate life memberships on the Board of Directors, causing this to be an issue up until this decade. Another way in which the Assembly moved to expand its position was the support of the sanctioning of Utah in 1962 because of the poor educational situation existing in Utah at that time. Critics of the NEA claimed that the union victory in New York City forced the sanction action by the Association, but regardless of the cause, the NEA gradually assumed a more militant posture with the Representative Assembly playing a more dominant role.

Jane Walker, a member of the Board of Directors from Pennsylvania, said: "At one time a classroom teacher or a Negro very seldom ever spoke from the floor at a meeting of the Representative Assembly. This is no longer the case. Everyone is given an opportunity to be heard."[62]

The recent meetings of the Representative Assembly have been wide open to all viewpoints, causing many old practices to be questioned and some to be discarded.

A case in point occurred at the 1966 and the 1967 conventions. William Carr, executive secretary of the NEA, indicated in 1966 that he was going to resign a year before his contract expired. This action triggered an interesting, but very assertive, move on the part of the Assembly. The Board of Trustees has always had the power of selecting the executive secretary, but the delegates moved to take this power away from the trustees and place it in the hands of the Executive Committee. The logic of this move is revealing in that it indicates the active role the Representative Assembly has assumed in recent years. The Representative Assembly either directly or indirectly elects eight of the eleven members of the Executive Committee, whereas the Board of Directors elects the majority of the people on the Board of Trustees. The implication becomes obvious. The Representative Assembly felt that the Executive Committee was more responsive to the will of the teachers than the Board of Directors, and that the Assembly should play a more active part in selecting the new executive secretary.

At this juncture, the Assembly found itself in a constitutional bind. Transferring the power to select the executive secretary from the Board of Trustees to the Executive Committee involved a change in the NEA Charter, and this could not be accomplished without congressional approval. Therefore, the delegates took two avenues of approach aimed at accomplishing their goal of making the organization more responsive to the dictates of the teachers.

The first approach involved blunting the power of the Board of Trustees in the selection of an executive secretary. Through floor action, the Assembly created a five-man screening committee whose sole purpose was to narrow the applicants for the position to three people, and at that point, the Board of Trustees would assume their legal position of making the final selection for the post of executive secretary.[63] The Board of Directors selected the screening committee, but the Assembly dictated the organization and composition of the committee. Two of the committee members could hold no official position within the Association, and one of these people had to chair the committee. The other three members had to be members of the Executive Committee.[64] The Assembly further stated that the successor to Carr must "have the prospect of ten or more years of vigorous leadership"[65] remaining, thus eliminating some of Carr's assistants.[66]

The second avenue of approach involved the Assembly's passing Resolution 66–26, which initiated action for a change in the Bylaws that would give the Executive Committee the power to select and fix the compensation of the executive secretary. The resolution passed with little opposition from the floor.[67]

The Representative Assembly continued to define further its policy-making authority at the 1967 convention held in Minneapolis, Minnesota. Resolution 67–26 passed with little opposition, preparing the way for a change in the charter that would permit the Executive Committee to select the executive secretary. The Assembly also passed Resolution 67–28 stressing the relationship of the Representative Assembly with the executive units of the NEA. It read:

> The Representative Assembly of the National Education Association hereby reaffirms its role as a policy making body as designated by the Charter and the Bylaws and hereby also reminds all executive units of the Association that their basic responsibility is to implement the policy and directives of the membership as expressed through the Representative Assembly. It further admonishes all of

the executive units of the NEA to be sensitive to the direction of the
Representative Assembly and to carry out its directives.[68]

The Representative Assembly's action of the past few years is a
continuation of the active spirit of teachers who have been constantly attempting to define their role in the Association. Fenner
and Wesley pointed out in many passages of their books the perpetual teacher questioning of the management of the NEA. Wesley
and Fenner's observations upon the evolution of teacher power
sound very similar to a reply made by Herschel C. Heritage, a director of the NEA from Iowa, when asked why the Assembly passed
Resolution 67–28:

> There were many possible reasons. Among these might be impa-
> tience of some members with the speed of change in so complex an
> organization; desire to make decisions; desire to exercise a personal
> influence; intolerance of youth for age; partial understanding of the
> the relation of the parts of an organization to the whole; desire of
> classroom teachers to assume more control in proportion to their
> numbers.[69]

Even though the Bylaws state specifically that the ultimate authority rests in the Representative Assembly of the NEA, one must
be cognizant that since the Assembly meets but once a year, some
other organizational body within the NEA must undertake or implement the mandates of the Representative Assembly. This function rests with the executive arms of the NEA, the Board of Directors and the Executive Committee.

The Board of Directors of the NEA

Article IV of the NEA Bylaws creates the Board of Directors.
Each state, commonwealth, and the District of Columbia has at
least one representative on the board. Each unit is entitled to an
additional director for each 20,000 or more active members. Therefore, the total membership of the Board of Directors in 1968 was
ninety-six people. Each state, commonwealth, and District of
Columbia elects its own board members without any restrictions
from the national organization. The term of office is for three years,
and no director can serve more than three consecutive terms.

Powers and Duties of the Board of Directors

The Board of Directors is subject in all ways to the Representative Assembly, but the board does "have in charge the general policies and interests of the Association except those entrusted to the Executive Committee."[70] The bulk of the Board's power comes from Paragraph f, Section 4, Article IV of the Bylaws, which states:

> The Board of Directors shall establish policies governing the publications of Reports and Proceedings of the Association. It shall receive, consider, and publish the annual reports of the executive secretary, the treasurer, the Board of Trustees, and the committees, commissions, and council, and transmit the same with recommendations to the Representative Assembly. It shall devise procedures for censure, suspension, or reinstatement of an affiliated association, and it shall submit them to the Representative Assembly for appropriate action. It may recommend to the Representative Assembly the creation or discontinuance of any committee, commission, council, or department. It may submit to the Resolutions Committee of the Representative Assembly any proposals as it deems to be in the interests of the Association.[71]

In addition to the aforementioned powers and duties of the Board of Directors, the Bylaws and Charter also grant the Board the following rights and tasks:

a) To elect annually one Trustee and one member of the Executive Committee.

b) To determine the time and place of the annual meeting after consideration of Executive Committee recommendations.

c) To elect the Budget Committee.

d) To determine the fiscal policies and procedures governing the general fund, except as otherwise provided for in the Bylaws.

e) To recommend to the Representative Assembly, on recommendation of the Board of Trustees, expenditures from the principal of the Permanent Fund.

f) To review and transmit financial reports to the Representative Assembly and a summary to the members.

g) To review constitutions and bylaws of departments.

h) To authorize departments to maintain offices at other places than headquarters of the Association.

i) To facilitate cooperation among the departments and with the Association.

j) To direct the disposition of the General Fund surplus.

k) To review and approve the budget for presentation to the Representative Assembly.[72]

In addition to the powers and duties specifically stated by the Charter and the Bylaws, there are many decisions that must be made that are not specified in the Charter and the Bylaws. The following are some examples:

a) Development and approval of plans for promotion of NEA membership.
b) Development of policies regarding the activities of state directors.
c) Recommendations for new or expanded service programs to the Representative Assembly.
d) Recommendations of long-term NEA goals to the Representative Assembly.
e) Recommendations for changes in NEA Bylaws.
f) Authorization to borrow funds.
g) Allocate funds for delegates' expenses and determine formula for distribution of same.
h) Authorization of loans to NEA departments.
i) Authorization for special benefit programs such as the NEA Mutual Fund and the Insurance Program for NEA members.[73]

Additional responsibilities of the Board of Directors not outlined by the Charter and Bylaws are:

a) Examine the present needs and the future trends in education.
b) Develop plans by which the NEA can give leadership and assistance in meeting these needs through its program and its service to members.
c) Recommend such plans to the Representative Assembly for adoption.
d) After decisions are made by the Representative Assembly, make general plans for implementing them, assigning detailed responsibility to the Executive Committee.
e) Make recommendations to the Representative Assembly as occasion may require to adapt the Association's structure to changing needs and circumstances.
f) Delegate to the Executive Committee from time to time those activities which can be handled more effectively by a smaller body.[74]

The Board of Directors Today

The Board of Directors plays a very vital role in the organizational structure of the NEA. It is one of the executive arms of the Association, and once policy has been made by the Representative

Assembly, the Board must implement this policy within the broad outlines designated by the Charter, Bylaws, and precedent. Wesley stated that the Board "is the deliberating and action agency of the Association."[75] Fenner added still another important function of the Board. She stated that the Board is the "official representatives of the NEA in their own states."[76] Since the Board is much smaller than the Representative Assembly, the Board meets three times a year deliberating and passing judgment upon the matters confronting the Association.

Each director is elected by Association members in his own state; therefore, the Board collectively represents a good cross section of the opinions held by individual Association members in their own states. Relative to this point, another significant role of the director is to serve as a communications link between the national Association and the individual member or Assembly delegate. Through this position the director can exert influence upon state or local Association members.

The Board also makes recommendations to the Resolutions Committee and the Bylaws Committee. At committee levels the Board functions well. The Board represents some of the best known people in the Association; many are staff members on state associations while others devote practically all of their spare time to Association matters. When some board members speak, therefore, they have a responsive audience. These committees are the key committees in the Representative Assembly, and any favorable decision made by these committees has a better chance of survival on the floor of the Assembly than do those ideas brought up on the floor of the Representative Assembly during the heat of debate.[77] Also such action by the committee would make it easier to oppose ideas considered unfavorable.

Over the past decade the Representative Assembly has made certain changes in the Bylaws restricting somewhat the power of the Board. Article IV, Section 4, specifically places the Board "subject to the authority and direction of the Representative Assembly." Article IV, Section 2, limits the terms of the Board to no more than three consecutive terms. During the last decade, there has been a great cry arise from the delegates that the NEA needs new blood and fresh, new ideas. Usually these criticisms have been aimed at the Board. The critics of the Board have apparently had an effect. The average length of service on the Board was 5.6 years in 1957; whereas it was only 3.5 years in 1967. Newer people are being brought into the ruling bodies of the Association.

Certain basic weaknesses exist within the organizational structure of the Board of Directors that are similar to the management of the business meetings of the NEA prior to the creation of the Representative Assembly. Membership of the Board is too large; the agenda cannot be completed at the regular meetings; and the cost of getting almost a hundred people together is considerable. The Board meets three times a year, and one of these meetings is held concurrently with the meeting of the Representative Assembly. The other two meetings usually occur in October and February. Henry Stoudt estimates that it costs the Association at least $10,000 per weekend meeting of the Board. In addition to the cost, the agenda is so crowded that not all of the business can be transacted.

These factors mitigate against the complete efficiency of the Board. The Board has difficulties meeting the day-to-day problems of running such a complex organization as the Association; therefore, a smaller unit must fulfill this need. This becomes the function of the Executive Committee.

THE EXECUTIVE COMMITTEE

Whereas the Board of Directors of the NEA has been a part of the NEA since its inception, the Executive Committee of the NEA can trace its beginning back to 1895.[78] The Committee consisted of only five members at that time and met but twice a year. The membership in the Executive Committee has increased to eleven through various changes in the Bylaws,[79] and in 1966–1967, the Committee met in formal sessions eighteen times.[80]

Article V of the NEA Bylaws creates the Executive Committee of the NEA. The Committee consists of eleven members: NEA president; NEA vice-president; immediate past president of the NEA; treasurer of the NEA; Chairman of the Board of Trustees of the NEA; two members elected from the Board of Directors of the NEA, one of whom must be a classroom teacher; and four members elected at large by the Representative Assembly, of whom two must be classroom teachers.[81] The president, vice-president, and the immediate past president serve on the Committee for a period of three years by virtue of their positions held in the Association. The Representative Assembly elects these three officers. The treasurer of the NEA is a member of the Committee. These people elected to the Committee have terms of three years and can serve no more than three consecutive terms. All of the Committee are ex officio members of the Board of Directors, and the Executive Committee can hold as many meetings as the Committee wishes.[82]

Powers and Duties of the Executive Committee

The Bylaws and Charter of the NEA grant the Executive Committee the following powers and duties:

a) To act on behalf of the Directors between meetings of the Board.

b) To review applications for membership, to censure, suspend, expel, or reinstate members in accordance with the Bylaws.

c) To review applications for affiliation and to censure, suspend, expel, or reinstate affiliates pursuant to procedures adopted by the Representative Assembly.

d) To recommend to the Directors the time and place for the annual meeting.

e) To distribute unallocated items in the budget; administer functions assigned by the Directors and to provide NEA funds to safeguard the state program in any jurisdiction having unified dues where an increase in dues would work unusual hardship.

f) To select members of commissions and councils of the Association and to determine their number, method of selection, and tenure.

g) To review a hearing conducted by the Committee on Professional Ethics and to affirm, reject, or modify the decision rendered by the Committee.

h) To review interim reports of the Association's finances.[83]

In addition to the powers and duties specifically mentioned in the Bylaws and Charter, the Executive Committee makes some decisions not specified by the Bylaws and the Charter. Some of these are as follows:

a) On recommendation of the Executive Secretary, personnel mat-
    ters: salary scheduling, retirement, appointments to higher
    levels of the staff, organization of headquarters staff and its
    units, and other personnel regulations.
b) Advertising rates in the *Journal*.
c) Employment of legal and other specialized services, except as
    assigned by the Bylaws to other officers.
d) Interim committees to deal with questions outside the scope of
    existing committees.
e) NEA relations to outside projects.
f) Report recommendations and actions of the Executive Commit-
    tee at each meeting of the Board of Directors.
g) Determine when to invoke or revoke sanctions and the nature
    of sanctions.
h) Remove and replace trustees to the NEA Insurance Trust.[84]

The Executive Committee Today

In 1957, Edgar Wesley called the Executive Committee an "interim board of directors."[85] This still remains true. In examining
the relationship between the Executive Committee and the Board
of Directors, one must be aware that the Executive Committee
members are ex officio members of the Board of Directors. The
Executive Committee, because of its size, meets quite frequently
throughout the course of a year, facing problems that need immediate attention. The Committee can make decisions on the problems confronting the Association, keeping within the broad framework of the policy making process of the Representative Assembly;
or it can act as a clearing house for the Directors and refer problems to the Board of Directors for further discussion or final decision. After discussion the Directors may make the final decision or
they can refer the matter back to the Committee for final action.[86]

Not all of the interchange between the Committee and the Board
of Directors is harmonious. A case in point is the discussion over the
site of the Board of Directors' meeting for February 1968. The Executive Committee suggested that the meeting be held at Washington, D.C., instead of Atlantic City, New Jersey, because of the
rather bad weather that had occurred in Atlantic City in previous
years. Many of the members felt that it was much easier to get to
Washington, D.C. than to Atlantic City in the middle of winter.
The February meeting traditionally was held at Atlantic City, co-
inciding with the annual meeting of the American Association of

School Administrators. The Board listened to the Committee's suggestion and rejected it. Then the Committee suggested that the Board could meet wherever it preferred. The Board decided to hold its meeting in Washington, D.C.[87] The issue is almost a trifle, but the implications are most significant.

The Executive Committee has a close relationship with the Representative Assembly. Thelma Davis said, "The Executive Committee feels a cooperative spirit with and a responsibility to the Delegate Assembly." This presses the Committee to find programs and projects that are in keeping with policies and resolutions passed by the Assembly. Also, the Committee must serve the Assembly in an educative capacity; that is, the Committee must disseminate all information available to the Assembly on current problems and issues confronting the NEA, so that the Assembly's decisions will be based on what best serves the Association.[88] The relationship between the Executive Committee and the Delegate Assembly may be heightened somewhat by the fact that eight of the members of the Committee are selected by the Assembly, and in recent years the delegates have not been reticent in reminding the Committee of this situation.

Conflict and inner criticism in an organization as large as the National Education Association are neither unhealthy nor unusual characteristics. That one group or another is attempting to gain control should not be construed as something nefarious. There has been a constant struggle going on between the legislative, executive, and judicial branches of our federal government since George Washington's second administration, and on the whole, the country has generally benefited from the struggles. So it is, on a much smaller scale, with the NEA. Like our country, the NEA has changed much over the past century, and the speed of change is increasing rather than decelerating. At one time, the NEA was a close-knit group of college presidents and school administrators who spoke for all of the teachers of the country. As membership began to increase, teachers demanded more voice in the organization. Today's teacher is well educated and very articulate, and he wants an even greater control over his organization. The rise of the Representative Assembly and the increase of teacher militancy are but two outward manifestations of changes within the Association. The Representative Assembly clearly is the legislative arm of the Association while the Board of Directors and the Executive Committee serve as the executive agencies of the Association. The Assembly, meeting but one week a year, makes the policy of the Association; the Board of Directors and the Executive Committee, which form a type of interlocking directorate to assure continuity, implement the policy of the Representative Assembly.

The Negro and the NEA from 1884 to 1926 | 2

*Herein lies the tragedy of the age: not that men
are poor—all men know something of poverty; not
that men are wicked—who is good? Not that men
are ignorant—what is truth? Nay, but that men
know so little of men.*   **W. E. B. DuBois**

These four decades represented a vigorous, hectic period of
growth for the United States, which saw life in this country affected immeasurably by the various elements of change. The Civil
War set in motion the rapid industrialization of the nation that
culminated in America's becoming the major industrial power in
the world by the beginning of this century. Simultaneously the
United States embarked upon some imperialistic ventures that
brought many nonwhite people under the American flag. Europe's
headlong rush for foreign lands and the subsequent political and
economic rivalries among these nations triggered World War I in
1914. Later the United States became involved in the conflagra-
tion and helped bring about an Allied victory in 1918. The war
had far-reaching influence upon the United States because this
country became the chief creditor nation in the world, thus as-
suring the United States' paramount position as a world power.

Domestically, this period was very turbulent. Labor and management strife was common and frequently violence occurred.
The flood of immigrants to the United States further compounded
the nation's difficulties. Farm mortgages were common, and college presidents, ministers, and entrepreneurs preached Social Dar-
winism. But many segments of the population demanded relief
from the pressures of a way of life that was practically unknown
to a people who had been basically agrarian prior to 1860.

This agitation led to the second great reform movement in American history, which bore fruit in the first fifteen years of this century. The government placed some restraints on big business; the courts began to uphold reform legislation; the graduated income tax and the direct election of senators became part of the Constitution; Upton Sinclair's literary efforts and public pressure improved standards in the meat industry; labor unions received a respite from antitrust litigation; and public school education reached a vast number of children throughout the nation. The progressive era renewed the individual's faith in the United States.

In the South the physical scars of the Civil War had begun to heal. Left on its own after 1877, the South faced overwhelming problems. Slowly it regained its prewar strength, but at the same time, the North and the West were making dramatic economic progress, placing the South in an almost untenable position. As a result, the reactionary element in the South became dominant in the last decade of the century; thus, the Negroes suffered great losses that reduced them to second class citizenship. This was accomplished in many ways: loss of voting rights, loss of political representation, entrenchment of Jim Crow Laws, denial of job rights, intimidation, general segregation, and lynchings.[1]

Tragically, the United States government was an accomplice to this situation by not protecting the Constitutional rights of the Negro. In 1896, the United States Supreme Court ruled against Homer Plessy, who had insisted upon riding in a white man's section of a railroad car. *Plessy v. Ferguson* had the impact of a federal law and gradually it became the accepted principle of the nation.[2] Consequently, the Negro found it necessary to work and live within a societal structure that greatly limited his freedom.

Out of this milieu came the most famous spokesman for the Negroes during this period. Booker T. Washington was a graduate of Hampton Institute and founder and principal of Tuskegee Institute, Tuskegee, Alabama. He advocated industrial and vocational education of the Negro, characterized by self-help and accommodation. Washington gained national prominence in 1895 when he gave a speech at the Atlanta Exposition outlining his basic philosophy. He became an advisor to presidents and worked with the leading industrial capitalists in an effort to carry out his concepts of Negro advancement.[3] During this time, Washington molded the shape of Negro education in the South in a manner that coincided with the viewpoint of most influential white Southerners.

Washington was not without his critics. To many Negroes he was the symbol of conservatism, and William Edward Burghardt DuBois became one of his most outspoken critics. DuBois, educated at Fisk and Harvard Universities, where he gained a rich liberal arts tradition, advocated that higher educaton would be more significant to Negro progress than Washington's emphasis on vocational and industrial training.[4] Militant in his attitude, DuBois was one of the early leaders of the NAACP, which was designed to protect and establish rights of Negroes.[5]

Since the South had many intrinsic economic problems, education in that region generally suffered. The doctrine of "separate but equal" compounded the tragedy, and consequently the educational rights of the Negroes suffered during this period. In 1865, most of the Negroes were illiterate. By 1900, illiteracy had been reduced to forty-five percent.[6] Whatever gains had been made were dwarfed by the economic, political, and social injustices inflicted upon the Negro. These injustices were most apparent in education. Strictly segregated, the basic educational inequalities between the white and the black children widened rapidly. For example, in the early 1900s, Georgia spent only twenty cents out of every educational dollar for Negro education even though half of the students were Negroes.[7] In 1902, the South spent twice as much money on education of white children as for the education of Negro children in proportion to the number of students in the school system.[8] At the end of the first decade of this century, Louisiana was spending 500 percent more for white children's education than for the Negro students.[9] This unwillingness to support Negro education caused severe problems, such as overcrowding, inadequate buildings, and poorly trained teachers.

The plight of Negro education would have been even more severe had it not been for the various philanthropic agencies such as the George Peabody Foundation, the Anna T. Jeannes Fund, the Julius Rosenwald Fund, and the John F. Slater Fund. Most of these organizations concentrated their money on two major areas: school construction and preparation of teachers.

James Dillard reported that the Slater Fund had helped establish 142 schools, which had 833 teachers. He also stated that this fund paid for twenty-five percent of the building costs and the salaries of these schools.[10] Dillard reported that the Rosenwald Fund had contributed over $200,000 toward the erection of 226 school buildings from September 1920, to January 1921.[11] By 1925, the Rosenwald Fund had contributed nearly two million dollars for the construction of 2,500 schools in fourteen southern states.[12] Total cost of these buildings was over ten million dollars. Tax money, contributions from white people, and matching funds to the Rosenwald Fund by Negroes accounted for the rest of the money. It is interesting to note that nearly all the funds insisted that the Negroes raise money for the various projects. Significantly, all of the Rosenwald buildings had some facilities for industrial training, thus emphasizing the two hallmarks of Washington's philosophy: self-aid and vocational education.

The Jeannes Fund was aimed at improving Negro teachers, who were trained in the necessary supervisory capacities so that they could go into the rural areas and help the teachers there. Generally this was the only supervision the rural teachers received. The impact of the Jeannes teacher could be seen at a meeting at Tuskegee Institute in 1931, where 313 Jeannes teachers met. They represented fifteen different states and supervised Negro teachers who taught over 500,000 students.[13]

Booker T. Washington and the philanthropic organizations had great influence upon Negro education in the South from 1884 to 1926. Washington advocated improving the Negro through the existing southern societal structure, and through this concept he was able to generate interest and financial support for his educational ideas. The philanthropic agencies worked within the southern ethos and acted as a catalyst in order to keep the Negro schools alive.

RELATIONSHIP BETWEEN THE NEA AND THE NEGRO

From 1884 to 1926 the National Education Association was

aware of the racial situation in the United States as some aspect of this topic was on the agenda of eighteen of its annual meetings. Quite frequently prominent Negro educators participated in the presentation of this matter to the delegates. Most of the addresses and discussions dealing with Negro education could be categorized under four major headings: (1) Negro education as a sociological value; (2) Negro education as related to the missionary zeal of Christianity; (3) the emphasis of the "separate but equal" aspects of Negro education; and (4) the acceptance of vocational education as the chief mode of Negro education. Most of the speakers emphasized one or two of these categories, but significantly, Booker T. Washington, who addressed the convention four times, covered all of these points.

Many of the educators argued for the sociological benefits of Negro education much in the same way their educational counterparts stressed the societal contributions of the common school movement during the period from 1830 to 1860. Conceding that the Negro had the ability to learn, these educators emphasized the positive societal implications of further Negro education.[14] G. R. Glenn, state supervisor from Georgia, stressed that education of Negroes would reduce the crime rate.[15] Booker T. Washington buttressed this opinion when he told the delegates that he only knew of six graduates of the fifteen leading Negro industrial schools who had been sent to jail.[16] In 1894, Richard R. Wright, principal of Georgia State Industrial College, struck a responsive chord with the NEA members when he told them that the graduates of the trade schools had never been involved in a strike.[17] This remark was greeted by applause from the NEA members. At the 1890 convention, a symposium on race relations was held in which education was viewed as the means by which the Negro could eventually be brought into the mainstream of society.[18]

Permeating many of the speakers' viewpoints on Negro education was the great emphasis upon the relationship between Negro education and the missionary zeal of Christianity. A. A. Gunby believed that educators must "take up the white man's burden" and educate the Negroes in America.[19] John H. Burrus equated social progress of Negroes with Christianity in this country.[20] Hollis

B. Frissell's two speeches to the NEA in 1900 and 1916 emphasized that the chief ends of Negro industrial education were to improve habits, character, and morality.[21]

Implicit in most of the addresses and discussions of Negro education was that the Negroes were separated from the rest of society
because of their race; consequently, some of the speakers emphasized the "separate but equal" doctrine even before *Plessy V. Ferguson.* Significantly enough, Booker T. Washington did this in
1884. W. H. Bartholomew advocated this principle in 1886,[22] and
J. A. B. Lovett further elaborated upon it four years later.[23] Only
Richard R. Wright raised any questions about this doctrine. He did
not attack this principle but pointed out some disadvantages of the
dual systems because the segregated systems allowed for no interchange of ideas, thus harming the Negro school system.[24]

While a few of the Negro educators advocated higher education
for Negroes, the major educational emphasis of the NEA was upon
vocational education for the Negroes.[25] Booker T. Washington was
the foremost advocate of this concept, and H. B. Frissell, principal
of Hampton Institute, concurred. It is significant to note that practically all of the educators, Negro and white, who spoke at the
NEA convention during this period supported the concept of industrial education for the Negro and frequently cited Tuskegee and
Hampton Institutes as excellent examples of Negro education.

BOOKER T. WASHINGTON AT THE NEA CONVENTIONS

The NEA was one of the first major organizations that gave
Booker T. Washington a national platform to present his views
upon Negro education. He spoke at the NEA conventions in 1884,
1896, 1904, and 1908. His basic philosophy was given in his first
two addresses, while the last two NEA speeches were considered as
progress reports of the status of Negro industrial education. It is
interesting to note that while his basic philosophy remained relative-
ly unchanged over the twenty-six year period, his platform delivery
changed somewhat. During this time, Washington's prominence
grew to a national level, enabling him to insert some gentle humor
in his speeches emphasizing the physical differences between
the races.

The NEA convention at Madison, Wisconsin, was his first opportunity to address the NEA. He called for the continued cooperation between the white and the Negro people, stressing that if the Negro were to be successful, he would have to cooperate with the white man because the white people controlled the property and the government. He was careful to emphasize that if the lot of the Negro improved, the rest of the society would also improve at a proportional rate.

He advocated that brains, property, and character would solve the racial problems of the South and that the reforms had to come from within the South and not forced upon the area from the outside. He told the delegates that the South did not " . . . like to obey orders that come from Washington telling them that they must lay aside at once customs that they followed for centuries, and henceforth, there must be one coach, one hotel, one school house for ex-master and slave."[26] He fully supported the "separate but equal" doctrine nearly twelve years before the Supreme Court issued its decision, *Plessy v. Ferguson*. To buttress his viewpoint on separate facilities, Washington pointed out that Alabama spent half of its educational budget on colored schools.

He emphasized the role of industrial education for Negroes in creating a new South. He believed that if the South spent money for the training of Negroes the entire region would prosper economically, thus benefiting white as well as Negro people. Washington cited the great need for more schools for Negroes such as Tuskegee Institute, which improved the lot of the Negro by giving him "something practical and useful to do.[27] His school stressed three goals: "First, to give the student the best mental training; secondly, to furnish him with labor that will be valuable to the school, and will enable the student to learn something about labor *per se;* thirdly, to teach the dignity of labor."[28]

He visualized his school as the basic tool that would improve the Negro economically, politically, and morally, and at the same time would keep the school in the basic southern societal framework that would ultimately lead to a better life for all people.

While examining Washington's speeches to the NEA, one cannot help but see the influence of Johann Pestalozzi upon Washington. Both worked with essentially the same kind of person—the poor downtrodden individual whom the world had passed. Pestalozzi emphasized the development of the head, hand, and heart as the key to the education of the individual. These became continuing themes in Washington's addresses. Through the full development of these faculties, Washington believed that the Negro could become an integral part of society. The hand was symbolic of the Negro learning a trade. The head symbolized the furthering of a skill whereby the Negro could do higher forms of work, ie., from a laborer in a steel mill to a craftsman working with the finished products of steel. Washington placed the most emphasis upon the development of the heart, which symbolized the improvement of the Negro's moral capacities. This was not hard to explain, for Washington was a visionary who frequently couched his reforms in the cloth of Christianity. He told the delegates:

> It seems to me that the time has come when we should arise in this matter above party and race or section into the atmosphere of man to man, Christian to Christian, citizen to citizen; for if the Negro who has been impressed and denied rights in a Christian land can help you, North and South, to rise to a better atmosphere of unselfishness and Christian brotherhood, he will have indeed a sufficient recompense for all he has suffered at your hands.[29]

Stressing love and humility and repudiating hate, he told his students never to feel superior to the white man because: "No race can go on cherishing hatred and ill-will toward another race without being lowered and degraded of all those elements that go to perpetuate a strong, growing and generous manhood and womanhood."[30] He skillfully combined a great faith in industrial education with a deep-rooted belief in Christianity. He felt that industrial education held the key to Negro progress and that progress was a law of God. He believed that the problems of the South could be worked out: ". . . in proportion as the Negro's skill, intelligence, and character can produce something that the white man wants or the white man respects;[31] hence, the value of industrial education."[32]
Then he linked progress with God:

> Think of it my friends; we went into slavery a piece of property and came out American citizens; we went into slavery without a lang-

uage and came out speaking the proud Anglo-Saxon language; we went into slavery with slave chains clinging about our wrists; we came out with the American ballot in our hands. Progress is the law of God and progress is going to be the Negro's guiding star in this fair land.[33]

Washington's address to the NEA convention in 1904 was a progress report of Negro education in the country. He used this speech as a means of answering those critics who advocated the view that education hindered rather than aided Negro progress. Washington claimed "whatever measure of education the Negro has received, he has paid and will pay more largely in the future."[34] He told how the white employer of the South constantly sought out the graduates from his school and pointed out that his students received an annual wage "three times as large which they earned before receiving any training at Tuskegee Institute."[35] He surveyed the economic aspects of the Negro in Virginia and Georgia and attributed much of the economic success of the Negro in Virginia to Hampton Institute. He showed that the Negro in Virginia owned "one-twenty-sixth of the total real estate," and in Georgia the Negroes paid taxes on land valued at nearly seventeen million dollars.[36] He cited other examples of Negro improvement and attributed them all to education.

The basic tenets of Christianity pervaded his whole speech and ended upon an evangelical note that indicated his deep faith in education as a means of improving the moral aspect of society:

My fellow teachers, let us, as we go out from this great gathering, teach the children of this land that in proportion as they lift up their hands to oppress and harm another race, in that degree will their soul be degraded and weakened; but in so much as they by word and action lift up the humblest and meanest and most unprotected of the human family, they themselves will be strengthened and broadened and made after the fashion of the Teacher of teachers, who when on earth became the servant to all, that in the end he might become the Master.[37]

Four years later at Cleveland, Ohio, Washington gave another progress report to the nation's educators.[38] He continued to emphasize industrial education as the key to the progress of the Negro and frequently cited the economic, social, and moral values of an industrial education. This was the last time that he addressed the NEA, but it was during the same time that his influence and philosophy were spreading and were being accepted by most of the influential white people in the United States.

During this period of American history the Negro had been successfully reduced to a second class citizen. This status was most apparent when one looked at the South's neglect of the Negro public schools. Had it not been for the various philanthropic organizations, Negro education would have suffered a more drastic fate.

Booker T. Washington was the chief spokesman of Negro education. Advocating a system of education that most white people could support, his views on industrial and vocational education for Negroes were implemented, and Tuskegee Institute became the symbol of educational progress of the Negro.

The NEA reflected the basic, conservative philosophy that pervaded the nation during this era. Problems of the Negro were discussed at many of the conventions, but actually the organization did nothing. The problems were viewed in an impersonal, almost detached manner, and the NEA, like most of the nation, seemed willing only to accept the fundamental beliefs of Booker T. Washington.

The NEA and the
Negro Teacher from 1927 to 1954 | 3

Procrastination is the art of keeping up with yesterday.
DON MARQUIS

The economic and social conditions that prevailed generally showed flagrant inequalities in all aspects of Negro life. Many Negroes migrated to the industrial cities of the North, while the majority of the Negroes who stayed in the South found themselves chained to a one crop economy that kept them at a bare existence level of living. If the Negro left the agricultural economy, generally he found that he was limited to menial positions because Negroes had been excluded from such basic skilled jobs as plumbing, carpentry, or bricklaying.[1] Usually the Negroes could do little about their plight because the normal avenues of democratic procedures had been closed to them. Their disenfranchisement had been thorough and complete.

During the 1920s and the 1930s the great economic depression engulfed the United States, causing the Negro predicament to become more severe. Since the agricultural areas were affected first, most of the southern states reeled under effects of reduction of prices and losses in markets. The worsening economic climate of the South gravely affected education in general and Negro education in particular.

A study conducted by the United States government in 1926 showed that over 2,200,000 Negroes were enrolled in segregated public schools in the South. The report indicated that there were only 425 public high schools in those segregated states which Negro students could attend. Attendance totaled 98,000 Negro children.[2] Many reasons were given for the scarcity of high schools: (a) lack of public support; (b) poor elementary education that mitigated against further education; (c) the early age in which certain states allowed Negro children to leave school to seek employment; and (d) negligent enforcement of compulsory attendance laws. In 1929, Virginia, South Carolina, Mississippi, and Louisiana had no educational requirements regarding child work permits, while four other southern states required only that a child know how to read and write before he acquired a work permit. Delaware and Washington, D.C., had the highest requirements of all segregated states. They demanded that a child complete the eighth grade prior to securing a work permit. The average compulsory attendance laws in segregated states required children from seven to sixteen to attend school; however, Negro students in only two of these states actually attended the minimum number of days required by the attendance laws.[3] Through these very lax laws, the states made it very easy for a Negro child to leave school and seek some kind of employment.

Charles H. Thompson showed that in 1930 the southern states were continuing to neglect Negro schools.[4] He claimed that the segregated states spent $44.31 annually per white child and only $12.47 a year for each Negro child. Furthermore, he pointed out that the segregated states spent only twenty-eight cents of every educational dollar for Negro education. Thompson also claimed that the Negro schools were vastly overcrowded and that the school term for Negro schools was shorter than the white school term. Attempting to redress this situation, Louisiana passed a law in 1935 that mandated the length of the Negro school term to six months.[5] Even with the passage of this law, the Negro school term was six weeks less than the white school term.

The educational statistics of 1940–1941 revealed that the educational picture in the South remained basically unchanged. Mordecai Johnson reported that the average salary for Negro teachers in a five state area of Mississippi, South Carolina, Louisiana, Arkansas, and Georgia was $295 a year.[6] He charged that these states spent only eight dollars annually per Negro child, whereas the national per capita educational expenditure was seventy-five dollars a year.

The "separate but equal" doctrine caused grave educational inequalities at all levels of education, and higher education was no exception. Negro colleges were inferior to their white counterparts. Stephen Wright claimed that only three Negro "universities" could justifiably claim the name in 1918.[7] In the segregated states it was virtually impossible for a Negro to gain entrance into a graduate or professional school, because these states did not maintain such schools for Negroes. If a Negro wanted to attend a professional school, he might receive an out-of-state tuition covering some of his expenses so that he could attend a school in a nonsegregated state. This allowed a few capable Negroes to secure advanced education without necessitating that the states eliminate segregation.[8]

THE NEGROES RESORT TO THE COURTS IN AN EFFORT TO END SEGREGATION

From 1896 to 1930, only three cases reached the United States Supreme Court regarding some aspect of racial segregation in the schools. None directly challenged the *Plessy v. Ferguson* decision and the Negro plaintiffs lost in every case.[9] During the 1930s, however, NAACP began a vigorous assault upon the segregated practices of education, and higher education became the immediate target. The legal advisors selected higher education since they felt that the "separate but equal" doctrine was more vulnerable because of the obvious comparisons with the colleges and the universities of the North and the West. Also the strategists believed that law suits against some southern public universities would cause other segregated states to establish professional schools without extended legal proceedings.[10]

The first significant case occurred in 1938 when Lloyd Gaines was denied entry into the University of Missouri Law School because of his race. Gaines initiated suit because no separate law school existed, and he felt that the out-of-state tuition failed to constitute equal treatment. Two lower courts upheld the University of Missouri, but the United States Supreme Court, in a six to two decision, reversed the lower courts' decision but without ruling against *Plessy v. Ferguson*. The court ruled that the state had to supply equal educational facilities for all and also indicated that the out-of-state tuition failed to meet the obligations of the state.[11] The decision had a great impact upon higher education in the South, for it marked the beginning of the establishment of professional schools for Negroes in a number of Southern states such as Missouri, Texas, Virginia, North Carolina, and Tennessee.[12]

After the completion of World War II, the Negroes stepped up their assaults upon segregated practices in higher education. In 1948, two important cases occurred that greatly weakened the foundations of the "separate but equal" doctrine. Herman Sweatt was denied entrance to the University of Texas Law School because he was a Negro who was eligible for entrance into a Negro law school in Texas. G. W. McLaurin was admitted to the University of Oklahoma because the courses he needed were not offered at Langston University, but he was segregated in the classroom, dining hall, and the university library. Both of these people initiated legal proceedings against the involved universities, and their cases were similar in that their lawyers placed great emphasis upon the intangible effects of segregation such as loss of prestige and social and psychological effects upon the individual because of segregation.[13] In 1950, the United States Supreme Court ruled in favor of the Negroes.

These cases ended the legal support of segregation in professional schools and showed that the court was willing to accept arguments against segregation based upon sociological and psychological evidence. This marked the successful weakening of the "separate but equal" doctrine and helped lay the groundwork for the NAACP's attack against segregation in the public elementary and secondary schools. These cases began in 1951.

When the NAACP began its attack upon the segregated public schools, tension increased rapidly. Herman Talmadge, governor of Georgia, said, "As long as I am Governor, Negroes will not be admitted to white schools."[14] The governor of South Carolina, James Byrnes, issued this statement: "We will, if it is possible, live within the law, preserve the public school system, and at the same time maintain segregation. If that is not possible, reluctantly, we will close the public school system. To do that will be choosing the lesser of two evils."[15]

By 1952 four desegregation cases, from Kansas, Delaware,

South Carolina, and Virginia, were pending before the Supreme Court. The next year a case from the District of Columbia was added to the docket. Thurgood Marshall, chief counsel for the NAACP, presented the arguments before the court. He attacked the "separate but equal doctrine" and cited the violations of the Constitutional rights of the Negroes, but he also referred to the recent cases regarding higher education and emphasized the intangible effects of segregation when he told the court, "Racial discriminations in and of themselves are invidious."[16]

THE RELATIONSHIP OF THE NEA
TO THE NEGRO TEACHER

In 1922, the NEA formed a Committee on Problems in Colored Schools. This was the first such organization in the history of the NEA, but unfortunately the committee accomplished nothing. In 1926, the NEA established with the Negro teachers a committee of ten to study the problems of Negro education.[17] Following this action, the NEA formed A Committee to Cooperate with the National Association of Teachers in Colored Schools.[18] Later at that convention, Dr. W. B. Hale issued greetings from the Negro teachers to the NEA. He paid tribute to the NEA: "Our Association joins the people of America with bowed heads, in reverence to the National Education Association that has revolutionized educational conditions in America."[19]

This was the beginning of a relationship between the two organizations that culminated in a historic merger nearly forty years later. In 1938, the committee was renamed the Joint Committee of the National Education Association and the American Teachers Association. From 1928 to 1954, the Joint Committee studied many facets of Negro education ranging from treatment of minorities in textbooks to support of federal aid to education.[20]

The Joint Committee usually met at least once a year and also gave an annual report to the NEA convention. During the late 1940s and early 1950s some of these reports were aimed at segregation within the profession. Potentially these reports were controversial, for they pointed out some basic issues that existed between the white and the Negro teachers; but the delegates

always adopted the reports with little or no comment and allowed
the Joint Committee's efforts to die a rapid and silent death.

With the creation of the Joint Committee, a few Negroes were
able to participate in some aspects of the NEA conventions; however, these people were not considered delegates to the Representative Assembly. Essentially this was the only real commitment
the NEA made with the Negroes until World War II. The war
placed the American treatment of the Negro in the spotlight,
causing many people to have some guilt feelings over this in-
justice. This writer suspected that many NEA delegates were also
embarrassed and bothered by the same matter, and at the 1943
convention they took some action in an attempt to square the
democratic teaching profession with reality.[21] Mr. Burton Henry
of California proposed the following resolution. "Be it resolved,
that in choosing a city for its conventions the National Education
Association shall see to it that only those cities shall be selected
where it is possible to make provisions, without discrimination,
for the housing, feeding, seating at the convention, and general welfare of all the delegates, and teachers regardless of race, color,
or creed."[22]

An immediate attempt was made to refer the resolution to the
Executive Committee for additional study, but numerous delegates
opposed this move. Miss Mary Ann Weeks of Missouri moved to
amend the resolution by striking out "without discrimination" and
inserting "dignified" before the word "provisions."[23] She told the
delegates that she had always been able to find good accommodations for Negroes, thus allowing the NEA "to bring to them the
benefits of our convention."[24] She feared that if the amendment
passed the NEA could not meet "where people need to hear this
subject discussed."[25]

Henry admitted that the NEA had not held its recent meetings
in a completely segregated city but that many cities maintained
varying degrees of segregation; therefore, he advocated that the
NEA adopt a policy "that we refuse to allow certain conditions to
exist in reference to our convention."[26] Henry cited the AFT conventions that were held in Washington, D.C., and Saint Louis,
Missouri, where discriminatory bars had been lowered while its

convention was in progress. Henry pointed out that the NEA could follow the union's example.

Miss Ethel Grubbs, a Negro teacher from Washington, D.C., backed Henry's resolution. She told the delegates of the problems of attending a convention in a segregated city: "I have to live miles away from the convention; I never get home during the lunch period to have any relaxation."[27] She objected to the word "dignified" because she felt it had no reference to her: "When you come to a convention and feel that remarks made about democracy do not refer to you, I feel that a real stand should be taken on the matter, once and for all."[28]

Mr. Robert White, a Californian, advocated tabling the resolution for further study "or else face the possibility of splitting the NEA wide-open."[29] Mr. James Haslam of Utah proposed a substitute motion: "That we look with disfavor upon any racial discrimination whatsoever."[30] Reaction was immediate and unfavorable, but much confusion existed among the delegates. A resolution, an amendment to the resolution, and a substitute resolution were pending before the delegates. Debate was closed and the president called for a voice vote on the three items. The delegates defeated the substitute resolution. The amendment to the original resolution suffered the same fate, while they passed Henry's resolution.

The debate proved interesting because the arguments would have relevance to the integration debates that engulfed the NEA after 1954. First, it is interesting to note that the drive for change came from the members and not from the leadership of the NEA. Second, it is quite significant that the delegates were aware of the AFT's integration position regarding selection of convention sites. Finally, some delegates feared that the NEA would be destroyed if it took a firm stand upon integration. This last point became a fully orchestrated chorus, skillfully played with many themes and variations after 1954.

For the next five years the integration matter lay dormant, but the NEA Board of Directors brought the matter up for reexamination when this body selected Saint Louis, Missouri, as the site for the 1950 convention. Chicago and Saint Louis were the only cities under consideration, and the Board ruled out Chicago when it realized that charges for convention rental facilities were greater in Chicago.[31] This brought immediate delegate reaction because many felt that Saint Louis could not meet the necessary requirements of the 1943 resolution. Mr. Irving Pearson, a state director from Illinois, raised some doubts about the selection at a Board meeting, July 4, 1949. Karl Berns, assistant executive secretary of the NEA, assured the directors that no racial discrimination would occur "in the convention hall, convention hall restaurant and meeting places, in public meeting places in hotels, and meal functions in the hotels."[32]

This assurance did not calm the delegates who opposed Saint Louis as the convention site, and the controversy boiled over onto the floor of the Delegate Assembly on July 7, 1949. Many of the delegates were unsure as to the course of action that they would follow. Mrs. Johanna Lindlof asked the NEA Parliamentarian about the Board's right to select the convention site. He replied that the NEA Bylaws grant this power to the Board, but if the delegates wished to change the Bylaws, they would have to give their intent to do so in 1949 so that the matter could be decided in the next convention. Mrs. Lindlof indicated that was not her plan, but she voiced a resentment of the Board's ignoring the mandate of the delegates: "I do not believe that you need a change in the constitution in order for the Board of Directors to take the orders of the Delegate Assembly in regard to the place where they must choose. We do not take the power away from them of choosing a proper place, but we have indicated a proper place to hold the conventions of the NEA."[33]

Later the Joint Committee of the NEA-ATA gave its report to the delegates and the Joint Committee brought up the matter again:

> In view of the increased participation of Negro delegates in the Representative Assembly and in the spirit of action taken at the Indianapolis meeting in 1943, concern was expressed that all members of the NEA be able to participate in future Representative Assembly meetings without embarrassment due to discriminatory practices which have existed in certain cities. The question was particularly raised in connection with St. Louis as a probable 1950 meeting place.[34]

Shortly after the Joint Committee report, Mr. Robert Clark from Pennsylvania moved to have the Representative Assembly ask the Board to reconsider Saint Louis as the site for the convention. Mrs. Anna Pike Haas seconded the motion. Mr. Pearson, a Board member from Illinois, supported the Board's position, pointing out that the cost factor was too high in Chicago and that Saint Louis was the only remaining city available for the convention. At this point, Mrs. Haas dropped a bombshell. She read a telegram from the executive secretary of the Philadelphia Convention Bureau inviting the NEA to hold its 1950 convention in Philadelphia and the bureau promised to "assist your national officers and local committees to the fullest extent."[35]

Mrs. Lindlof supported the resolution, but in doing so, she also advocated a more dominant role of the Representative Assembly:

> We are the people, the representatives of the people of the NEA, and if we here request the Board of Directors or whoever it is to decide according to the rules to hold a convention in a proper kind of place where democratic ideals can be carried out, where no discrimination will be practiced against any of the delegates or any of our visitors, I cannot believe but that we have that power here, and that our Board of Directors will be guided and act according to that resolution.[36]

Mrs. Russell of New York added that at a recent AASA conference in Saint Louis a very prominent Negro educator from the University of Chicago could not find suitable accommodations because of his race. She told the delegates: "I think that in that case we should very seriously consider that we do not accept the concept of comparable accommodations on a segregated basis for any members of this organization in any place in which we go."[37] At this point, the delegates voted acceptance of Mr. Clark's resolution.

The next day the delegates continued their assault upon the Board's right to select the future convention sites. Mrs. Haas proposed an amendment to the NEA Bylaws that added the following statement to the end of the first sentence of Article VI, Section 1: ". . . provided, however that in choosing the site of these meetings only the cities shall be considered where it is possible to make provisions without discrimination for the housing, feeding, seating at the meeting, and general welfare, of all the members of the Association."[38] This amendment to the Bylaws would lie before the NEA for a year and would be decided upon by the delegates to the Representative Assembly in 1950.

That evening the Board of Directors met to discuss the request of the Representative Assembly to reconsider the site for the 1950 convention. Karl Berns assured the Board that no discrimination would be practiced in any of the convention facilities at Saint Louis. Mrs. Haas was invited to read her telegram from Philadelphia officials asking the NEA to come to that city in 1950. Some discussion followed as to the difficulty of finding any city completely free from discrimination. Since the Board of Directors had already selected Saint Louis, some directors felt the NEA had a moral obligation to fulfill its obligation. H. V. Cooper of Mississippi made a motion to keep Saint Louis as the 1950 convention city. A roll call vote followed in which forty-two directors supported the motion, and four abstained.[39] Then the directors closed ranks by indicating that they would do everything in their power to make the 1950 convention the most successful in the history of the Association.

Immediately after the 1949 convention, the Executive Committee ordered the NEA staff to make a survey of all the major convention cities in the United States in order to determine which cities could meet the amendment to the Bylaws proposed by Mrs. Haas. The staff reported that few cities met the requirements; therefore, the Executive Committee proposed a substitute amendment to the Bylaws that it hoped would retain "the spirit and the purpose of the original amendment without involving us in possible legal complications by trying to select a convention city which cannot live up to the will of the original amendment."[40] This substitute amendment read as follows: ". . . that in choosing the site for the meetings only those cities shall be considered when it is possible to provide a maximum degree of equality for the housing, feeding, seating at the meetings, and for the general welfare of all the members of this Association."[41]

This amendment was introduced at the 1950 convention and precipitated a sharp floor fight, but the debate showed that Mrs.

Haas' backers were speaking as individuals and not as members of their state delegations.[42] Instead, the powerful state delegations rallied to the defense of the Executive Committee and the Board of Directors. Many delegates feared that if Mrs. Haas' amendment were passed, the number of possible NEA convention sites would be drastically reduced, thus causing harm for the Association. Mrs. Grubbs opposed the substitute amendment and pointed out that no one could really define "maximum degree of equality." After she spoke, six people representing different sections of the country supported the Executive Committee's position. The strongest blow against Mrs. Haas' amendment came when Robert Clark, who in the 1949 convention sponsored the Representative Assembly's motion for the Board of Directors to reconsider its decision concerning the 1950 convention site, abandoned his previous position and supported the organizational stand. Clark admitted his error in opposing the Board because segregation existed in most areas of the country, thus making it impossible to implement his motion; therefore, Clark supported the substitute amendment prepared by the Board of Directors and the Executive Committee because the amendment would continue to further democracy in the country: "I look upon this amendment, as now amended by the Board of Directors, as one way in which this great Association can keep its eyes high, look far into the future, and achieve an increasing measure of the sort of democracy we all want. I, therefore, would like to put myself, if it will clear myself a bit more, behind the amendment."[43] The president, Andrew Holt from Tennessee, put the substitute motion before the delegates, and they passed it with no further debate.

The arguments regarding segregated facilities of the convention cities represented a basic uneasiness many of the delegates felt concerning the relationships between the NEA and the Negro teacher. While this issue had captured much of the delegate interest, the Association, in a less spectacular way, was moving to involve more Negroes in NEA activities. NEA membership had always been open to Negroes, and some had been participating in NEA conventions during the 1940s.[44] The Representative Assembly's membership included thirty-seven Negroes at the 1949 convention.[45] Most of these people came from the North and the West. Although a Negro

teacher from the South could belong to the NEA, he was excluded
from representation in the Association since many state associations
had membership bars that denied a Negro teacher membership in
the state and local associations.

The Joint Committee of the NEA-ATA had been working on
this matter since 1949. Finally in 1951, the Joint Committee proposed to the NEA Executive Committee the creation of "a second
state association if members of that association are not eligible to be
active members of the already recognized affiliated state association."[46] Thus the concept of the dual affiliates was born. After a
short study to make sure that the dual affiliates did not conflict with
the Bylaws, the Executive Committee implemented the request,
thus allowing representation of nine Negro state organizations during the 1951 convention.[47] The following year the Negro delegation
increased to 150 members,[48] and a Negro, George Gore, was elected
as one of the eleven NEA vice-presidents.[49] By the end of 1953,
Alabama, Arkansas, District of Columbia, Florida, Georgia, Kentucky, Louisiana, Mississippi, North Carolina, Oklahoma, South
Carolina, Tennessee, Texas, Virginia, and West Virginia had established dual affiliates with the NEA. Willard Givens, executive secretary of the NEA, voiced the uneasiness many delegates seemed to
share over the creation of the dual affiliates when he recommended
the continuation of these organizations in the southern states:
"That until the day arrives when all teachers are eligible to belong
to one state association, the present form of relationship will be
continued."[50] This arrangement seemed to be the only way in
which the NEA was willing to cope with the racial situation at the
state and local levels.

This period witnessed the beginning of the successful efforts of
the Negroes to gain some redress from segregation through legal
proceedings. The Gaines Case, *Sweatt* v. *Painter,* and *McLaurin* v.
The Oklahoma Board of Regents paved the way involving the
desegregation of public elementary and secondary schools in the
United States.

During this period the NEA made some very cautious progress
that involved the Negro teacher in Association activities. The Joint
Committee of the NEA-ATA provided a dialogue between the black

and the white teachers. The 1943 resolution requiring integrated cities as convention sites was a spontaneous burst of democratic progress. The creation of the dual affiliates in 1951 brought more Negroes into the Association, but the dual affiliates also served as a harsh reminder of the realities of segregation.

The NEA still remained a conservative organization. The changes that did occur came from the members and not from the leadership of the organization. In fact, the Executive Committee and the Board of Directors blunted the 1943 resolution quite effectively when they selected Saint Louis as the 1950 convention site. This action brought to the surface a basic unrest some delegates had concerning the governing bodies of the NEA. This seems to be a recurring characteristic of the NEA, and delegate dissatisfaction ebbs and flows depending upon the particular issue.

Finally, one must note the silence of the NEA in regard to the battle over the desegregation issue that had engulfed the nation by 1953. The NEA had not uttered one word on this matter even though some influential people in the South had threatened to destroy the public school system if desegregation occurred. Since the NEA had a vested interest in public education, this silence was ominous because it offered a portent of the future.

The NEA and the Black Teacher from 1954 to 1960 | 4

There is danger in reckless change; but greater danger in blind conservatism.   HENRY GEORGE

DEVELOPMENTS IN 1954

On May 17, 1954, the Supreme Court of the United States issued a momentous decision, *Brown* v. *The Board of Education,* striking down racial segregation in the public schools of America. This edict reversed the "separate but equal" doctrine that had existed since 1896 and emphasized that segregation deprives children of the equal education opportunities in a democratic society. In the majority opinion, Chief Justice Earl Warren reasserted the basic American principle that all men are created equal.

Generally, Americans hailed the decision as long overdue. *Time* magazine called it the most important ruling since the Dred Scott decision in 1857 and claimed that the decision would affect the lives of over twelve million children in twenty-one states.[1] Dr. Harold Taylor, president of Sarah Lawrence College, referred to it as one of the most important decisions ever reached by the Supreme Court.[2] *Nation's Schools,* in an editorial, called the edict "a significant marker" on the road to equality.[3] Dave Gillespie, editor of the *Gaston Citizen,* a newspaper in Gastonia, North Carolina, told Edward R. Murrow, that "all parts of the country, not only the South, should do some real soul searching."[4] Dr. Arthur Adams, president of the American Council of Education, while hailing the decision, raised a significant point: "An important question," asked Dr. Adams, "that must be answered is how will the areas affected accept the decision?"[5]

This question had particular relevance since forces in the South were already being organized to oppose the high court ruling. Senator Richard Russell of Georgia attacked the court for assuming legislative duties unwarranted by the Constitution, and his state, under the leadership of Governor Herman Talmadge, prepared legislation for the creation of a state wide system of private schools.[6] Mississippi and Louisiana planned similar action to circumvent the court. The governor of Virginia organized a thirty-two man commission to study ways to avoid desegregation legally.[7]

William A. Early, president of the NEA and superintendent of schools in Savannah, Georgia, said that he expected the public schools to continue regardless of the legislature's action. Then, speaking as superintendent of schools of Savannah and not as president of the NEA, Early said that the dual system will "operate until they receive specific instructions from the State Attorney General's office."[8]

While the opinion of the court appealed to the spirit of American fair play, however, it is doubtful whether most people really grasped the revolutionary significance of this ruling until much later. For example, the Rotarians of Savannah, Georgia, heard of the decision while having their weekly luncheon. The *New York Times* reported that some applauded while most seemed unconcerned. One person remarked, "It's a good thing. We can now practice the true Christian principle of brotherhood."[9]

The 1954 NEA Convention

Six weeks after the historic court decision, the NEA held its annual convention at Madison Square Garden in New York City. The weather was hot and it rained almost every day, but neither the heat nor the lingering smell from the recently departed circus seemed to dampen the spirits of the nearly 20,000 people who attended the meetings.[10] Ralph Bunche, Grayson Kirk, Ralph Sockman, and Samuel Brownell addressed the convention, and the delegates wrestled with the pressing problems confronting the organization. Federal aid for school construction enjoyed the highest priority and was closely followed by academic freedom in the classroom. Higher teachers' salaries remained a perennial demand of the group.

William G. Carr, executive secretary of the NEA, began the business meetings of the Representative Assembly on Monday evening, June 28. His report covered the entire spectrum of Association business, but in the last quarter of his presentation he specifically highlighted three unresolved matters requiring attention of the NEA. They were: (a) the work of the Reece Committee that was investigating tax exempt foundations and associations; (b) the recent decision of the Supreme Court regarding segregation; and (c) the outlook for federal aid to education.

Concerning segregation, Dr. Carr briefly reviewed the decision and placed the NEA at the vanguard of progressive action by proclaiming:

> The Association is already on record as flatly opposed to any form of educational discrimination. The Supreme Court has now ruled, in substance, that to require segregation is to discriminate. The Platform of the Association also requires that teachers should suffer no discrimination because of race or color. Furthermore your Platform has for many years carried a declaration that each school should provide a complete system of public schools from public funds.[11]

Carr also pointed out that the court did not tell the litigants how the decision would be carried out. He expected the guidelines to be forthcoming within the next year; therefore, he advised that the Association delay further action on this matter until the court issued specific plans for implementation of the decision. He said: "The Representative Assembly of 1955 will be in a position to know how the national Association may, upon request, assist our state and local associations to give effect to our well established policies in line with the decrees of the court."[12]

The Representative Assembly came to grips with the resolution on segregation in the public schools on the morning of July 2. This resolution was one of thirty-four resolutions presented to the delegates that morning, and it did not consume any more of the delegates' time than did the discussions over the resolutions concerning teacher retirement and social security or state and White House conferences on education. All of the resolutions cleared the Assembly in less than four hours.[13]

Benjamin Fine of the *New York Times* reported that, "The segregation resolution caused sharp debate in the Resolutions Committee," but only two criticisms arose when floor debate began. Herbert
A. Marshall, a delegate from South Carolina, said that the resolution was premature because "the court had not handed down a decree as to how or when or if this is to be done."[14] He asked the
Assembly to withhold action, but since this was not placed in the
form of a motion, the delegates ignored his request.

What little debate there was on the resolution occurred between
Dr. Robert Wayne Clark of Pennsylvania and Francis W. Beedon,
chairman of the Resolutions Commitee, concerning the wording of
the first phrase of the resolution. Although Clark won his point, the
exchange between the men was polite, and afterwards Beedom admitted that the resolution was probably improved.[15]

The opening phrase of the resolution as proposed by the Resolutions Committee read: "Pursuant to the recent decision of the
Supreme Court of the United States with regard to racial segregation."[16] Clark wanted to remove this phrase in order to show, "That
the thinking of the educational profession of America depends in
no degree, and in no manner upon the decision of the Supreme
Court."[17] Clark eliminated this phrase and presented his amended
version to the convention. The delegates immediately accepted the
resolution with only two state delegations, Mississippi and South
Carolina, dissenting.[18]

The approved resolution read:

> The principle embodied in the recent decision of the Supreme Court
> of the United States in regard to racial segregation is reflected in
> the long established provisions of the Platform of the National Ed-
> ucation Association. The Association recognizes that integration of
> all groups in our public schools is more than an idea. It is a pro-
> cess which affects every state and territory in our nation. The Associa-
> tion urges that all citizens approach this matter of integration in
> our public schools with the spirit of fair play and good will which
> has always been the outstanding characteristic of the American peo-
> ple. It is the conviction of the Association that all problems of in-
> tegration in our schools are capable of solution by citizens of in-
> telligence, saneness, and reasonableness working together in the in-
> terests of national unity for the common good of all.[19]

Reaction to the NEA Integration Resolution

This marked the first time that the NEA took an official stand on segregation in America. The South was well represented at the convention, and both the president, William Early, and the president-elect, Miss Waurine Walker, lived in Georgia and Texas respectively. Significantly, the delegations from forty-six states voted for the resolution and many of these states had segregation within their confines. It should also be recalled that in 1954 the NEA had fifteen states maintaining dual educational organizations.[20] The *New York Times* congratulated the teachers on their stand against segregation and said that perhaps now children might "learn mutual tolerance in many schools where they formerly have not had that lesson."[21]

Close examination, however, reveals that the Association recognized only that integration "is more than an idea" but "is a process" affecting all of the states of the United States. The resolution did not endorse the Supreme Court decision, but, as Dr. Carr did in his opening address to the Assembly, it skillfully placed the Association ahead of the action of the Supreme Court.

A better understanding of the official reaction of the NEA results from examining the *NEA Journal's* report of the convention highlights. The magazine made only a few references to the Supreme Court decision on the segregation resolution accepted by the delegates, and they were generally buried within the magazine.[22] The text of the Supreme Court decision was printed but with no comment at all.[23]

Only one reference to the Supreme Court ruling appeared in the minutes of the Board of Directors and the Executive Committee, and this occurred in an indirect manner. Originally, John Foster Dulles was to have been the major speaker at the convention, but because of international matters he had to withdraw. The minutes showed that Richard Nixon, Henry Cabot Lodge, and others were contacted to give the keynote address but all declined; therefore, the Executive Committee decided to have Carr include in his report to the Assembly comments about the Reece Committee, the Supreme Court decision, and federal aid to education. Carr outlined his comments about the Reece Committee and school desegregation, and the Committee approved them.[24]

DEVELOPMENTS IN 1955

As indicated previously, soon after the court issued its decree on school desegregation, opposition arose in defense of the status quo. Of course, most reports after 1954 focused attention upon the integration of students, while far less attention was given to the integration of teachers. But by 1955, this matter was beginning to assume significance. J. Rupert Picott, NEA vice-president and executive secretary of the Virginia Education Association, a Negro organization, reported that the teachers in Prince Edward County had not received their contracts for the 1955–1956 school year.[25] West Virginia closed nineteen Negro schools and fifteen black teachers lost their positions.[26] Many Negroes in the rural sections of Missouri were not rehired for the forthcoming school year. The attorney general of Georgia planned to use the loyalty oath that all teachers had to sign as a means of eliminating teachers favorable to integration. All teachers were to swear to be loyal to the constitutions of Georgia and the United States. A person believing in the court decision on integration or belonging to the NAACP would be considered disloyal and be dismissed.[27] Herbert Doddy reported that many states in the deep South were placing the positions of black teachers in jeopardy, and in doing so, "These states are defying the Supreme Court of the United States, the highest law in the land, and denying the democratic spirit of fair play and equal opportunity."[28] The year following the 1954 court decision generally showed that cities with large Negro populations and tenure laws had at least made token integration; but in smaller communities, this was not the case. In rural areas Negro teachers were actually losing their jobs. For example, the West Virginia superintendent of schools sent out the following directive to the local districts: "Where attendance falls below the minimum, schools might be closed, pupils sent to another school and pay of the teacher in the school closed discontinued."[29]

Myron Lieberman, a professor from the University of Oklahoma, maintained that the NEA must take action in the forthcoming convention to give aid to the black teachers who had lost their jobs over the integration crisis.[30] He charged that neither the NEA nor any of its affiliates took any active role in the Supreme Court cases on segregation of the schools and stressed that this inactivity was "a serious abdication of professional responsibility on the part of the Association."[31] He proposed that the NEA adopt a strong stand against racial segregation in the country.

The 1955 NEA Convention

Amid this background, the NEA convention met at Chicago, Illinois, July 3–8. Almost 4,800 delegates attended and total attendance reached 10,000 people. The theme was "America's Main Power: Educated Manpower," and President Waurine Walker addressed the convention upon this subject. Adlai Stevenson, former governor of Illinois, and Harold Stassen, advisor to President Eisenhower, gave the principal addresses.

Major emphasis of the convention was securing federal aid to education, and Stevenson devoted his whole speech to the topic. In a speech interrupted many times with applause, Stevenson proposed that the federal government spend at least four billion dollars a year on aid to public schools.[32] When he concluded, the convention accorded him a standing ovation.

The NEA Building Fund and plans for the centennial of the NEA also occupied important places upon the agenda. At one point in the convention, President Walker interrupted the proceedings and announced to the delegates that the NEA Building Fund had just reached $3,000,158.34, which amounted to sixty percent of the overall goal for the building fund. John H. Starie called this interruption "one of the most dramatic moments in recent NEA history."[33]

Dr. Carr gave a long address to the convention on the state of affairs of the NEA.[34] About forty percent of the report concerned the day-to-day business transactions of the Association, while at least twenty percent related to some aspect of the relationship of the NEA with the federal government with chief emphasis upon the need for federal aid.

He touched briefly upon the segregation issue by pointing out to the delegates that the Supreme Court had remanded to the federal district courts the task of determining the schedule of school desegregation. He told the delegates that last year's convention had accepted a resolution on integration and concluded his remarks on the subject by saying:

> Thus the position of the Association is already clear. It is in my judgment very doubtful whether further declaration of policy is necessary at this time. It would be a deception for your executive secretary to give an annual report which ignored recent decisions. It would be equally unfortunate to allow them to monopolize our attention. Many things need to be done in American education. Success in these matters will require a greater national unity in our profession.[35]

This comment was most significant because it represented the basic NEA position on this matter. Recognizing the inherent dangers of this issue, Carr asked for Association unity, and in doing so, he indicated that the NEA would pursue less controversial subjects such as federal aid to public education, while placing on the shelf the active quest for integration in the Amercian public schools.

This concept was borne out when the Representative Assembly received for debate NEA Resolution Number Five: Integration in the Public Schools. Clyde Phillips, chairman of the Committee on Resolutions, proposed that the following resolution be adopted by the convention:

> The National Education Association recognizes that integration of all groups in our public schools is a process which concerns every state and territory in our nation.
> The Association urges that all citizens approach this matter of integration in a spirit of fair play and good will which has always been the outstanding characteristic of the American people. It is the conviction of the Association that all problems of integration in our schools are capable of solution at the state and local level by citizens of intelligence, saneness, and reasonableness working together in the interest of national unity for the common good of all.[36]

After Phillip's resolution was seconded, Walter Ludwig, a delegate from New York, moved to amend the resolution by adding to paragraph one the following amendment: "Of particular concern is the application of the principle of equality of opportunity in the appointment of teachers and other personnel."[37] This amendment had reference to the problems of black teachers in some states since the Supreme Court decision. Phillips disagreed with this amendment, pointing out that the platform already contained a clause protecting the individual teacher from discrimination. Elmer Tron, from New York, opposed Ludwig's amendment by arguing, "that the Committee on Resolutions has studied this matter very carefully, and that they attempted to avoid any friction by a careful wording of the resolution."[38] Dr. William L. Green, executive secretary of the North Carolina Teachers Association, a black organization, supported Ludwig's position. He said that the amendment would help ease the teacher shortage in many of the areas confronted by this matter. William Eshelman, vice-chairman of the Committee on Resolutions, rose to lend organizational support to Phillips. Eshelman advocated peace and unity with the Association. He argued:

> I would like to appeal to you that in America, in the NEA, we need a lot of unifying influence rather than devisive influence and even though we believe in this particular amendment because we have it in our Platform, pointing it up at this particular time would in our opinion have nothing but a divisive effect, and we cannot afford to divide a great organization like the NEA.[39]

President Walker closed debate and the delegates defeated Ludwig's amendment. John W. Buckner, of Illinois, attempted to change the first sentence of the resolution to read, the National Education Association "approves" rather than "recognizes," but this was defeated very easily with practically no debate.[40] C. B. Nuckoll supported the original resolution and suggested "that we leave it as it is. . . . and go down the street together and we will work out the problem in the name of all American children."[41] Walker called for a vote, and the delegates accepted the resolution in a voice vote.

Reaction to the NEA Integration Resolution

Feelings ran very high during the debate on the resolution. Benjamin Fine reported the resolution pleased no one. He said,

"The people of the North did not believe that it went far enough while the South insisted that it went too far." This was, however, as far as the organization chose to go with integration at this time for fear of dividing the Association.

The extent to which the Association played down the segregation crisis within its ranks can be seen by an examination of the 1955 *NEA Journal*. The magazine did not carry any articles concerning the Supreme Court decisions and its impact upon the country. It did not make any reference to the plight of many black teachers, some of whom were NEA members, who were affected by the consequences of the court decisions. A few pages were devoted to the Chicago convention, but the editor scrupulously avoided anything deemed controversial.

Each issue of the magazine contained about two pages devoted to current educational news called "News and Trends." This was the only section of the magazine that touched upon the subject, and these items appeared without any editorial comment. In May 1955, the column reported that in the regional meetings of the American Association of School Administrators, the members agreed upon nine resolutions concerning public education in America, and one of the nine was the same resolution passed by the 1954 NEA convention.[42] The September 1955 column had a four paragraph report on the Supreme Court remanding to the federal district courts implementation of the desegregation cases.[43] The October column carried short releases upon the resolutions passed at the 1955 NEA convention. It featured resolutions on teachers' salaries and fundamental freedom of teachers but did not mention the integration resolution.[44]

Regardless of the NEA's official stance on integration, which for all intents and purposes was one of calculated silence, the convention at Chicago showed that division of the ranks existed. The resolution passed was virtually the same as the one passed in 1954. The debate was longer, however, and the militants began, though ever so slightly, to rock the "New Ark." Dr. Carr recognized the danger of the issue when he asked for unity within the Association. Numerous other people took up the call and their pleas prevailed, thus keeping intact the original resolution proposed by the Commmittee on Resolutions. The organizational forces were still in control, but it was obvious that rough seas were ahead for the NEA "Ark."

DEVELOPMENTS IN 1956

Most states that practiced segregation prior to *Brown* v. *the Board of Education* refused to comply with the court or made only token efforts at school integration. Alabama, South Carolina, Georgia, Florida, Louisiana, and Mississippi continued their hard core policy toward integration, while in three states, North Carolina, Virginia, and Tennessee, one or more school boards made some plans for integration.[45] William A. Bender spoke of the resistance of the South by citing Mississippi as a typical example: "The naked truth is that Mississippi does not want to do so [integrate] and has no intention of making a move to that end now or in the years of the future."[46] J. Rupert Picott reported that no city or county in Virginia had desegregated.[47]

The plight of the black teacher generally reflected the total picture of integration in these areas. Preston Valien reported that sixty Negro teachers were dismissed in Kentucky, and at the same time, black teachers lost their positions in Moberly, Slater, and Hannibal, Missouri. Oklahoma integrated no Negro teachers, but on the other hand 165 Negro teachers lost their positions. Nineteen Negroes lost their jobs in Texas and no integration of faculties occurred.[48]

In South Carolina, black teachers underwent similar problems but with a different twist taken by school officials. Teachers had to fill out applications with questions asking whether they supported integration or whether they or any of their relatives belonged to the NAACP. If they answered in the affirmative, the school district provided them with prepared resignation letters, which they had to sign. In addition to this, the form was self-incriminating in that it was a crime to belong to the NAACP, punishable by a fine of $100. In Orangeburg, South Carolina, eleven teachers and one principal lost their jobs in this manner.[49]

In North Carolina, things were almost as bad. The state tenure law was abandoned, and subsequently all teachers had to reapply for their positions. Any teacher supporting integration found his teaching position in danger.

The 1956 NEA Convention

Within this backdrop of unrest, footdragging, and absolute contempt of the Supreme Court's decision, the NEA met in its annual convention at Portland, Oregon, July 1 to July 6, 1956. Almost 4,400 delegates were on hand with total attendance reaching nearly 9,000 people. John Lester Buford's presidential address focused upon the theme of the convention, "Proud to Teach." Eric Johnston, president of the Motion Picture Association of America, and Lee DuBridge, president of California Institute of Technology, gave the main addresses.[50]

On July 4, William Carr gave his annual report to the delegates. He centered his report around "the ten major events in the work of the Association during the past year."[51] Seven events dealt with the growth of the NEA or the advancement of the profession; two items pertained to federal aid to education; and the last important event stressed public relations. Not once did Dr. Carr mention segregation in the United States. In fact, none of the speakers who addressed the convention made reference to the segregation issue.

Official silence did not quell the people who wanted the NEA to take a more positive stand on integration. On June 30, Myron Lieberman, a delegate to the convention representing the Oklahoma Association of Negro teachers, chaired an informal committee whose major purpose was to bring about a stronger NEA stand against segregation. His committee advocated three major points that they hoped to have the Association adopt. They were: (a) the NEA must support integration; (b) the NEA must establish a $50,000 defense fund to aid teachers who have lost their jobs because of views on integration; and (c) the NEA must condemn hiring practices based upon racial or religious beliefs.[52] Lieberman intended to present these demands to the Committee on Resolutions but conceded that they did not have much of a chance. He vowed that a floor fight was inevitable.[53]

This seemed to be the consensus of his supporters, as they began to draw battlelines for the floor fight. While obviously not enjoying numerical superiority within the organization of over 600,000 active members, 25,000 Negro teachers were members of the Association while over 75,000 Negro teachers were affiliated with the NEA. William Green, executive secretary of the North Carolina Teachers Association, a black organization consisting of over 10,000 teachers, indicated that he was prepared for a floor fight.[54] Other people began to use a word hitherto not mentioned in regard to an integration resolution. If the NEA were to adopt a strong stand against segregation, this action would provide a strong "moral" example to other civic and educational groups within the country.

The people advocating a strong integration stance by the NEA might have had much moral commitment on their side, but they did not have key positions within the organizational structure of the convention. W. W. Eshelman was the chairman of the Committee on Resolutions, and no one doubted his position on the matter. It was he who spoke in defense of the 1955 resolution stressing peace and unity in the Association. The organization was well prepared to cope with this challenge.

Organizational control became evident when the Department of Classroom Teachers, the largest department within the organizational structure of the Association, met July 2, and adopted an integration resolution similar to the one adopted by the convention in 1955. The DCT defeated an amendment that stated, "The process of integration . . . be basic to the American way of life."[55] Some delegates referred to the DCT's position as "weak and pussyfooting.[56] This was the first test of the organizational forces. At this point, Benjamin Fine recognized the power of the organization when he said, "It appears unlikely that the NEA will change its stand."[57] The following day the Committee on Resolutions accepted a mild resolution on integration. The Representative Assembly passed the resolution as written without any debate from the floor. The bitter floor fight just did not materialize. The advocates of a strong resolution did not get any organizational support from the delegates just as they had failed to secure support in the preliminary stages of the battle. Never before had the Association been as divided over an issue, and many delegates feared that a stronger stand against segregation would destroy the Association.

Reaction to the NEA Resolution

The Association had been spared, but at a heavy cost. The issue was dead only for 1956. The proponents of a tough stand against segregation vowed that they would be back in Philadelphia at the 1957 convention. The Georgia delegation wanted the official records to show that twenty-two delegates voted for the resolution, thirty-nine voted against the resolution, while fifty-five of the delegates were not present for the final vote.[58] F. D. Moon, executive secretary of the Oklahoma Association of Negro Teachers, said, "Non-segregation is the law of the land. How can the NEA ignore this fact?"[59] The most severe criticism leveled at the NEA came from *America,* a weekly review:

> NEA is shooting for the 1,000,000 member mark. They ducked the great moral issue of segregated schools. For fear of losing members and not attracting new ones, the NEA sidestepped this question with what can charitably be called a very mild resolution, toothless enough to draw ayes from the stalwart white supremacists. NEA has thus missed a unique opportunity to stand up and be counted at the very moment when statesmanship of education was sorely needed . . . NEA can blame the nearsightedness of its governing clique.[60]

If an individual had read carefully the *NEA Journal* during 1956, he would not have been surprised at what transpired at Chicago during the convention. No article on integration occurred during the year. Probably the major story of the year was the defeat of the Kelley Bill in the United States House of Representatives.[61] The bill provided for large grants of federal aid to education. The article pinpointed many villains, such as the United States Chamber of Commerce, the National Association of Manufacturers, and the American Farm Bureau; but James McCaskill reserved his special wrath for the Powell Amendment attached to the bill. This amendment provided that no federal funds would go to states or districts maintaining segregation. He said, "The Powell Amendment more than anything else was the major contributing factor to the defeat of the Kelley Bill."[62] The editor chose to place this statement in heavy black print to emphasize it. The author also pointed out, "Keep in mind, however, that the adoption of the Powell Amendment prevented Southern members who favored the bill from voting for it."[63]

Federal aid to education was a controversial issue in the 1950s and probably many people believed that something had to be done to aid the public schools. The NEA did have a resolution in regard to segregation in the schools, and it did have a platform concerning hiring practices of personnel without regard to racial or religious differences. Apparently the governing body within the NEA felt no conflict of interest existed when it went all out for federal aid to education.

The "News and Trends" column throughout the year placed heavy emphasis upon NEA activity in regard to federal aid to education. This column also emphasized the activities of the World Confederation of Organization of the Teaching Profession, which Dr. Carr actively supported. The January column carried a short release reporting that in Virginia a referendum would be held calling for changes in the state constitution to decide whether children had to attend an integrated school. The article offended no one because both the advocates and the opponents of the referendum received six lines of space to present their views.[64] The following month, the column carried a brief statement that the referendum had won by a two to one majority.[65] No editorial comment followed concerning the grave implications of this matter. In September, the column made brief mention of the integration resolution passed at the convention. It stated, "After careful consideration of the conflicting points of view regarding the racial discrimination in the schools, the Association reaffirmed its position taken in 1955."[66]

DEVELOPMENTS IN 1957

The NEA celebrated its centennial in 1957. During its first century, the NEA had become the largest professional organization in the United States with a total membership reaching a little over 700,000 people. The Association's plans for a new multimillion dollar building in Washington, D.C., symbolized the progress of the teaching profession over the past 100 years and the expectations of the organization for the next century.

The NEA's huge organizational forces enabled it to serve teachers in many ways unknown to its members of fifty years before. During this interval the Association became the largest educational lobby in the nation and in the year of its centennial marshalled forces for a great drive to secure federal aid to education. Teachers benefited greatly from the publishing activities of the organization. During this same time the research division made significant contributions to the advancement of education and the improvement of the teaching profession.

Of course Washington, D.C., became the scene for the initial celebration honoring the NEA. President Eisenhower appeared at a testimonial banquet where he gave a glowing tribute to the organization. During the course of his presentation, President Eisenhower stressed the need for federal aid to public school construction.[67] The audience received his comments warmly. Four days later, the NEA family heard Howard Hansen direct the National Symphony Orchestra and the choir of Howard University in the world premiere of "Song of Democracy," which the NEA had commissioned Hansen to write commemorating the NEA centennial.[68]

Many periodicals of 1957 carried articles on the birthday of the Association, and two educational journals, *School and Society* and *Progressive Education,* devoted their entire publications to the NEA.[69] Both presented a critical examination of the Association, and they emphasized the NEA's stand upon the integration issue in America. The editor of *School and Society* accused the Association of trying to straddle the integration problem[70] while Lloyd P. Jorgenson charged that the NEA was ignoring the issue.[71]

William G. Carr defended the Association. He gave a glowing account of the NEA contributions to American education.[72] In the process he alluded to some of the internal problems of the organization and how he regarded them:

> NEA has demonstrated to the nation that unity and diversity can exist in one body. How much unity in America may be credited to the NEA, no one can say; but certainly the NEA's influence as one of the unifying forces should be respected and intelligently compromised when issues meet a showdown. Above all it should be noted that "diversity within unity" of the nation's teaching profession must carry an impact throughout its schools to successive generations of citizens.[73]

Carr continued by stressing how the NEA became the spokesman of education through its constant defense of teachers everywhere:

The NEA gives attention to the rights of teachers as citizens. Its Defense Commission investigates where there are issues involving the right of teachers to teach the truth as they see fit and to live by standards of respectability and civic responsibility set for citizens generally. The Defense Commission has set precedents by its reports on cases exposing abuses where local and state associations could not cope with the situation. Some of these reports have clarified for the whole nation issues involved in keeping our schools free—for we all hold that students cannot be free to learn where teachers are not free to teach. Thus, the NEA protects the personal welfare of the teacher when investigation shows them to be right, helps them to build a respect for the profession and wider understanding of how vital teachers' rights and securities are to the freedom of the people.[74]

Jorgenson and Lieberman disagreed with Dr. Carr's position. Jorgenson argued that many teachers in the United States were having very grave problems caused by their position on the integration crisis. He indicated that some states and many local and school districts employed several common forms of discrimination: (1) abolition of state tenure laws to allow for dismissal of black teachers; (2) intimidation of teachers who advocated integration; (3) employment on a racial basis; (4) membership in the NAACP as reason for dismissal; and (5) gerrymandering of school districts to preserve segregated districts.[75] Lieberman stressed that the NEA had the ability to investigate some of these charges through the Association's Committee on Tenure or the Committee on Professional Ethics, but he charged that these committees remained silent when asked to investigate such injustices.[76]

From 1954 to 1957 there was only one case regarding alleged racial discrimination that the NEA officially investigated. The California State Educational Association charged that some teachers in Clay, Kentucky, refused to meet with integrated classes. The NEA Commission on Defense of Democracy examined the charges and found the accusations to be false. The commission dismissed the charges.[77]

On the national scene, events still moved slowly against segregation. Many states ignored the Supreme Court decision, and a few states made only token integration, but Charles H. Thompson saw some encouraging signs.[78] He pointed to the changes in the Gallup Poll from 1954 to 1957 showing people's opinions regarding integration. In 1954, fifty-four percent of the people voiced approval of integration while forty-one percent expressed disapproval. By 1957 only thirty-one percent of the people questioned did not approve of integration while those people expressing approval increased to sixty-three percent. He also said that Negroes were developing good grass-roots leaders who were no longer being terrorized by acts of violence. Thompson reported that black ministers were going to jail because of their disagreement with the laws.[79] Most of the federal judges had upheld the legality of integration. Slowly the emphasis seemed to be changing from the questioning of the legality to the deep questioning of the morality of segregation. A new phase of the struggle was beginning.

The NEA held its annual convention at Philadelphia, Pennsylvania, the city of its birthplace. This convention was significant because it marked the official centennial anniversary of the Association. The United States Post Office Department evinced interest in the convention by placing on sale July 1, a three-cent stamp commemorating the NEA birthday. Many delegates made a pilgrimage to the Athenaum Building, where the NEA was founded in 1857.

Over 6,100 delegates attended the convention, whose theme was "An Educated People Moves Freedom Forward." Total attendance was nearly 20,000 people, and they heard major addresses by Richard Nixon, James B. Conant, and Bruce Catton. Federal aid to education occupied the center stage of attraction. Vice-President Nixon indicated that the chances for a federal aid bill in 1957 were not good and attributed segregation as a major culprit.[80] He indicated, however, that the administration would continue its support for federal aid and urged that the educators go home and begin campaigning immediately for a federal aid to education law.

The delegates took Nixon's advice. They voted a dues increase to ten dollars a year, thus increasing the NEA budget by over $3 million annually. Much of this budget increase was earmarked for a massive campaign to pressure Congress into passing federal aid. In fact, a grassroots organization to improve federal and state relations was a recipient of $500,000, while an additional $500,000 went to the public relations program designed to spotlight the need for additional appropriations to education from the federal government.[81]

So the convention moved almost placidly toward its concluding day in a birthday spirit characterized by near unanimity on the major topics. The spell was abruptly broken on the last day of the convention when the integration resolution came up for acceptance by the Representative Assembly. Until this time, integration was not on the agenda. In fact, only Vice-President Nixon had even mentioned it. When debate occurred, however, *Nation's Schools* referred to it as "an open display of the fifth of July fireworks."[82] The *New York Times* said, "The school integration split the National Education Association wide open today."[83]

The chairman of the Committee on Resolutions, Alma Theresa Link from Wisconsin, proposed the same resolution on integration as issued by the NEA conventions of 1955 and 1956. C. B. Nuckolls, a principal from Ashland, Kentucky, seconded the motion, and the fireworks promptly erupted. Zade Kenimer, a Georgia delegate, requested a roll call on the resolution and was turned down. Arthur Rice said that the Georgia delegation was split on the issue and a roll call was a means to identify publicly just where each Georgia delegate stood on the issue.[84] George Snyder, a California delegate, called the present resolution "innocuous" and proposed to amend the resolution by adding to the end of the resolution these statements:

> Believing that integration of all groups in the American public school is part of the concrete of that education which moves freedom forward, the Association recommends that all teachers assume special responsibility for the study, discussion, interpretation, and democratic action in regard to problems of group conflict; that state and local organizations serve as agents of reconciliation in resolving differences and that the good offices of the NEA and its departments be used in every possible way to promote good will and understanding necessary to peaceful change.[85]

Helen E. Holcomb of Washington seconded Snyder's amendment and Paul Whitehill, a New York delegate, spoke on behalf of the amendment. He chided the Resolutions Committee for proposing an amendment essentially the same as those passed in the two previous conventions and reminded the delegates that the convention's theme, "An Educated People Moves Freedom Forward," would have a hollow meaning unless they accepted Snyder's changes to the original resolution.[86]

William W. Eshelman rose to the defense of the original resolution. Eshelman employed the same arguments as he used in the 1956 floor debate, only this time there seemed to be a greater sense of urgency when he stressed Association unity:

> I personally feel, and I believe that it is the feeling of a large por-tion of the Representative Assembly that this statement on integra-tion is one of the real things that has kept the NEA together as a united force in solving one of the most perplexing problems in our society. As we go into the second century, I feel it would be good if we continue this statement to keep the Association together and definitely solve the problem. They are being solved at a very satis-factory rate, and this resolution definitely says a few things that will help us a great deal.[87]

Debate on the amendment was closed and a voice vote was taken. The amendment was defeated. Snyder called for a rising vote. The vote showed that the amendment lost by a fifteen to one ratio.[88]

Whitehall immediately countered with another amendment that struck out the words "which concerns" for the words "earnestly to be sought in" in the first paragraph so that the resolution would read: "The National Education Association recognizes that the unity of all groups in the public schools is a process earnestly to be sought in every state and territory in our nation."[89] At this point the organiza-tion brought out their biggest gun used to date in the integration controversy: George Deer, delegate from Louisiana, was the first member of the NEA Board of Directors to speak from the floor of the Assembly upon this subject. Deer advocated gradualism and argued that no outside resolution would solve the matter, for it must "be dealt with by those people who know it and understand it."[90] C. B. Nuckolls followed Deer and poured more water upon the spreading flames of discontent. In a rather emotional appeal, Nuckolls cried for fellowship, brotherhood, and understanding. He, too, advocated the gradual approach to the problem:

> I still have faith in America. I have faith in all its citizenry. I have faith in the people in the North and in the South. I really believe, being from the South, that the Southern people, and especially the South, will cooperate. It may take time, it is a process of develop-ment. But if we will be patient and work together, it will come about; that good will and harmony for one and all people will be seen in this solution and a total integrated program.[91]

Two more people spoke for Whitehill's amendment, while one person from Virginia attacked the change in the original resolution. Debate was closed. Whitehill's amendment was defeated by a rising vote. Then the delegates approved the original resolution proposed by the Resolutions Committee, and for the third successive year, the NEA's official position on integration in the public schools remained the same.

DEVELOPMENTS IN 1958

The events that occurred between the NEA conventions of 1957 and 1958 were swift and explosive, causing the spotlight of public attention to become fixed upon public education. In September 1957, the United States Congress passed the first civil rights bill since the Reconstruction Period following the Civil War. The bill pertained only to voting rights and fell short in other areas, but it was the first bill on civil rights in eighty-two years, and many people regarded it as the necessary first step toward equal political rights for Negroes. The second event that had profound influence upon education occurred not in the United States but in outer space. The Soviet Union had successfully orbited a satellite, thus shaking American confidence in the nation's technological primacy. The man on the street wondered how this country had been bypassed and asked, "Who is at fault?" Education gradually became the culprit. Critics such as Arthur Bestor had been pointing out that public education contained many weaknesses, and during this time these critics were joined by a new and powerful voice: Hyman Rickover. Public education became the target for a massive national inquiry into the failure of the United States to keep pace with the Soviet Union. But the difficulties had just begun to mount. Little Rock, Arkansas, became the symbol of the old, refusing to bend to the new way of life. Educators became totally enmeshed in this conflict, finding themselves unable to arrive at any complete accord upon this matter.

The 1958 NEA Convention

The NEA held its annual convention in Cleveland, Ohio, June 28 to July 4, 1958. Almost 4,700 delegates comprised the Representative Assembly. "Our Future Goes to School Today" served as the theme of the convention, and Lyman V. Ginger presented his presidential address upon this topic. Leroy Collins, governor of Florida, Max Lerner, professor of Brandeis University, and James Conant addressed the delegates. William G. Carr's annual report consisted virtually of a financial report to the delegates, placing emphasis upon the increased services of the NEA caused by the previous year's dues increase.

Continued emphasis upon acquiring federal aid to education prevailed. This topic occupied the major part of the delegates' attention. Lee Metcalf, coauthor of the Murray-Metcalf Bill, told the receptive delegates that there was nothing wrong with the schools that money could not solve.[92] During the last few days of the convention, the Association opened up a "briefing office" whereby the teachers received information as to how they might mobilize the people back home to lobby for federal aid.[93]

The integration resolution was not presented to the Assembly until the last day of the convention. Ben Kellner, chairman of the Resolutions Committee, presented the resolution for adoption, and C. B. Nuckolls seconded the motion. Since no discussion occurred, the resolution passed easily. The NEA had adopted for the fourth consecutive year the same resolution pertaining to integration in the public schools.

At the end of the Friday afternoon session, the next-to-the-last of the entire convention, Walter Ludwig jolted the Assembly away from the interest upon federal aid. He proposed that "the Representative Assembly recommend the appointment of a research committee to study problems of integration in our schools, at local, state and federal levels."[94] Also, he asked that this committee report to the Representative Assembly in 1959 with specific recommendations. This was a new tactic employed by Ludwig and potentially a dangerous one because of its emphasis upon a study at local and state levels of government.

Charles J. Sudduth, a Negro principal from San Pablos, California, seconded the motion while the delegates were still recovering from the verbal bombshell. Apparently, Ludwig and his followers planned the action well, because the first three people who spoke defended Ludwig's position. Then Ludwig rose to elaborate further upon his proposal:

This is a request for a study, a survey, and a report. Making a study is no new task for the NEA. For many years, the Association has set a high professional standard by research studies in many fields . . . We propose in this motion that during the coming year the Association commits itself to another area of study, the problems of integration in our schools. This would be no limited regional or sectional study. It would examine the progress of integration of all groups in our public schools. . . . Only the NEA can make the study needed because only the NEA embodies all the public educational interests on the local, state, and national levels. Only the NEA can bring together the resources needed for such a study, teachers, administrators, school boards, with the understanding and patience of the Association's committees and experts. . . . I know some of you are saying, "This would be a controversial study." Yes, it does move into the field of controversy, but in the Platform that we earlier adopted in the Assembly, we approved, on page eleven of that Platform, a statement which recognizes the teacher's need and his right to deal objectively with controversial issues. Should we not set the example for the individual and isolated teacher by being willing to deal, as an Association, with a controversial question?[95]

C. B. Nuckolls opposed Ludwig's position, indicating why he always supported the Association:

Kentucky uses its resources, its people, its planning, its cooperative efforts in all its areas. We [the Kentucky Teachers Association, a Negro teachers group] merged with the Kentucky Education Association a couple of years ago—all of our associations in Kentucky are merging—and we have here in this Assembly many representatives from Kentucky who are sent up by the Kentucky Education Association and by various classroom teacher Associations.[96]

He viewed segregation as a local problem capable of solution by people fully aware of the local situation.

Stanley Stromswold, a Michigan delegate, placed the Association above all other matters and struck a responsive chord with the Assembly. He argued that the study committee would do more harm than good. Although claiming he would do all in his power to build a democratic society, Stromswold added, "I do not believe that I will do this by weakening the influence of the NEA in the South."[97]

All during the debate, Guy Jewell, a delegate from Maryland,

attempted to stop debate on the motion or to kill the motion alto-
gether by using various parliamentary techniques. He finally was
successful; but at that moment, a Georgia delegate, William Winn,
threw the convention into further uproar by moving for an adjournment because a quorum no longer existed.[98] All during the debate,
Leonard Buder, a newspaperman representing the *New York Times*,
reported seeing Southern delegates leaving the convention floor.[99]
When the roll call began, "the Southern exodus quickened."[100] Much
confusion existed as the chairman of each state delegation attempted
to get his delegates together for the important count. President
Ginger finally announced that a quorum did not exist and that the
meeting was adjourned until Friday morning. The tally showed
only 1,876 delegates present for the roll call while 2,343 delegates
were required to conduct official business of the NEA.[101]

This walkout was the most drastic action yet taken by the delegates opposing a stronger integration posture of the Association,
and it indicated the extent of the serious division within the Association. Apparently some question existed as to whether enough delegates would return to the final session of the convention so that the
convention might be concluded. Ginger reflected the gravity of the
situation when, after announcing adjournment of the afternoon
session, he implored the delegates to be in their seats for the final
evening session: "But if this delegation, this NEA Convention, is
to complete its business, you must be seated by delegations tonight
in order to complete the business."[102]

The convention met in its final meeting Friday evening in a com-
paratively peaceful mood. In the interval between the stormy afternoon meeting and the final meeting in the evening, the New York
delegation met and agreed to withdraw the motion for the establishment of a study committee, thus saving the convention from further
turmoil. Most of the session was devoted to an interview of James
Conant by the delegates of the Assembly. This lasted for almost
two hours. As the meeting neared conclusion, Ginger called for a
roll call in order to conclude the business items from the last session.
Ginger called upon Ludwig in this manner: "I understand that
Mr. Ludwig has asked for permission to withdraw the motion
made this afternoon—is that correct, Mr. Ludwig?"[103]

Ludwig responded by deploring the action of those delegates who blocked the democratic process by walking out on the afternoon meeting. But he indicated that he did not want the final session of the NEA to end the same way and so he withdrew his motion under three conditions:

> First, with the consent of the New York delegation which has been polled and given and the delegation asked that this be presented. Second, with the understanding that what was a strong presentation this afternoon from a considerable body of the Delegate Assembly in a procedure which if followed through democratically, might have given a mandate to the Board of Directors; with the understanding that with this in mind, the administrative officers of our Association present to the Board of Directors for consideration what was here offered. Third, the motion is withdrawn, provided that the seconder, Mr. Sudduth of California agrees. I think he is prepared to give his consent.[104]

Ginger repeated these three points, and Ludwig agreed to their correctness. Ginger recognized Sudduth, who withdrew his second to Ludwig's motion. Within minutes after this action, Ginger adjourned the 1958 NEA convention.

Reaction to the NEA Integration Resolution

The NEA was still intact after the conclusion of the 1958 convention, but increasing strains were beginning to show upon the century old organization. The same integration resolution had been passed by the Assembly, but nobody seemed happy over the outcome. The group pressing for a tougher organization stand on integration threw the convention into turmoil by asking for a study committee, thus causing a majority of delegates to stalk out of the convention. Leonard Buder reported that the convention ended on a "bitter note" over the integration controversy.[105] A Southern moderate expressed his feelings over the conclusion of the convention this way: "The desegregation controversy in the hard core states is more touchy than at any time since the Supreme Court ruled that segregation is unconstitutional. Everything that has happened since September when we had that trouble at Little Rock has set back by ten or twelve years what might otherwise have been accomplished.[106]

DEVELOPMENTS IN 1959

During the period that the NEA was agonizing over the integration crisis, the moral issue of integration was reaching significant proportons. A number of religious organizations within the United States had begun to make formal pronouncements in opposition to segregation, support of the Supreme Court decision, or condemnation of segregation. The National Council of Churches reported that between 1954 and 1958 twenty-seven Protestant denominations officially spoke out in support of the Supreme Court decision. Many were from the South, such as Florida Council of Churches, Southern Baptist Convention, Kentucky Council of Churches, and the New Orleans Council of Churches.[107] Reverend Billy Graham denounced segregation at an integrated service held at Fort Jackson, South Carolina, attended by over 60,000 people.[108]

Probably the strongest pronouncement from a church group in the United States came from the Catholic bishops of the United States at their annual meeting held at Washington, D.C., in November 1958. The bishops found segregation in direct opposition to the basic moral and social precepts of Christianity and urged its eradication from the society:

> Can enforced segregation be reconciled with the Christian view of our fellowman? In our judgement it cannot and this for two fundamental reasons.
> (1) Legal segregation or any form of compulsory segregation, in itself by its very nature imposes a stigma of inferiority among segregated people. Even if the obsolete court doctrine of "separate but equal" had been carried out to the fullest extent so that all public and semi-public facilities were in fact equal, there is none the less the judgement that the entire race by the sole fact of race and regardless of the individual qualities, is not fit to associate on equal terms with any member of another race. We cannot reconcile such a judgement with the Christian view of man's nature and rights.
> (2) It is a matter of historical fact that segregation in our country has led to oppressive conditions and a denial of human rights for the Negro. This is evident in the fundamental fields of education, job opportunities, and housing.[109]

The significant thing to be aware of is that by 1959 many church groups in the United States had begun to make definite commitments in the field of civil rights. The moral issue of integration had begun to buttress the attack against segregation. These religious denominations represented essentially the same cross section of people that the NEA represented, but up to this point the NEA had neither endorsed the Supreme Court decision of 1954 nor condemned segregation as practiced in many states and localities in the United States. Events were occurring rapidly that required the NEA to take some action, however limited, in the integration dispute.

Prince Edward County in Virginia closed its public schools and Little Rock, Arkansas, officials moved in the same direction, while many school districts with similar problems caused by integration waited to see if closing of public schools would be successful.[110] In addition to the threat of public school closings, the Little Rock school authorities threatened to fire forty-four teachers, of whom about one-fourth were Negroes, because of their mild support of school integration.

The American Association of School Administrators, a powerful department within the organizational structure of the NEA, met at its annual convention in Atlantic City, New Jersey, in February 1959. The delegates passed a resolution that maintained: "That adjustment consistent with the Supreme Court ruling on school segregation is a process, complex in nature and deep seated in social and cultural conflict, which calls for calm judgment, tolerant understanding, careful planning, and concerned effort by lay citizens as well as educational leaders."[111]

For the first time, the Board of Directors and the Executive Committee of the NEA discussed the integration problem at their regular meetings. In the October 1958 meeting of the Board of Directors, NEA President Ruth Stout reported upon the five crucial issues facing the NEA. They were: (1) integration; (2) curriculum; (3) children we educate; (4) legislation; and (5) membership.[112] The following day the Board of Directors issued a statement on integration that the Board approved as the official statement of the NEA regarding integration. The statement was the same resolution adopted by the Representative Assembly on integration from 1955 to 1958. Nine Directors from different geographical areas spoke in favor of the statement. They were: George

Deer, Louisiana; Claude Purcell, Georgia; Virgil M. Rogers, New
York; Joseph Van Felt, Virginia; Robert Neil, Tennessee; John C.
Evans, Jr., Utah; Sampson G. Smith, New Jersey; Margaret C.
Schowengert, Missouri; and Donald F. Cline, Nebraska.[113] At the
February 1959 meeting, Mrs. Antonia Crater, a director from Oregon, read a copy of the integration resolution that the Oregon delegation intended to present to the Resolutions Committee for consideration. Mrs. Crater indicated that if the committee failed to
accept this resolution, the delegates intended to present the resolution on the floor of the Representative Assembly.[114] No official discussion followed Mrs. Crater's presentation.

The Executive Committee discussed the Oregon resolution, and
George Deer shunted the whole issue aside by telling the Committee
that "this problem [integration] is not one that professional organizations can handle."[115] The Executive Committee was composed of
eleven members, five of whom had definitely committed themselves
toward support of the Representative Assembly's integration resolution. Francis Beedon and William W. Eshelman were past chairmen
of the Resolutions Committee. George Deer had always opposed a
more liberal stance, while Margaret Schowengert supported the
Board of Director's official statement in 1958. Lyman Ginger was
a past president of the NEA and supported a mild statement even
at the 1960 convention. The advocates for tough organizational
stand on integration could expect little aid from the Executive
Committee.

Even though the Board of Directors endorsed the resolution of
the Representative Assembly, forty-four teachers in the Little Rock
school system received support from the Association when the Little
Rock school board attempted to fire those people who held mild
views on integration. The Association did not attempt to stress
its support of these teachers, for very little was said in the actual
business sessions of the Assembly concerning NEA intervention.
Ruth Stout indicated in her presidential address that she and Dr.
Carr sent a telegram to the teachers indicating complete Association support. Forrest Rozzell, executive secretary of the Arkansas
Education Association, praised the Association's action on the floor

of the convention during the debate on the integration resolution. The NEA offered to pay almost $250,000 in unpaid salaries to those teachers whose positions were threatened and pledged continued financial support to those whose contracts were not renewed in the following school year.[116]

The 1959 NEA Convention

The NEA met in its annual convention at Saint Louis, Missouri, June 28 to July 3, 1959. The weather was typical for that time of the year in Saint Louis—hot and humid.[117] The atmosphere inside Kiel Auditorium, however, was still closer and more tense, for integration was the chief topic of the delegates' conversation and debate.[118] Of course, the organization continued its push for federal aid to education, but it could be sensed that the division within the ranks caused by the integration hassle had to be healed before the Association made its final drive toward federal aid.

Ruth A. Stout, president of the NEA, attempted to heal the wounds during her presidential address on the first day of the General Assembly meeting. The title of her address was "Breakthrough to Reality" and was symbolic because Miss Stout became the first NEA president directly to confront the delegates with the integration problems as they related to the Association. She felt that the closing of public schools in some areas of the country was "one of the most tragic events in the history of the nation."[119] Carefully she pointed out that the NEA Platform buttresses the preservation of a democratic society by calling for the maintenance of free public schools. Moving on to the protection of teachers' rights, Miss Stout said: "As members of our professional association, we also have a concern that teachers be protected in terms of their professional rights and their rights as citizens. As teachers and citizens we have a responsibility of teaching respect for the law, and of respecting law ourselves, not static but dynamic law."[120] She maintained that education held the key to the integration dilemma:

> The difficulties involved in integration of the public schools are merely a manifestation of a much deeper social, cultural, and legal difficulties. Clearly there is a gap between what some mean by

rights of democracy and what others mean by the same term. These
differences must be dissipated. But differences of feeling, attitude,
opinion, and conviction cannot be legislated. Changes in these are
in the realm of "unenforceables." In the educative process lies the
only hope ultimately, for the change genuine enough to be endur-
ing and consistent with democratic theory.[121]

Then she referred to the impending debate:

> As we consider later this week the resolutions on this very crucial
> problem, let us be sure that what we say will have the effect of what
> we want it to have. If we cannot be sure of this, let it be left un-
> said. Too often we impute cause and effect relationships where they
> do not necessarily exist. Too much is at stake at this moment, in
> terms of the welfare of the children of the nation; the respect with
> which the democratic society may be held in other nations, in
> fact, its very survival, for us to say anything that would be better
> left unsaid.[122]

Dr. Stout ended her discussion of the integration controversy by
supporting the 1958 NEA resolution on integration and pleading
for unity within the ranks:

> I beg you to remember that we are representatives of fifty states
> and the territories, that we do have differing opinions and problems,
> that we have differing degrees of the same problems, and differing
> attitudes and backgrounds of experience. We do also, I believe I can
> safely say, have the same ultimate goals. The resolution of 1958,
> however, is not the sounding of brass and tinkling cymbal that some
> would have us believe. . . . Whatever action we take in this conven-
> tion must be such as to permit all professional teachers and affili-
> ated organizations to continue their memberships and services of
> the National Education Association.[123]

The next day the Resolutions Committee held hearings upon
the resolutions, pending presentation to the Representative Assembly later in the week. Over 700 people packed the conference room
to hear the arguments over the integration resolution. People regarded this action as the prelude to the floor fight. Forrest Rozzell,
executive secretary of the Arkansas Education Association, and
Edward Henderson, executive secretary of the Florida Education
Association, spoke strongly for a moderate resolution. Henderson
pulled no punches. He clearly indicated what would happen if the

NEA adopted a strong resolution on integration: "The present resolution indicates some knowledge of the problem, but it does not make it more difficult for us to defend our leadership. I can afford this resolution, but if I go home under a more vigorous statement, I must repudiate my membership in the National Education Association or lose my ability as a leader."[124]

Opposition to the mild resolution came from Fred Clark of Stockton, California; Charles Sudduth, a principal from San Pablo, California; and Walter Ludwig, a social sciences teacher from Mamaroneck, New York. Clark claimed that the 1959 convention theme, "Quality Education Opens Windows on the World," was contradictory in regard to the integration issue. He suggested, "Education Should Open Some Doors Right Here at Home."[125] Sudduth charged that a mild resolution was a victory for the segregationists.[126] Ludwig wanted the NEA to recognize that a "crisis" existed.[127] The advocates of a mild resolution prevailed, and the same integration resolution of the past three years cleared its last obstacle prior to its presentation to the Assembly.

The advocates of a strong resolution received another serious blow on July 1, when the New York delegation met at the Statler Hotel and decided to support the Association's integration resolution by a vote of 142 to 2. Furthermore, the delegation replaced Ludwig in the 1960 NEA Resolutions Committee.[128] When Leonard Buder reported this action, he concluded, "It is a consensus here that the Assembly will reaffirm the present position."[129]

The split between the factions remained, however, and was not any closer to solution than prior to the start of the convention. The organizational leaders felt that the fate of the Association depended upon solving this crisis without further antagonizing the members from the South; therefore, they followed two avenues of approach aimed at reconciling the two factions and solving the problem that had plagued them since 1954. The Resolutions Committee, with the aid and advice of the Board of Directors, decided to recommend to the Assembly the integration resolution adopted previously by the Association.[130] Recognizing the unfair treatment of teachers in some areas of the country and the threat to the public school system in the country by threatened closings, the committee decided to deal with these problems in two different resolutions entitled, "Public Education in America," and "The Teacher as a Citizen." In this way the committee considered the unfair treatment of teachers and the threat to the public school system "in a general content, rather than specifically in relation to integration."[131] The committee added a final paragraph to the resolution dealing with education in America, which took note of the closing of public schools in the country:

> Solutions to the problems which face public education must maintain and strengthen the priceless heritage of free educational opportunity for every American child. Any movement which would dismiss this vital asset would deprive future generations of their birthright and the nation of their badly needed services. As the Platform of the Association has long stated, the survival of democracy requires that every state maintain a system of free public education, and safeguard the education of all children. Free public schools are the cornerstone of our social, economic, and political structure. The free public school system is not expendable.[132]

The committee spoke of unfair treatment of teachers in the last sentence of the final paragraph of the resolution dealing with the teacher as a citizen: "The Association believes that support of those teachers whose status or rights have been unfairly menaced or impaired is a major obligation of professional organizations."[133] Both of these resolutions passed without any debate, but when Ben Kellner presented the committee's resolution on integration, fireworks erupted. President Stout made a motion for its adoption, and Charles Deubel from New York seconded the motion. Walter Ludwig offered a substitute motion:

> The National Education Association believes in equal educational privileges for all children without distinction based upon race, religion, or national origin, either in the opportunities extended to the pupils or in the selection of their teachers.
> The Association urges all those in authority in government, no less than the average citizen, to abide by the laws including the "new charter" of human freedom—the 1954 decision of the Supreme Court in the school desegregation cases. The Constitution of the United States is what the judges say it is. Decisions of the Supreme Court may not be successfully defied without great damage

to the body of the American people. Respect for law, an outstanding characteristic of our people, must be preserved.

We commend those teachers, school administrators, and other citizens who by their efforts have made orderly integration possible. We recommend that professional organizations affiliated with the National Education Association be urged to integrate and that no such organization discriminate on account of race. It is our conviction that problems of integration in our schools are capable of solution at local, state, and national levels by citizens of intelligence, saneness, and reasonableness working together in the interests of national unity for the common good of all.[134]

James Cullen, chairman of the New York delegation, defended the original resolution on integration and disavowed his delegation from any minority report "done without the prior consent of the New York state delegation."[135] Charles Sudduth followed with a vigorous attack on the "weak and outmoded" NEA resolution and asked for support of Ludwig's substitute motion. At this point someone asked for a recess for lunch. This was a point on which everyone could agree.

When debate resumed, Ludwig found some of his forces had diminished. He charged intimidation on the part of several states. He claimed that when he proposed this motion, several people from the Joint Committee of the NEA-ATA had agreed to speak for the motion, but since that time some of the Negro delegates "have been visited by some of the members of the states' white delegation. They will not speak this afternoon."[136] Ludwig continued his attack: "The old resolution says integration is a concern to every state and territory. What we need to decide and what the public has a right to know is "Does the NEA believe in integration?" The committee's resolution does not say. The substitute resolution gives a clear and forthright yes."[137]

After Ludwig's plea for a change, seven people representing different geographical areas in the United States defended the original resolution. Some of the arguments were familiar while others were astounding in their naïveté; but all supported the status quo. Isabel Epley of Pennsylvania stressed that the NEA Code of Ethics already made the Association's position clear. Robert Williams of

Virginia advocated complete trust in the ability and judgment of the Resolutions Committee. Vivian Powell, a member of the Resolutions Committee, believed that eventually the NEA would have to adopt a stronger resolution on integration, but not in 1959. Mrs. Daintry Allison of North Carolina charged that Ludwig and his followers really knew nothing at all about the subject, and Matthew Gaynor advocated procrastination:

> Let's go home and work there to get our local problems ironed out. Let us give the states a chance. Let's give them time. They know what the problems are. Let us give the NEA staff and the Board of Directors of the NEA a chance to study this problem. . . . Let the Board of Directors begin their study. Let's see what we can come up with in the way of recommendations, and perhaps next year we might be able to take a more deliberate and sensible stand than is being made here through the substitute resolution.[138]

Debate was closed and the delegates defeated Ludwig's substitute motion by a voice vote.

Mrs. Maxine Smith of Oregon promptly countered with four amendments proposed by the Oregon delegation. These were more moderate than Ludwig's resolution, but Earl Hanson, a member of the Resolutions Committee, opposed them for two major reasons. First, he claimed that this squabble over integration endangered the chances for the NEA to secure federal aid to education. In listing his second reason, Hanson brought forth the perpetual fear haunting many people, which was that "a different approach [on integration] might eventually result in the liquidation of public education."[139] He also indicated that the NEA Board of Directors had started a study of integration. President Stout called upon Dr. Carr to elaborate upon Hanson's statement concerning the study on integration. Carr replied succinctly:

> Madam President, this is the motion passed by the Board of Directors a few days ago: "That the staff be instructed to prepare a careful review of all available studies of educational problems involved in school integration, that a report thereon, after review by the Board of Directors, be made available to the members of the Association." The work on this will begin as soon as we clean up after this convention.[140]

If Carr's dramatic announcement was intended to quiet the restless convention, it apparently failed. Three people followed him with strong statements for a more positive stance of the NEA regarding integration.

Forrest Rozzell supported the moderate stand. In a speech that consumed almost ten minutes, he reviewed the crisis in Little Rock and Arkansas, pointing out that the Arkansas Education Association occupied the forefront fighting for the preservation of public schools in that state.[141] He praised the NEA for coming to the aid of the teachers purged by the Little Rock school board, and in a dramatic gesture introduced the president of the Little Rock Classroom Teachers Association. He announced that she received a contract for the 1959-1960 school year in the Little Rock school system, giving complete credit for this achievement to the NEA. He said, "The NEA could not have done any more to help us under these so-called 'stronger' resolutions than it did under the resolution proposed by the Resolutions Committee."[142] Rozzell closed by calling for a vote of confidence in the NEA by defeating any amendments to the resolution proposed by the Resolutions Committee: "If you have faith in the integrity of your professional leadership as represented by the Resolutions Committee and leadership in Arkansas and the rest of the South—if you have confidence in the judgement of the leadership, you will vote to reject all of these proposed amendments and stand by the recommendations of the Resolutions Committee."[143] At the conclusion of his plea to the delegates, Rozzell received a standing ovation from the Assembly.

Debate continued. Ohio indicated almost unanimous support for the Resolutions Committee. The delegates from Washington and Oregon continued their support of the Oregon amendments. At this juncture, William Green from North Carolina gave a moving speech in defense of the amendments.

Green was a spokesman from a very large segment of black teachers who belonged to the NEA. He cited the creation in 1952 of dual state organizations that allowed over 30,000 Negro teachers to become full members of the NEA. Since that time, he continued, the number of dual organizations in the NEA had decreased from

twenty-one to eleven. Then he indicated that the remaining eleven
states maintaining dual organizations ought to grant to their black
members the same rights that ten of their neighbors granted to their
black members of the Association. Dr. Green did not advocate Negroes leaving the Association, as apparently some people feared, but
he did charge the NEA of "welshing on the deal":

> We fought this battle against discrimination through other organiza-
> tions until 1952 and you told us through your Platform, before you
> got into the business of special resolutions, that our right to fair
> treatment qualified us. You said you would fight for us, and when
> we declare war, you run up the white flag; it is not a fair deal. . . .
> I am not afraid of being unemployed until I get a chance to draw
> my social security. I tell you they have feared fear—that is all. If you
> are qualified you can stand on your own professional qualifications
> and be employed as an educator. The voice you heard from the
> South [Rozzell's] was not a voice of educational leadership, it was
> the voice of compromise and political intimidation.[144]

The fight raged on and tempers became frayed. James Cullen
blasted the Oregon delegation for further disruption of the convention because of their presentation of the integration amendments.
Mr. Cullen's comments were the strongest condemnation issued to
date from the floor of the Representative Assembly concerning the
integration debate. Cullen said:

> The state of Oregon has come here with amendments, and it is a
> fact and the people ought to understand that in the whole state of
> Oregon there are less than twenty-five to thirty colored teachers.
> If that state of Oregon, and I know that they are sincere in their
> proposals, if they want to do something along this line, they certainly
> can make a contribution by going in and recruiting some of the fine
> colored teachers who are having difficulty in the southern states.[145]

Dr. Keith Goldhammer of Oregon calmly replied: "Many of us in
the state of Oregon are attempting to do something about the problem of hiring displaced teachers from the South . . . and we do need
the strength of the NEA resolution as we propose to amend it."[146]

The time had arrived to vote on the amendments. Each of the
four amendments was read to the delegates. Each was turned down.
Then the Assembly considered the original resolution proposed by
the Resolutions Committee. It passed by a voice vote.

After the integration resolution had been passed, Dr. Carr asked to speak to the Assembly. The delegates granted him permission. Carr expressed great pride in the two-hour debate, stating that he found it symbolic of democracy in action. He reiterated that the NEA accepted no type of discrimination among its members, stressing that the NEA resources were available to any teacher "unjustly treated as the result of a local problem."[147] He also emphasized the need to preserve the public school system in the nation. He saved the most important argument for his final point. This point was the overriding fear that many delegates expressed concerning a strong integration resolution's impact upon the destiny of the Association:

> And lastly, I think you have said to us who work for you on the staff that the NEA remains now, as it was when we came to St. Louis, a strong and united body determined to deal with its own problems in its own way, and to make its own contribution to that unity in our nation which is indispensable if the whole institution of freedom is to survive. You have said that the unity of the NEA is important to each and everyone of you; that your staff should strengthen and broaden that unity, not just for the Association itself, but also because the unity of teachers in the nation is essential to the unity of the nation itself.[148]

Reaction to the NEA Integration Resolution

Criticism of the NEA convention's treatment of the integration problem rolled in after the conclusion of the annual meeting. The *New York Times* simply stated that the action of the delegates "marked the fifth consecutive year that the Representative Assembly had accepted substantially the same resolution on integration."[149] The *St. Louis Post Dispatch* remarked editorially:

> The goal of the NEA ought to be, it seems to us, to do its part in implementing with all "deliberate speed"—to use the Supreme Court's word—the national policy that racial discrimination has no place in tax supported education. That this national policy is not everywhere accepted everyone of course knows. But it spreads from mouth to mouth as the latest news from Little Rock bears witness. If the NEA as a vast professional organization of education can help with a reasonable, fair, and constructive statement, well and good. Surely there would be no harm in a moderate effort, undertaken in a spirit of good will and good faith. Let it always be remembered that the word "educate" comes from two Latin words, *e* and *duco*

meaning "to lead out." Whenever educators cease "leading out" they cease being educators.[150]

William W. Brickman was even more caustic of the Association's deliberations at Saint Louis: "The NEA stated their conviction in a half-hearted, weak-kneed manner. Not only did the NEA whisper inaudibly its message to the American public on the subject of racial school integration, but it perpetuated segregation in its own organizational ranks."[151]

Finally out of Minneapolis, Minnesota, there came a voice that the Association could ill afford to ignore. The American Federation of Teachers at its annual convention assailed the NEA for its weak stand upon integration. The union charged that the NEA "abdicated its claim to leadership and guidance of teachers in the nation." The AFT delegates passed a resolution "giving determined support" to the desegregation decision.[152]

Whatever its literary quality, a poem written by John Dane for *Progressive Education* in 1957 captured the basic attitude many critics held toward the NEA's treatment of the integration problem:

NEA COUNSEL

A currently bandied expression,
Directed toward the teaching profession:
Why concede to the Councils
On the issue of desegregation?

Raise a shaft of opinion.
Shatter dominion,
Of hallowed white father,
And timid black children.

But as is the custom,
With children of education,
They introduce teachers to innovation,
And WALK—bypassing bus stations.

The leaders of children,
Are children themselves,
Come of age in the Constitution.

> But the expression remains,
> Why the NEA refrains from answering,
> The currently bandied question,
> Asked by the teaching profession,
> No opinion—no action,
> On the issue of school desegregation. [153]

THE POSTURE OF THE NEA JOURNAL
ON INTEGRATION FROM 1954-1959

A review of the *NEA Journal* during the years from 1954 to 1959 reflected the basic stand taken by the Association at its national conventions. No major articles appeared either about integration problems in general or specific problems regarding teachers who suffered injustices because of their viewpoints about integration in the public schools. A few short news articles appeared in the "News and Trends" column, and they touched upon some of the issues affecting public education. If a person totally unacquainted with the integration crisis as it affected the public schools read the *NEA Journal* or even the "News and Trends" columns for this five-year span, he would have acquired a very sketchy knowledge of the integration-segregation clash in the United States. For example, not one item concerning integration appeared in the 1958 *NEA Journal*. Also, when the magazine reported upon the conventions, the fight over an integration resolution was never mentioned. Probably the biggest stories occurring in the magazine over this period were the centennial articles and the coverage of the Association's constant quest to secure federal aid to education legislation.

Although no articles pertained to the integration movement, some pictures of Negroes appeared in the *NEA Journal* from 1954 to 1959. Buried deep in the November 1955 issue was a photograph of a group of NEA members who had taken a trip to Israel. F. D. Moon was one of the members.[154] In 1956, the magazine carried pictures of the Congressmen who supported the Kelley Bill. A Negro was one of the Congressmen.[155] In an article concerning the NEA Headquarters, a picture showed a black clerk in the NEA office.[156] No pictures of Negroes appeared in 1958, but in 1959, three different editions of the magazine carried pictures of Negroes. One showed a black maintenance man at NEA Headquarters;[157] another featured a Moroccan boy in an article about UNICEF;[158] and the third picture showed African delegates attending a WCOTP conference.[159]

In 1954, the NEA adopted its first resolution upon integration and public education in the United States. The next year, the delegates made a few slight changes in the resolution, and this became the official NEA statement upon integration for five consecutive years. During this interval, pressure mounted for the Association to take a more positive stand on the subject because of many events that had been occurring in the nation. These events had a direct relationship with public education and the NEA. The organizational forces, which controlled the convention machinery, successfully blocked any change in the resolution but at an ever increasing cost to the NEA, measurable in terms of the Association's loss of prestige and faltering unity. The 1958 and 1959 conventions featured heated and bitter debates highlighted by the conservative members walking out of the convention in 1958 and charges of NEA "welshing" in 1959. For the first few years of the struggle the leaders of the NEA attempted to ignore the issue; but when this could no longer be done, they rallied support of the Association by appealing to some basic fears of the NEA rank and file. These fears were that if a strong resolution were passed: (1) the free public school system would be endangered; (2) a federal aid to education bill would be threatened; and (3) the Association would be in danger of destruction because of the threatened exodus of the conservative members. It must be recognized that these fears had basis for fact, but the conservative members of the Association, from the North and South alike, exploited these fears, and the leaders of the Association accepted these ideas and used them to perpetuate the status quo.

By 1960, however, the pressures for change did not disappear, and the challenge for achieving a new approach to the integration matter without destroying Association unity remained. The NEA's prime task for the forthcoming decade was to develop a fair and adequate solution to the integration problem, thus building a broader base of support for the organization.

Integration in the NEA from 1960 to 1963 5

When you get too big a majority, you're immediately in trouble. SAM RAYBURN

Regardless of the Supreme Court decision, integration moved very slowly. Since 1954, six border states and the District of Columbia had integrated forty-nine percent of their Negro students. At the same time, the eleven southern states had desegregated a negligible .162 percent of their black student body.[1] Most of the large cities in the border states had desegregated, and token desegregation had occurred in some of the southern states.[2] Alabama, Georgia, Mississippi, Louisiana, and South Carolina still refused to desegregate, thus maintaining "separate but equal" facilities for 1,392,000 Negro students in that five-state confine.[3]

The South continued its parliamentary assault upon school integration by attempting to circumvent the 1954 decision. Early in 1960, Senator Herman Talmadge introduced a constitutional amendment aimed at restoring the states' exclusive control of education. Senators from Virginia, Mississippi, and Alabama cosponsored the bill.[4]

During the same year, black students from Greensboro, North Carolina, enacted a new civil rights technique that spread to many sections of the United States, thus giving the nation a new word in its vocabulary: the "sit-in."[5] Aimed at breaking down segregation at the major chain stores' lunch counters, Negro and white students conducted "sit-ins" from Florida to Ohio, and these began to stir the nation's interest in civil rights.

The NEA Board of Directors continued to ponder the integration problem. John A. Palmer from California brought up Walter Ludwig's motion made at the NEA convention in Cleveland concerning the Board's study of integration. Palmer suggested the Board's adoption of the motion so that it would not become an issue at the 1960 convention; Dr. Carr, however, was cool to the idea since he claimed that all relevant factual information about segregation already existed.[6] George Deer "wondered if there might be a survey of studies already made on integration."[7] But Palmer made a motion that the Board officially adopt a study, and Miss Hazel Blanchard seconded his motion. The Board passed it with no further debate.

Later in the year, the Board defined the exact terms and methods of the study, stipulating that "each study will be summarized briefly without any editorial comment."[8] In this manner, the Board narrowly limited the investigation's scope to little more than an annotated bibliography dealing with education and integration. In February 1960, Dr. Sam Lambert, research director of the NEA, presented a preliminary report to the Board. The directors approved it and directed Lambert to complete the study prior to the annual NEA convention.[9]

The 1960 NEA Convention

The 1960 NEA convention was held at Los Angeles, California, June 26 to July 1. Over 5,700 delegates attended the proceedings and heard major addresses given by Lee Metcalf, Democratic Congressman from Montana and cosponsor of an NEA approved federal aid to education bill; Senator John Sherman Cooper from Kentucky; and Miss Pauline Frederick, an NBC news commentator. The convention theme was "A United Profession Enhances Quality in Education," and William W. Eshelman developed this theme in his presidential address. He emphasized the projected membership growth of the NEA and proclaimed a slogan indicative of the Association's aspirations: "A Million or More by '64."[10]

National politics pervaded the entire convention as the delegates were aware of the forthcoming national Democratic convention at Los Angeles. Metcalf traced the development of the federal aid to education bill, and, not too subtly, placed the Democratic party on education's side. Senator Cooper was less partisan in his presentation; he said, however, that a federal aid bill would be passed during 1960.

William Carr addressed the delegates on the first business session, stressing five major topics: (a) membership; (b) public information; (c) educational goals and programs; (d) international activities; and (e) federal support.[11] He made no reference whatsoever to desegregation.

Regardless of Carr's omission, segregation was the hottest issue at the convention. A New York delegate asked, "If the nation's educators won't stand up to this now, who will?"[12] A southern delegate said, "Lots of teachers in the South haven't any tenure. Contracts run from year to year. Get out of line on that issue and whish."[13] A lively floor fight seemed imminent.

Even prior to the Assembly's debating the issue, Carr and Eshelman found themselves on the defensive because of the charges leveled by Edward Irwin, a national vice-president of the AFT. Irwin challenged the NEA to compare its civil rights record to that of the AFT,[14] for the AFT had suspended all of its segregated affiliates in 1956.[15] In 1960, the NEA still had eleven state affiliates and many local affiliates that maintained racial bars to membership, thus making the NEA very vulnerable to attack.[16] On the first day of the convention, Carr and Eshelman answered Irwin at a press conference. Eshelman said that dual state affiliates existed because of the necessity of law.[17] Carr stressed that every member of the NEA had equal rights and upheld dual associations because: "If the Association insisted upon integrated state groups in some sections, it would mean that all teachers . . . would be unable to belong to the NEA and would lose membership."[18]

The integration resolution came up for passage during the final day of the convention. In a lengthy meeting, lasting five hours, Eshelman found himself practically under seige, especially as the debate wore on past dinner time. Tempers flaring, the California and Arizona delegations, which led the fight for a strong integration resolution, bombarded him with almost "every parliamentary maneuver in *Roberts Rules*."[19] The situation was exacerbated further by Eshelman's inability to see the California delegation, which was seated in the rear of the convention hall. This prompted some sharp exchanges between the chair and the California delegates.

The arguments employed during the debate were not new. Some speakers presented calm, logical representations while others were florid and emotional. At least one, given by Dr. L. D. Pitts, was eloquent. The significant factors, however, were the intensity, length, and delegate involvement of the debate.

The tussle showed that the NEA was still badly split over the issue. The delegates from California, Oregon, and Arizona spearheaded the drive for a stronger NEA stance on integration. Their basic argument was that the Association had to get into step with the rest of the nation and support the 1954 decision. The proponents of the existing resolution based their defense upon four major points: (a) the correctness of gradualism; (b) segregation was an exclusive problem of the South; (c) a strong integration resolution would hurt the cause of the Negro teacher; and (d) a deep fear that a strong resolution would split the Association.

The debate witnessed, for the first time, many leading NEA personalities getting involved in the floor fight, and all but one of them supported the organizational stand. George Deer and Miss Mabel McKelvey, members of the NEA Board of Directors from Louisiana and New Hampshire, respectively, supported the Resolutions Committee. Three past presidents, Lyman Ginger, Dr. Ruth Stout, and John Lester Buford, argued for the 1959 resolution.[20] John Palmer, a member of the Board of Directors from California, was the highest ranking NEA member who supported a tougher integration stance.

Miss Elizabeth Ann Meek, chairman of the Resolutions Committee, proposed the same integration resolution that the Assembly accepted in 1959. George Deer seconded this resolution and told the delegates why they must pass it. These reasons were elaborations of the 1959 arguments: (a) the people advocating a tougher position just did not understand the complex problems involved; (b) integration was a matter for courts to solve; and (c) resolutions of a strong nature would only harden opposition to local desegregation. In closing, he echoed previous Southern sentiments: "This resolution which our Resolutions Committee has presented to us has been generally accepted in those areas. We have operated under it for the past four years. It has made it possible in our communities for us to support the National Education Association and its program."[21]

John Koerner, an Arizona delegate, attempted to amend the resolution. His first amendment stated: "That the National Education Association pledge continued support to the United States Supreme Court decision and school integration."[22] Somewhat later in the debate he introduced a second amendment stating: "That the NEA acknowledge and commend those communities which have made progress toward ending the practice of segregation in their schools."[23] The first amendment produced such a reaction that it consumed almost half of the entire time the Assembly spent upon the whole matter of integration. Charles Sudduth supported Koerner, citing examples of white and Negro teacher dismissals, public school closings, and intimidation of teachers who advocated integration. He stressed that the NEA had to lend its strength to the Supreme Court decision in order to help bring about real equality in the nation.[24]

Lyman Ginger supported the original resolution. Tracing his educational experiences in Kentucky from 1950, he pointed to the racial progress made when the races worked together without outside pressures. He charged that the desegregation problem would not be solved by a stronger NEA resolution.[25] In closing, Ginger played upon a basic fear that plagued many delegates:

> I, too, am interested in equality in education as well as quality, but at the same time, I see nothing but trouble and difficulty to say to people who are working with this problem in the South that we are going to force you by our opposition to do something that your own community will not accept. Ladies and gentlemen, I contend in closing that a resolution conceived on the Atlantic seaboard, christened on the Pacific Ocean, and then forced upon any group of people anywhere will do nothing but defeat the great purpose of the National Educational Association.[26]

After Ginger's concluding remarks, three people spoke against the amendment. Mrs. Margery Alexander Thompson, a North Carolinian echoed Ginger's statements concerning the need for cooperation of the races without outside pressures. Miss Isabel Epley, chairman of the Commission of Professional Ethics, stressed that racial problems were covered under the NEA Code of Ethics. Mr. Claude Welch of Kansas told the Assembly that his state delegation opposed any amendment to the resolution.[27]

John Lester Buford felt that any amendment would only make the problems of the Southern Negro more difficult. Agreeing that the conditions in the South were not good, he emphasized that things would have been more serious had not the white teachers supported their Negro colleagues. He illustrated his remarks:

> The schools of Little Rock are open. Nashville school system integrated without closing their schools. Bad as it is in Virginia, there are ten divisions, counties, or cities which have integrated. North Carolina without undue incident integrated five systems. This great state recently chose a moderate for a governor. It was the teachers of North Carolina who led the fight to defeat an extreme segregationist candidate. How best can we help? Let's not in our attempt to do justice by our Negro friends, inadvertently deny them the strongest support they have, the support of the white teachers who do belong to the NEA.[28]

Delegates from Ohio, Minnesota, Missouri, and Tennessee supported Koerner's amendment, stressing the need of NEA to back the Supreme Court decision. They indicated that NEA ought to get in step with many of the other national organizations that had already supported the court decision.[29]

About halfway through the debate, L. D. Pitts, executive secretary of the Georgia Teachers and Education Association, a Negro organization, delivered a moving speech. Admitting his reluctance to address the convention because many of his "dear friends" would not understand him, he told the Assembly that the course of the debate mitigated against his continued silence. Pitts alluded to the presentations of the NEA past presidents and charged that the leaders of the Association failed to understand the circumstances under which a Negro had to live in the South. When the NEA officials come to the South, Pitts said, "They get off a white train and live in a white hotel in the South; they are ushered around, as it must be, by the officials in the South."[30] Implying that the framers of the integration resolution suffered the same myopic condition, he said the NEA "cannot any longer refuse to take a position . . . the present resolution does not . . . say that the NEA believes."[31]

Shortly after Pitts concluded his remarks, Eshelman took a voice vote on the amendment. It lost. Illinois and Oregon delegates demanded a roll call, forcing the chair to accede to their demands. A recess followed that enabled the delegation chairmen to poll their members. This period was very tense, and through it all, Eshelman maintained his composure and exhibited a sense of humor that helped to reduce the tension. The roll call showed that the amendment passed 1,933 to 1,780.[32] At that moment, the situation changed dramatically. Charles Deubel, a member of the Resolutions Committee, proposed to amend the amendment through substitution. Eshelman conferred with the parliamentarian who allowed that Koerner had to submit his second amendment for debate and final vote prior to consideration of Deubel's motion. Koerner introduced his second amendment, and the delegates passed it with very little debate. Then Deubel countered with his substitute motion, which in effect cancelled out the amendments just passed by the Assembly. This caused confusion on the floor of the Representative Assembly, assigning the parliamentarian a very important role at this stage of the debate.

Deubel's amendment added one additional paragraph to the original resolution:

> The Association commends the communities which have handled their problems regarding desegregation in such a manner to assume their responsibility to maintain public schools and their obligation to recognize the political and professional rights of their teachers. It commends also the officers and directors of the National Education Association for their vigorous and effective support of state and local educational associations when the professional rights and status of the teachers were unfairly menaced and for having prepared and published the forthcoming National Education Association report, *Studies of Educational Problems Involved in School Integration.*[33]

Pointing out that some members felt that NEA had to take a stronger stand on the issue, Deubel urged the Assembly to pass this amendment while admitting: "This resolution is a compromise resolution. It is a bit stronger than the one you have printed [the original resolution prepared by the Resolutions Committee], and it is not quite as strong as some of the amendments that you have before you or will have before you before the day is over."[34]

Robert F. Williams spoke after Deubel and attacked Koerner's amendments. He said that the Virginia delegation voted overwhelmingly against them, and indicating the gravity of the situation, Williams charged, "We came here vertically but because of what you have done to us, we will have to go home horizontally."[35]

Dr. Stout defended Deubel's motion because it was more consistent with NEA policy. She denied that the NEA's refusal to adopt another integration resolution limited forward movement, although she admitted the validity of Pitt's arguments concerning the lack of understanding for the Southern Negro. Stout, however, held out some hope for progress when she told the delegates, "The democratic processes are slow, else we would not be debating this year after year."[36] Briefly reviewing the NEA Platform, she concluded, "We recognize that many of the points which some people would like to have included in the integration or desegregation resolutions are not only implicit but explicit in our resolutions."[37]

Some delegates wondered why the Resolutions Committee had prepared two integration resolutions, so Miss Meek attempted to clarify the matter:

> I want you to know that the Editing Committee, the people up here, presented the two resolutions to the entire Resolutions Committee. We presented the one printed in your report; we also presented the one Mr. Deubel read to you a few minutes ago. It was not our decision, the decision of the Editing Committee, which one to put in the report. The Resolutions Committee, representing every state, voted to put in last year's resolution in the report. They rejected this one [Deubel's amendment] by a twenty-one to twenty-four vote. We wrote the second resolution which has been moved to substitute, after the open hearing the other day when we sensed that the NEA perhaps wanted a change.[38]

By this time, the debate had dragged on for over three hours, and some of the delegates indicated a willingness to reevaluate their previous positions. Eshelman called for a standing vote on Deubel's motion and it passed. The California and Arizona delegations continued the debate for at least another thirty minutes after discovering some flaws in the chair's parliamentary procedures, but the proponents of a strong resolution were defeated again.[39]

The 1960 NEA resolution on desegregation in the public schools reads:

The National Education Association believes that integration of all groups in our public schools is an evolving process which concerns every state and territory in our nation.

The Association urges that all citizens approach the matter of desegregation in the public schools with the spirit of fairness, good will, and respect for law which has always been an outstanding characteristic of the American people. It is the conviction of the Association that all problems of desegregation in our schools are capable of solution at the state and local levels by citizens of intelligence, saneness, and reasonableness working together in the interests of national unity for the common good of all.

The Association commends the communities which have handled their problems regarding desegregation in such a manner as to assume their responsibility to maintain the public schools and their obligation to recognize the political and professional rights of teachers. It commends also the officers and directors of the National Education Association for their vigorous and effective support of state and local education associations when the professional rights and status of teachers were unfairly menaced and for having prepared and published the forthcoming National Education Association report, *Studies of Educational Problems Involved in School Integration.*[40]

The first two paragraphs of the 1960 resolution were slightly changed from the previous resolutions. It declared that integration is an "evolving process" rather than a "process" and substituted "fairness" for "fairplay." The title was changed from Integration in the Public Schools to Desegregation in the Public Schools. The third paragraph commended the communities that kept the schools open during the integration crisis while recognizing "the political and professional rights of the teacher." The resolution also commended the national, state, and local organizations for protecting the rights of the teachers when these rights "were unfairly menaced." Finally, it commended the Board of Directors for authorizing and publishing *Studies of Educational Problems Involved in School Integration.*[41]

Reaction to the NEA Desegregation Resolution

As an aftermath to the bitter struggle, the Board of Directors met in an effort to avoid such debates in the future. Lyman Ginger proposed that the Editing Committee meet with the Negro and white leaders of the southern affiliates in order to arrive at an integration resolution acceptable to all. His motion carried without any deliberation.[42]

Ironically, the Georgia Education Journal assured its readers that the resolution remained "substantially the same" as in the past,[43] even though the *New York Times* considered it somewhat stronger than previous pronouncements.[44] The *Pittsburgh Courier,* however, blasted the NEA for its stance on integration:

> The misnamed National Education Association stood pat at its Los Angeles Convention on its policy of maintaining separate jim crow chapters of Negro teachers in eleven states. Dr. William Eshelman, NEA president, asserted that the jim crow set up "is as much a necessity of law as anything else," declaring "public schools must remain open all over the country." The NEA is thus on record as virtually backing the position of the most reactionary southern white elements who have bitterly fought the 1954 Supreme Court decision since it was handed down. The policy is in contrast to the rival American Federation of Teachers (AFL-CIO) which years ago revoked the charters of segregated radical locals in the South and practices the integration it preaches.[45]

At the annual AFT convention, a union spokesman labeled the NEA's continuance of dual organizations as a "shameful neglect of the principles of democracy."[46] The union urged the NEA to follow the AFT's example of eliminating segregated locals.[47] The teachers' union also endorsed the "sit-ins," recommending support of these protests because they "are peaceable expressions of protest by young people against environmental handicaps as they seek self-respect, recognition, and dignity."[48]

At the same time, the AFT expressed a willingness to battle the NEA. The field was to be New York City, and the immediate prize was the bargaining rights of 40,000 teachers. The union considered that the NEA had three basic weaknesses that could be exploited: (a) the NEA was a company union; (b) the NEA had failed to make a clear stand on desegregation; and (c) the NEA practiced segregation within its own ranks by maintaining dual affiliates.[49]

Posture of the "NEA Journal" during 1960

During 1960, the *NEA Journal* carried only two articles that were even remotely associated with the integration crisis. One article pertained to a black teacher in the school system of Philadelphia, Pennsylvania.[50] Two months later, an article appeared about minorities in the classroom, making no reference to Negroes.[51] During the year, the magazine showed only three pictures of Negroes. One of these was in relation to the article, "Edna Griffin—Big City Teacher," while the other two were unrelated to the racial problems in the nation.[52]

DEVELOPMENTS IN 1961

The pace of Negro progress improved somewhat in 1961 because of President John F. Kennedy's appointment of several Negroes to government posts: Thurgood Marshall as United States circuit judge and Carl T. Rowen as deputy secretary of state for Public Affairs. George Weaver received an appointment as assistant undersecretary of Labor,[53] while John B. Duncan became the first Negro appointed as commissioner of the District of Columbia.[54]

Public school integration increased at an imperceptible rate. The border states and the District of Columbia had integrated almost fifty-three percent of their Negro students, while the South had integrated less than .3 percent of its black student body.[55] Desegregation occurred for the first time in twenty-nine school districts, with token integration in Atlanta, Dallas, and Galveston.[56] Complete faculty integration took place in Washington, D.C., while Maryland and Kentucky also made progress in that area.[57] Some Negro displacement occurred in Texas, Oklahoma, and West Virginia.[58]

Many of the desegregation battles continued in the federal courts. A Louisiana law permitting the establishment of private schools to avoid desegregation was overturned. Another United States Court stopped school officials of Prince Edward County, Virginia, from using public funds to maintain a private school system. Desegregation lawsuits spread northward as the school districts of New York City and Chicago faced legal action concerning de facto segregation.[59] The United States Supreme Court ruled against an Arkansas law that required a teacher to list all associations that he had belonged to or had contributed to since 1955.[60]

The 1961 NEA Convention

The Association held its annual convention at Atlantic City, New Jersey, June 25 to June 30. Almost 5,000 delegates transacted the Association's business. Dr. Jonas Salk and Frank Thompson, a congressman from New Jersey, presented the main speeches. Miss Clarice Kline addressed the delegates upon the theme of the convention: "A Charge to Keep." Avoiding all controversial subjects, her speech was the usual combination of platitudes and quotations. Dr. Carr told the members about the extended services of the NEA, and he used colored slides to accompany his presentation.

The NEA continued to court federal aid as the delegates ground out their perennial resolution concerning the need for government money. Their spirits were buoyed by a message from President Kennedy in which the president felt that Congress would pass the Morse-Thompson Bill by late summer.[61]

Behind this facade of innocence lurked a general feeling of uneasiness caused by the aggressiveness of the AFT. Many delegates were concerned about the vulnerability of the New York City and Detroit affiliates, since each had less than 1,200 members and had been in a state of disarray for years. This situation was true for many urban affiliates because the rurally dominated NEA had generally ignored urban education.

George Jones, former executive secretary of the ATA, explained how the Association clung to this agrarian philosophy. He maintained that the NEA always emphasized its professional status. Intrinsically, this appealed to a rural teacher because, through NEA membership, the teacher automatically acquired additional community prestige. Jones also charged that many superintendents required that all of their teachers belong to the NEA as a requisite for employment. These two factors—a belief in professional status and mandatory membership—were the major reasons why the NEA was predominantly rural in its outlook.

On the other hand, the NEA failed to appeal to the urban teacher because of the impersonal relationship existing between the teacher and the community; therefore, the teacher was more interested with the tangible benefits, i.e., salary, working conditions, and classload. In short, the teacher was interested in what the NEA could do for him along material lines, and prior to the 1960s, the urban teacher found very little NEA involvement in his area.[62]

This becomes apparent in Table 2, which shows the membership of the NEA in relationship to the Association membership in urban areas. In 1961, the NEA had attracted the largest number of urban teachers in its history, but this was still only twenty-two percent of total NEA membership.

Because of the NEA weaknesses in the urban areas, some members had been urging an establishment of a Division of Urban Services to function in the same capacity as the Division of Rural Services, which had been serving the rural teachers since 1936.[63] Study began upon this request when the Representative Assembly allocated $50,000 toward the initiation of a project aimed at determining ways in which the NEA could aid the urban affiliates. Some delegates thought the sum was too small, so they attempted to double the initial funding of the project. Dr. Carr opposed this effort, and his wishes prevailed.[64]

Table 2

Comparison of Total Membership of the NEA from
1954 to 1961 with Memberships in Urban Areas
with Population of 100,000*

Year	Total NEA Membership	Membership in NEA in Urban Areas with Population of Over 100,000	Percentage of Members
1954	561,708	102,782	18
1955	612,716	110,272	18
1956	659,190	117,641	17.7
1957	703,829	115,299	16.4
1958	616,707	105,270	17
1959	667,120	117,479	17.5
1960	713,994	143,070	20.2
1961	765,616	169,464	22.1

*The various NEA Handbooks from 1954 to 1961.

In another move to counter the AFT, the delegates called for professional negotiations, although the Resolutions Committee carefully couched the resolution in nonunion language. Assuming that all differences could be solved in a dignified manner, the resolution "precluded" the strike as a weapon in the solution of teacher-school board disputes.

The AFT also played a significant role in an intrastate tussle between the Virginia Education Association and one of its affiliates, the Arlington Education Association. The VEA suspended its Arlington affiliate when it voted to integrate its membership. Within a few days, Carl Megel sent a telegram to the AEA attacking the VEA upon its "prejudicial and unAmerican resolution" and inviting the AEA to affiliate with the union. Edward Kennedy brought this matter to the attention of the delegates and proposed the following motion:

> That the Representative Assembly instruct the president to set up a special committe to study the implications of the actions involved between the two professional organizations and make recommendations for a just and ethical solution and further, that the Arlington Educational Association be commended by the body for their courageous leadership in the state of Virginia by uniting their professional organization without regard to color.[65]

A lively debate ensued pitting members of the white, southern associations against delegates from the North and the West. Robert Williams from Virginia called for a roll call, and a South Carolinian, Edward Culpepper, seconded the motion. When the votes were counted, the results overwhelmingly endorsed the Arlington Education Association by a 3,457 to 722 margin. Alabama, Georgia, Mississippi, Louisiana, Virginia, North Carolina, and South Carolina entered their "no" votes into the Association's records.[66]

A consistent trend toward integration within the NEA was lacking, however, since earlier the organization had refused to enter the conflict over the closing of the Prince Edward County school system, a subject which was brought up by Walter Ludwig. The main fight was still to come: the debate over desegregation in the public schools.

The chairman of the Resolutions Committee presented the desegregation resolution to the Assembly:

The National Education Association views with deep concern the problems which accompany the evolving process of desegregation in the public schools in response to the changed legal status of the public schools initiated by the Supreme Court decisions on desegregation. Because this process involves fundamental questions of human rights as well as central issues of professional status, it is fitting that the Association restate the principles that guide it in approaching these problems:

1. Support of democratic principles and of the free society which embodies them.

2. Respect for law as an inescapable condition for maintaining an orderly society.

3. Protection of individual rights as the first and highest duty of democratic governments.

4. Support and protection of orderly processes in protesting unfavorable laws.

5. Recognition of the dangers inherent in unrestrained and unlawful protests of judicial decisions.

6. Maintenance of free public education served by a free and dignified profession.

In light of these principles, the Representative Assembly hereby requests the officers and directors of the Association to plan and initiate actions which will:

1. Assure the maintenance of free public education.

2. Promote good will, fairness, and respect for law.

3. Offer possibilities of reducing hostility.

4. Alleviate anxieties among teachers and officials who administer the public schools.

5. Support local and state associations which seek to protect teachers whenever their professional rights and status are unfairly menaced.

6. Openly commended, for efforts to improve conditions, local and state officials of public school systems, directors and officers of local and state organizations, teachers and administrators of public schools, and private citizens.

The Association commends the communities which have handled their problems regarding desegregation in such a manner as to assume their responsibility to maintain the public schools and their obligation to recognize the political and professional rights of teachers. It commends also the officers and directors of the National Education Association for their vigorous and effective support of state and local associations when the professional rights and status of teachers were unfairly menaced. Particularly it commends the alertness of the officers and directors in establishing a fund from which interest free loans could be made to teachers whose salary payments were delayed because of problems involved in desegregation. The Association recognizes that Americans of good will in every state are seeking, within the areas possible for them, to support the integrity of public education and the principles to which the National Education Association is devoted. The nation is indebted to these loyal citizens who display in their lives the highest American ideals.[67]

William Bishop traced the evolution of the desegregation resolution's rewording. He reminded the delegates that the Board of Directors issued a directive calling for the Editing Committee and the representatives of the southern associations to meet in an effort to solve the impasse. This meeting produced an agreement that the executive secretaries of the dual affiliates submit two documents to the Editing Committee: one called a point of view and the other a proposed resolution. After completing this, the Editing Committee met with the dual associations and worked out a compromise resolution. In this manner, the NEA hoped to avoid another bitter struggle.

Discontent became evident immediately after Bishop completed his address. William Simons, a District of Columbia delegate, moved to amend the resolution by adding the phrase "Support the United States Supreme Court decision of desegregation of public schools" after the word "will" in the first sentence of the resolution's second paragraph.[68] Sik Kum Taui of Hawaii seconded the motion and the fight began. Simons, Taui, Larry Flynn, representing the Overseas Education Association, and Miss Ann C. Chereb of New York spoke for the amendment, thus indicating broad support for the change.

W. W. Eshelman defended the Resolutions Committee's decision, but then, five people representing Maryland, Minnesota, Alabama, New York, and Illinois supported Simons' amendment. Robert Stanford told the convention that his delegation passed in caucus "substantially the same" amendment as proposed by Simons.[69] Franklin Brainard from Saint Paul, Minnesota, said that the Saint Paul division of his organization voted overwhelmingly to support the Supreme Court. The other three men echoed his sentiments. The president of the Department of Classroom Teachers reminded the Assembly of the DCT's support of the Resolutions

Committee. Pressure for change continued to mount as Arizona and Missouri delegates argued that the NEA must uphold the court decision without any equivocation. Bert Ishee, a North Carolinian, backed the Resolutions Committee and hit upon two familiar points: (a) the delegates who supported this amendment had no personal experience in this matter; and (b) the problem could be solved through gradualism. Feeling that the committee's resolution took his basic points into consideration, he urged the members to support "the strongest resolution ever to come out of the Resolutions Committee—one which offers guidelines which will help us in this complex, difficult, and vitally important problem."[70]

This tide of opinion continued to favor the amended version of the resolution. Arizona, Michigan, and California delegates indicated that each of these states had already adopted resolutions favoring the Supreme Court decision. After the endorsement of these states, ten more people spoke on the amendment, and seven of them upheld it. Howard Mattlin of New York reviewed the reasons for the amendment, placing them into five general categories: (a) patriotism; (b) American image; (c) a selling point in the United States competition with the Soviet Union; (d) NEA image in the United States; and (e) morality. He emphasized the final point:

> I don't think that anyone here can vote against the amendment and feel that he has committed a moral act. . . . If the NEA had wanted to support this it would have made a one sentence resolution and none of this would have been needed—that one sentence would have been what the amendment really is. I think that if we face up to this reality as adults, the amendment is the only thing that makes the resolution a moral resolution for all of us.[71]

At this point the prospects of the amendment looked good, but Richard Batchelder from Massachusetts raised a question, causing some of the delegates to reevaluate their position:

> Is the amendment before us to pledge support of the Supreme Court decision or does the amendment before us place NEA and its officers and directors in a position in which we must plan and initiate action which will carry out the Supreme Court decision?
> . . . While I would accept the Supreme Court decision, I am

not so sure that this Delegate Assembly or great Association should be put in a position where we should try to enforce the Supreme Court decisions of the land.[72]

The delegates applauded him. Miss Kline read the amendment again. George Deer asked that she repeat it because "a great many of us in this auditorium are seeing this quite differently after Mr. Batchelder's remarks, than we saw it before."[73] Miss Kline complied and Deer moved to close debate. The delegates agreed. She called for a vote on the amendment, and the Assembly defeated it. Then the Assembly defeated Simons' request for a roll call vote. Ohio and Illinois delegates attempted to add two more amendments but were unsuccessful.[74] Finally, Harold Holstein proposed to amend the original resolution by placing this sentence: "The National Education Association pledges continued support of the United States Supreme Court decision on school desegregation," between the first and second sentence of the first paragraph of the original resolution. Batchelder seconded the motion, and it was passed with practically no debate.[75] Louisiana, Mississippi, Georgia, Virginia, Alabama and South Carolina recorded their "no" votes on the Association's minutes.

The amended desegregation resolution read:

> The National Education Association views with deep concern the problems which accompany the evolving process of desegregation in the public schools in response to the changed legal status of the public schools initiated by the Supreme Court decisions on desegregation. The National Education Association pledges continued support of the United States Supreme Court decision on school desegregation. Because this process involves fundamental questions of human rights as well as central issues of professional status, it is fitting that the Association restate the principles that guide it in approaching these problems:
>
> a. Support of democratic principles and of the free society which embodies them.
>
> b. Respect for law as an inescapable condition for maintaining an orderly society.
>
> c. Protection of individual rights as the first and highest duty of democratic governments.
>
> d. Support and protection of orderly processes in protesting unfavorable laws.

    e. Recognition of the dangers inherent in unrestrained and unlawful protests of judicial decisions.

    f. Maintenance of free public education served by a free and dignified profession.

In the light of these principles, the Representative Assembly hereby requests the officers and directors of the Association to plan and initiate action which will —

    a. Assure the maintenance of free public education.

    b. Promote good will, fairness, and respect for law.

    c. Offer possibilities of reducing hostility.

    d. Alleviate anxieties among teachers and officials who administer the public schools.

    e. Support local and state associations which seek to protect teachers whenever their professional rights and status are unfairly menaced.

    f. Openly commend, for efforts to improve conditions, local and state officials of public school systems, directors and officers of local and state organizations, teachers and administrators of public schools, and private citizens.

The Association commends the communities which have handled their problems regarding desegregation in such a manner as to assume their responsibility to maintain the public schools and their obligation to recognize the political and professional rights of teachers. It commends also the officers and directors of the National Education Association for their vigorous and effective support of state and local associations when the professional rights and status of teachers were unfairly menaced. Particularly it commends the alertness of the officers and directors in establishing a fund from which interest-free loans could be made to teachers whose salary payments were delayed because of problems involved in desegregation. The Association recognizes that Americans of good will in every state are seeking, within the areas possible for them, to support the integrity of public education and the principles to which the National Education Association is devoted. The nation is indebted to these loyal citizens who display in their lives the highest American ideals.[76]

The debate lasted only two hours and was more subdued than the previous arguments over this topic.[77] Apparently much of this was due to the Board of Directors bringing the representatives of the Negro and white associations together in an effort to work out a compromise resolution. The compromise resolution arrived at by the committee did not endorse the Supreme Court decision,

thus triggering Simons' attempt at amendment. Simons' forces were
well organized and represented a good cross section of the country
except the South. The South, supporting the original resolution,
offered nothing new to the gradualism argument, but the Southerners did not, however, resort to their usual threat of bolting the
Association. Interestingly enough, Simons' amendment was killed
by Batchelder's asking whether the amendment would require the
NEA to enforce the Supreme Court decision. Subsequently, this led
to the acceptance of a slightly more moderate amendment, which
Batchelder seconded.

Batchelder's entry into the desegregation debate presents some
interesting aspects worthy of comment. Up until 1961, officers of
the Association, i.e., past presidents, members of the Board of
Directors or the Executive Committee, and personnel of the Resolutions Committee, led the floor fights against the modification of
the integration resolutions. Usually the rest of the people involved
represented the rank and file who never rose in the NEA hierarchy.
Batchelder, however, was an exception as he was on the threshold
of leadership. During the 1961 convention, he was elected to the
Executive Committee, a position he held until 1967. In 1965, he
became the president-elect of the Association and assumed the
presidency the following year.

Reaction to the NEA Desegregation Resolution

Although the amended resolution marked the first time that the
NEA endorsed the 1954 court decision, the immediate reaction of
the Negro community was not completely favorable. The *Pittsburgh
Courier* compared the NEA to a Rip Van Winkle who had slept
on the desegregation issue until:

> Finally on June 30, this organization of 765,000 school teachers,
> after a two hour debate in Atlantic City, voted to support the
> Supreme Court 1954 decree, but voted down stronger resolutions
> . . . Well, it is better to improve integration at a snail's pace than
> not at all, but we did expect faster action from a group with a
> vested interest in education and patriotism.[78]

Reaction came from the South, as George Deer expressed the
area's general unhappiness with the resolution:

Southern delegates have insisted that the Association accept the mild statement on this question which has been on the books since the 1954 convention at New York. They have had the support of the Resolutions Committee and the Delegate Assembly in the past years. At this convention, the Resolutions Committee offered again a resolution which had full support of the southern groups. This, however, was amended on the convention floor so as to give a stronger statement in support of the Court's stand on this matter . . . The southern delegates were unhappy over the amendment.[79]

Meanwhile, the Louisiana Attorney General ordered all Louisiana teachers who belonged to the NEA to drop their membership in the Association or face dismissal. He based his decision upon a state law forbidding any teacher to hold membership in an organization supporting integration.[80]

Posture of the "NEA Journal" during 1961

The *NEA Journal* reflected the new position of the Association during 1961. While no major articles concerning the integration crisis appeared, the "News and Trends" column carried some items about the desegregation conflict. It carried the decision of the Board of Directors to grant interest free loans to New Orleans teachers whose schools were unable to meet the payroll because of the integration strife.[81] The NEA desegregation resolution was featured prominently in the September issue of the magazine.[82] Two months later, the column reported that the Louisiana Attorney General had modified his stand upon teacher membership in the Association. Dismissals of teachers who belonged to the NEA were dropped. This occurred through the "efforts of the Louisiana members and affiliates of the NEA and by the Baton Rouge attorneys associated with NEA legal counsel in the District of Columbia."[83]

Relationship Between The Integration Resolution And Southern NEA Membership

Since the NEA endorsed the Supreme Court decision, examination of southern NEA membership is necessary to determine whether the resolution has had any effect upon membership. Examination of Table 3 reveals that NEA membership in 1954 was 561,708 members, of whom 148,729 members came from this eleven state area, accounting for twenty-seven percent of the total NEA membership. NEA membership increased to 765,616 people seven years later, while the southern states had 183,369 members or twenty-three percent of the national NEA membership. Only Louisiana and Mississippi had fewer members in 1961 than in 1954. Otherwise, the only other definite membership loss, caused by an NEA dues increase, occurred in 1958. The net membership gains of the other nine states more than offset the losses in Mississippi and Louisiana. The membership figures showed that the threatened defection of members had not yet developed, but the next few years would be crucial.

Table 3

Total NEA Membership from 1954 to 1961 with Individual State
Membership for that Same Period for States Maintaining
Dual Organizations*

Organization								
	1954	1955	1956	1957	1958	1959	1960	1961
NEA	561,708	612,716	659,190	703,829	616,707	667,120	713,994	765,616
Alabama	17,318	17,771	19,001	18,546	15,787	17,752	19,294	19,955
Arkansas	7,005	7,417	7,451	7,613	7,129	7,031	8,757	9,142
Florida	6,792	7,962	10,235	11,204	11,787	13,741	15,271	17,606
Georgia	16,820	17,770	18,759	20,682	16,510	20,469	20,816	21,636
Louisiana	8,833	9,700	9,452	8,097	5,633	5,666	6,269	7,009
Mississippi	4,222	4,241	4,516	4,575	2,561	3,069	3,436	3,857
North Carolina	21,136	23,579	25,621	26,879	22,395	25,826	27,065	28,524
South Carolina	7,894	9,167	9,680	9,814	6,932	8,095	8,778	10,047
Tennessee	21,521	22,460	23,551	23,137	18,818	19,766	21,170	22,874
Texas	21,889	24,435	25,924	27,730	23,822	23,951	26,076	27,155
Virginia	17,309	19,172	21,248	21,576	16,779	16,260	17,221	18,604

*NEA Handbook, 1954 to 1961.

For the time being, no states left the NEA. Perhaps this exodus did not occur because the NEA said nothing about the elimination of dual affiliates. Still maintaining racial bars to memberships, these eleven states were unaffected by the NEA's integration resolution. Generally the South had dragged its feet since the 1954 decision, thus limiting integration in the deep South to a token effort. On a lesser scale, the southern members of the Association could affect the NEA integration resolution similarly, thus the southern teachers could ignore the NEA edict just as the southern people had generally ignored the 1954 Supreme Court decision. The key to the problem became the dual affiliates, for as long as they existed, teacher desegregation in the NEA would not really be a reality; therefore, the next stage of the NEA integration conflict will center around the elimination of the dual affiliates.

DEVELOPMENTS IN 1962

A very slight increase of school integration occurred in 1962. The border states and the District of Columbia integrated a little over half of their black students, while the South had yet to desegregate even one percent of its black student body.[84] Desegregation occurred in forty-nine school districts for the first time. Integration moved faster in higher education than in its elementary and secondary counterparts. Of the 285 state supported colleges and universities in these regions, 163 schools had somewhat integrated by the beginning of the new school year.[85]

Regardless of the many peaceful examples of school integration, James Meredith's entry into the University of Mississippi gained the most attention during 1962. It caused another direct confrontation between federal and state officials, triggering disorders and mobilization of the National Guard. With the aid of United States officials, Meredith finally enrolled, but conditions at the University remained tense. Things became so bad that the Executive Committee of the Southern Association of Colleges and Schools notified the university that it intended to recommend loss of accreditation because of political interference into the affairs of the school. The Association of Higher Education, a department of the NEA, gave complete support to the accreditation agency.[86]

AFT Victory in New York City

While the struggle over integration dominated the national attention, the NEA had developed a new problem that temporarily relegated its internal integration dispute to a secondary position so that the Association might cope successfully with the rising threat of unionism. The AFT inroads into the urban areas frightened the NEA leaders and members alike, causing them to react faster than they had ever reacted to the integration crisis.

The immediate attention focused upon New York City, where the United Federation of Teachers, an affiliate of the AFT, was attempting to organize the teachers. The time was ripe for such a move, as the city schools had been a constant arena for internecine conflicts since the 1940s. The secondary teachers had the same salary scale as the elementary teachers, but the requirements for the former were higher, thus causing conflict; the teachers chafed under bureaucratic administration; steady political pressure from outside sources affected the district: buildings and equipment deteriorated; racial unrest increased rapidly. The teachers struck in November 1961, and, finally, won an agreement for a bargaining election. The UFT was the only teacher organization that actively campaigned for the election. In the summer of 1962 the teachers voted overwhelmingly in favor of the election.

The NEA had previously established a regional office in the city, but the Association faced great odds in conducting a successful fight against the union. Perhaps the NEA would have been wiser to have selected a battleground a little more favorable for the Association's success in the first major test of strength against the AFT, for the NEA had not exhibited any membership strength in New York City in over two decades. In 1961, the NEA had only 881 members, which was a net increase of 221 members in nine years. This was an infinitesimal figure considering that the district had nearly 46,000 professional employees eligible for NEA membership.[87] In addition to membership difficulties, the NEA had other problems. The AFT placed the Association immediately upon the defensive by attacking its civil rights record. The Catholic segment of New York disagreed with the NEA's position on aid to private schools, and the Jews charged the NEA of anti-Semitism because in the 1950s the NEA had banned Jewish teachers from NEA-sponsored tours that passed through Arabic countries.[88]

Myron Lieberman pointed out that the AFT recognized the significance of a victory over the NEA. New York City had more teachers than the ten smallest states in the country, and since New York was the communications center of the nation, the union was assured of national news coverage. This would do much to spread the word of the AFT throughout the United States.[89]

Three organizations competed for the teachers' vote. The UFT represented the AFT, while the Teachers Bargaining Organization, a hastily formed coalition of elementary and secondary teachers, supported the NEA. The third group was the Teachers Union, a left wing splinter group with no national affiliation. During the campaign, the NEA attempted to maintain a professional image, whereas the UFT assumed a very aggressive position.[90]

The NAACP supported the UFT, and Herbert Hill, national labor secretary of the NAACP, said:

> The NAACP has always exposed and fought discrimination and segregation in unions and in other organizations. . . . By the same token we have never hesitated to raise our voice in support of unions which are for racial equality. Such an example of demonstrated good faith and diligent application exists today in the American Federation of Teachers whose New York City local is right now on the ballot seeking to win bargaining rights for the New York City classroom teachers.[91]

When Hill compared the civil rights record of both organizations, he concluded that the NEA practiced segregation in the South as evidenced by the existence of dual state and local affiliates.

On December 16, 1961, officials counted the votes. The AFT affiliate won by a great margin. The UFT received 20,045 votes, while the TBO got only 9,770 votes. The TU came in last with only 2,575 votes.[92] The *NEA Journal,* commenting on the union victory, said: "The New York Teachers Bargaining Organization and its component groups are to be congratulated for an excellent campaign which they were required to compress into a very few weeks to achieve unity on behalf of the teaching profession in New York City."[93]

In order to counter further AFT successes, the NEA moved to

build up their city affiliates. After a six month study, the Board of Directors established the Urban Project. The Board resolution creating the project indicated the urgency of the program: "There is immediate need for the NEA to establish a new and rigorous program of services which will seek to develop active local association programs throughout the country."[94] The *NEA Journal* said that the Urban Project "will mark a renewal of the Association's policy to help its members to meet their problems."[95]

The Urban Project was very broad in scope and was aimed at improving the welfare of the city teacher and rejuvenating the central core of the city. Dr. John Norton, director of the six month study, said that the project would "help solve school dropouts, reduce juvenile delinquency, and eliminate slums."[96] Dr. Carr denied that the project was a direct result of the AFT victory in New York, pointing out that it had been initiated by the Representative Assembly in 1961; however, T. M. Stinnett, said, "The rapid strengthening of the Project was influenced by the battle over New York City."[97] It is significant to note that shortly after the organization of the Urban Project, "legal counsel was retained . . . to provide special assistance on current urban problems, including such areas as professional negotiations."[98]

The 1962 NEA Convention

The NEA held its annual convention at Denver, Colorado, July 1 to July 6, 1962. For the first time since 1957, civil rights was not the major topic of delegate discussion, having been replaced by the NEA's small, but aggressive rival—the AFT. Total membership of the Delegate Assembly reached 6,000 people, a new high. Even though this number was greater than practically any AFT affiliate in the nation, the union cast a huge shadow upon the convention. William Carr and James Carey, president of the International Union of Electrical Workers, gave the principal addresses.

Carr spoke to the delegates prior to the beginning of the business session of the Representative Assembly. He titled his speech "Turning Point." He examined the four major crises of modern NEA history wherein the Association had to make major decisions that profoundly altered NEA history. The first turning point, as Carr saw it, occurred in 1920 when the NEA created the Representative Assembly, which democratized the Association. The second major crisis was during the 1930s when the "NEA treasury was as flat as a flounder."[99] The organization responded to this situation by making plans for the future, i.e., the establishment of the Educational Policies Commission, the Future Teachers of America, and the Committee on Educational Finance. World War II signaled the third crisis within the NEA. The NEA rose to the occasion by playing a vital role in the creation of UNESCO and WCOTP. During this same period the Professional Rights and Responsibilities Commission and the National Committee of Teacher Education and Professional Standards were organized by the Association. The fourth period of stress occurred during the early 1950s. Again, Carr told of NEA response to the crisis: "It built a nine million dollar Headquarters; more than doubled its membership; doubled its services; set up joint committees with magazine publishers and school board members; . . . won a number of dramatic battles to protect rights of teachers; opened four regional offices . . . and greatly expanded programs of the Department of Classroom Teachers."[100]

Then Carr embarked upon the current major crisis facing the NEA. He pointed to urbanization and unionization as causes of the crisis. He admitted that the Association had not dealt "effectively with the needs and problems" of urbanization. Linking the educational problems in the cities with the declining union membership, Carr indicated that the unions viewed the teaching profession as a potential source of swelling union membership. He told the delegates that the Association reacted to the union threat by creation of the Urban Project and reiterated the basic principles of the NEA: the NEA is a professional organization and the Association is a democratic organization, independent and all-inclusive. Carr asked the school boards to cooperate by employing professional negotiations. Finally, he asked the teachers to become involved in association work, emphasizing professional negotiations as the means of this involvement.

James Carey spoke as a member of the "Public Education Tomorrow" symposium. He chided teachers for clinging to their narrow definition of professionalism, pointing out that newspapermen are considered professional but yet they belong to a union. Then he launched into the reasons why teachers were turning to the unions:

poor pay and lack of job security. Carey taunted the NEA on its lack
of success in the New York City election: "The NEA decided on a
test of strength in New York City. The NEA decided for the first
time that it would risk a contest of collective bargaining strength.
But the United Federation of Teachers affiliated with the American
Federation of Teachers, AFL-CIO, overwhelmed the NEA."[101] Indi-
cating that the fight was just beginning, he warned the delegates,
"The labor movement is prepared to match any contribution of the
NEA to improve the standards of school teachers anywhere in these
United States."[102]

Carey's speech was aggressive but not antagonistic. This marked
the first time that most teachers had ever seen one of the nation's
leading professional union men. It required some temerity for Carey
to speak at the convention, as he certainly was in alien territory.
Newsweek said that there were some instances of heckling, and the
NEA Proceedings indicated that he was interrupted once during
his speech.[103] T. M. Stinnett attributed the heckling to a "labor
plant."[104] Carey's speech clearly indicated that the NEA could no
longer afford to ignore the AFT, and the escalation of the fight
loomed immediately upon the horizon.

As a result, the NEA moved to cope with the AFT by adopting
two resolutions that the members hoped would aid them in the
struggle. One dealt with professional negotiations and the other
called for professional sanctions, euphemisms for collective bargaining and the strike.[105] The two resolutions were carefully worded
so that the NEA would not sound as militant as a union, but the
resolutions did give an indication of the future direction of the Association.

Since the AFT rivalry, Carey's address, and the resolutions on
professional negotiations and sanctions dominated the convention,
the delegates had little time for the desegregation resolution. The
entire matter took less than fifteen minutes, and although the desegregation resolution was amended, the change was insignificant.[106]

The dispute between the Arlington Education Association and the
Virginia Education Association came before the convention, and no
debate occurred on this matter. President Ewald Turner gave a brief
history of the trouble, telling the members that a NEA Study Committee had investigated the problem as requested by the Delegate

Assembly. The Committee issued face-saving recommendations for the Virginia Education Association, but nevertheless stated that if a local association exercised its option, i.e., changed membership qualifications allowing Negroes to belong, "all local affiliates should be equally eligible for state association membership."[107] The AEA accepted the recommendations of the committee, while the VEA remained silent upon the issue.

Posture of the "NEA Journal" During 1962

The impact of urban education affected the *NEA Journal*. During the year, almost every issue of the magazine examined some aspect of education in the cities. The magazine initiated a series called "Stirrings in the Big Cities," which examined the educational problems of eight major cities in the nation. The editor began to take a hard look at some of the real issues of urban education, resulting in the loss of some of the magazine's naïveté. New terms were added to the reader's vocabulary via fine articles on the disadvantaged child, school dropouts, and ghetto education. As the realistic view of education grew, the number of Negro pictures also showed a proportionate increase. The magazine carried fourteen pictures of Negroes in 1962. Most of them showed black students and teachers as integral parts of desegregated classrooms. Still another picture featured Dr. Carr and three other educators viewing the Berlin Wall. One of these educators was a Negro.[108]

The Effect of Unionism and Civil Rights Upon the NEA

The subtleties of these pictures could not escape the careful reader, for it signaled the beginning of a new period for the Association. The external pressure brought to bear upon the NEA by the AFT, and the internal pressure brought upon the Association for a change in its civil rights posture were two of the chief elements forcing the change. Change for an organization the size of the NEA can be a slow, difficult, and, sometimes, traumatic experience. Many NEA members and leaders were still wary about professional negotiations, the use of sanctions, and the desegregation role of the Association, for these were new, almost foreign problems, which a predominantly rural membership found difficult to comprehend. Relative to this position, T. M. Stinnett claimed that during the 1950s the NEA operated the same as it always had even though the world was changing at a rapid pace.[109]

The Association's attitude toward civil rights and its new interest in urban education were two cases in point that substantiated Stinnett's criticism. The NEA required seven years to endorse the Supreme Court decision of 1954. When endorsement finally came, the delegates, rather than the NEA officials, provided the impetus. The treatment of urban education was the same, as the NEA leaders virtually ignored educational problems of the cities. Membership fell while the educational plight worsened. The AFT victory stirred the NEA out of its lethargic state, and the Association, out of necessity, had to prepare to battle the union. By 1962, leaders and liberal members recognized that the major educational problems in the nation exisited in the cities; consequently, the NEA began to move hesitatingly into this arena, a move that required what amounted to a change of Association philosophy.

The major emphasis of the NEA would be upon the competition with the AFT; but this could not be separated from the internal struggle over civil rights, for the two issues dovetailed during this period, making it impossible to proceed in one area without affecting the other. The AFT had its strength in the major urban areas of the nation. Usually these schools had a large percentage of black teachers who could play an important role in any bargaining election. Under these circumstances, the AFT exploited the Achilles heel of the NEA: dual organizations in the South.

DEVELOPMENTS IN 1963

Integration of public schools moved slightly forward in the 1963–1964 school year. According to the *Southern Education Report,* the border states and the District of Columbia had integrated almost fifty-five percent of their black student body, while the South still had not integrated one percent of its black students.[110] Racial bars were eliminated in 161 school systems, thus accounting for the largest number of school districts to desegregate since 1956.[111]

The Fairfax Education Association of Fairfax County, Virginia, removed all of its racial restrictions for membership. This NEA affiliate, representing almost 3,000 members, voted 2,090 to 405 to follow the example of its neighbor, the Arlington Education Association. The membership change became effective in the beginning of the 1963–1964 school year.[112]

The Prince Edward County schools remained closed, denying education to 1,700 black children. As a result of the school closing, the AFT and the NEA attempted to provide some type of education. The AFT teachers from Philadelphia and New York had already taught some of the Negro students during the summer of 1963.[113] The NEA became involved through the establishment of the Prince Edward County Free School Association, making the first major contribution of $2,000 to that organization.[114] When the Free School Association opened its doors, the superintendent said, "Without the help of the NEA in recruitment and screening of teachers the Prince Edward Free Schools could not have gotten under way at this time."[115]

Another professional organization had its civil rights problems during 1963. The NAACP picketed the American Medical Association's convention because only one-fourth of the Negro doctors could belong to the AMA; furthermore, the NAACP claimed that only four southern county medical associations permitted black membership. These restrictions caused the loss of patients because of the Negro doctors' inability to practice in many hospitals. The AMA remained silent upon the issue.[116]

The *New York Times* disclosed that the American Nurses Association had a similar problem, but contrary to the AMA's reaction, the ANA had moved toward desegregation of its affiliates as early as 1946. The Colored Graduate Nurses became part of the ANA in 1950, and during the next decade, only one state association failed to desegregate. The ANA gave that affiliate one year to integrate or face expulsion.[117]

The 1963 NEA Convention

Detroit, Michigan, was the scene of the annual NEA convention held from June 30 to July 5. Almost 6,800 delegates transacted the NEA's business, which focused upon three major issues: proposed sanctioning of Utah; the desegregation resolution; and extremist attacks upon educators. Mrs. Hazel Blanchard devoted much of her presidential address to the latter subject, while William Carr, in his annual address, emphasized professional negotiations, intelligent use of sanctions, and federal aid to education. He made a fleeting reference to "the march of events in civil rights."[118]

The other principal speakers were not reticent about civil rights. Dr. Eugene Carson Blake reminded the delegates that 1963 was the one hundredth anniversary of the Emancipation Proclamation and warned that the Negroes would not wait much longer for social progress: ". . . the Negro community is tired of waiting any longer and will wait no longer. Teach this to your contemporaries, your teachers, your school boards, your communities. Teach this to your pupils. This had better be understood."[119] Francis Keppel, United States Commissioner of Education, spoke of the educational problems facing the nation's nonwhite population and challenged educators to improve the lives of the disadvantaged Americans through the creation of meaningful educational programs. Keppel chided the NEA for its late entry into this particular field:

> This Association and others have for years issued policy statements about education. This attention to educational problems has been gratifying to many members of the profession, but it must be recorded that public confidence in the profession and the profession's contribution to the larger issues of public policy have not been measurably increased. Perhaps this is because policy development, to mean anything, requires personal involvement in the turbulent waters of public decision making. Such involvement is, of course, the very essence of a democratic society.[120]

Discussing the educational problems of the large cities, Dr. Samuel Brownell, superintendent of the Detroit Public Schools, asked the NEA to help achieve equal opportunity for the Detroit children: "We need the support of the educational association in helping us to attain our objective of equal opportunity for all, just as your educational leadership is needed on this problem nationally."[121] Dr. Thomas H. Lantos, economic consultant to the California Education Association, gave a dynamic speech called "Closed Minds in an Open Society." He touched upon the major educational issues in America, relating them to the NEA. He pulled no punches when he discussed civil rights and challenged the Association to face the racial problem realistically and to work toward its elimination. Indicating that the NEA had received much adverse criticism over civil rights, Lantos urged the Association to adopt a more liberal stance so that it could earn the respect of the people throughout the nation:

> In the last few days, newspaper readers in this country have been made aware of the fact that the NEA is not immune to this problem. It does not become the organization, which represents what is claimed to be the leading profession, to lag in its own willingness to face up to the issue of human equality. It is neither by accident nor collusion that a number of speakers who have preceded me on this platform have called upon the NEA, as I do, to put its own house in order, and earn the right to be called the leading profession.[122]

Thus, the NEA's internal struggles over desegregation became a major issue, after lying dormant since the 1961 convention.

The civil rights dispute, however, had to share equal attention with the Utah sanctions' controversy. Early in 1963, the Utah Education Association imposed sanctions against Utah because of the state's failure to finance education adequately. By convention time, no settlement had been reached; therefore, many delegates expressed a willingness to impose national sanctions, but the Executive Committee opposed this action.[123] The Board of Directors concurred, but the Board was also aware of the Assembly's strong prosanctions sentiment. At a Board meeting, a state director asked Carr whether the Representative Assembly could overturn the decision of the Executive Committee.[124] Carr replied that the Assembly was "supreme."[125]

Recognizing the possibility that the Assembly could veto the action of the Executive Committee, Carr tried to head off any such delegate movement in his opening address to the convention. He emphasized, "No useful purpose could be served by imposing national sanctions while current negotiations for settlement are in process."[126] But the Department of Classroom Teachers moved toward open revolt when it advised its members not to seek employment in Utah.[127] Reportedly, this action caused Carr to reply, "You leave us with no room to maneuver or compromise."[128] At that point, the organization began a campaign to bring the members back in line. Prior to the beginning of the sanctions' debate, Mrs. Blanchard asked Carr to give a complete history of the negotiations with Utah. With restraint as his theme, Carr gave a careful presentation, reiterating the Executive Committee's intention of imposing sanctions if negotiations failed.[129] Carr's purpose was clear: to act as a brake upon the Assembly.

Carr was successful and the delegates accepted a weakened resolution, commending the Executive Committee for its action and granting to the Executive Committee the right to impose sanctions if the impasse continued.[130] This resolution was astounding because the Executive Committee already possessed this power.

During the debate over the Utah situation, an interesting link between the integration and the sanctions' floor battles became evident. The cast of characters and the organizational techniques employed were similar. Some of the people who argued for a strong integration resolution also supported the sanctioning of Utah, while those who wanted to go slow on integration, advocated a more cautious approach to sanctions. The New York and California delegations generally backed a strong stand on both of these matters. Earl Hanson, chairman of the Resolutions Committee, and Guy Jewell, chairman of the Editing Committee, opposed national sanctions. These men had also figured prominently in the past integration battles. They had consistently supported the Resolutions Committee, which advocated a cautious approach to integration. In previous conventions, the NEA past presidents spoke against amendments to the integration resolution; in the sanctions' argument, Miss Kline urged support of the Executive Committee.[131] The comparison does not end here. In the 1961 convention, Richard Batchelder's interjection into the integration debate killed a stronger amendment. Batchelder was elected to the Executive Committee the same year, and a few years later, became NEA president. During the sanctions' fight, Braulio Alonso gave a powerful speech against national sanctions, causing the delegates to rally behind him.[132] Alonso became a member of the Executive Committee in 1963 and became NEA president in 1967.

Overlapping the argument over sanctions, the civil rights issue appeared on the NEA agenda almost every day of the convention. On July 2, Joseph Avellone, an Ohio delegate, introduced the following amendment:

That the NEA go on record as fully supporting President Kennedy's civil rights legislation, and that it respectfully urge the representatives in Congress to vote for and vigorously support the legislation proposed by the President and also urge the members of the United States Senate to do all within their power to prevent a Senate filibuster which would debar the legislation from coming to a vote on the floor of the Senate.[133]

Edward Holloway, also from Ohio, seconded the motion, and the delegates passed it without any debate.[134]

On the next day, Lyman Ginger proposed the Board of Director's resolution pertaining to dual affiliates:

Having commended affiliates which have removed racial membership barriers, and noting that while significant progress has been made toward the ending of discrimination in professional associations much remains to be accomplished, the National Education Association urges those state and local associations where racial membership restrictions are still in effect to establish consultative committees to facilitate their removal.

While there are no racial restrictions for membership in the National Education Association, the 1963 Representative Assembly, believing that the Association should assist its affiliates to deal with this issue, offers the good offices of the Association:

1.   To assist state and local associations where racial restrictions remain to establish consultative committees which may facilitate their removal.

2.   To sponsor cooperatively with state and local affiliates meetings, workshops, seminars, or other activities in the field of intergroup and human relations, or on other topics, which will help to remove racial barriers in professional education associations.

3.   To work with state affiliates where restrictions still exist to grant local associations the right of local option within the framework of the state association until such time as the state itself can remove such restrictions.

The 1963 Representative Assembly also requests that the Joint Committee of the NEA and the American Teachers Association consider whether and under what conditions it would be desirable and feasible to merge the two associations, and report its recommendations in one year or less.[135]

This amendment was aimed at resolving the disputes over dual affiliates. Ginger also indicated that the Joint Committee of the

NEA-ATA supported the resolution of desegregation of public schools, recommending its adoption without any change.

When Ginger stopped speaking, Pat Tornillo, a Floridian representing the National Council of Urban Education Associations, moved to amend the Board's resolution. This broke the uneasy quiet prevailing since 1961 and precipitated a bitter floor fight. Significantly, it marked the beginning of a new stage in the civil rights battle—the move to eliminate dual affiliates. Tornillo said: "I would like to amend the motion presented by the NEA Board of Directors by striking out the following: "establish consultative committees to facilitate their removal," and by substituting the following: "take immediate steps to open their membership doors to all teachers regardless of race, color, or creed."[136] Eugene Peschel of California seconded the amendment. At that point a question arose concerning a lack of a quorum. Tornillo believed that one did not exist. The chairman of the Rules Committee agreed and advised the president, who adjourned the meeting until that evening. The evening session was strictly ceremonial, so the amendment did not come up for debate until the next day, July 4.

After Tornillo read his amendment again, George Deer attacked it, claiming that it would place 300,000 southern teachers in an untenable position. Pleading for gradualism, he argued that the teachers had to work in a social structure that they had inherited. Then he implied that the acceptance of this amendment would cost the NEA dearly: "Now if you adopt this amendment, you will be saying to nearly 300,000 of your fellow teachers, white and Negro, "We just do not care much about your professional situation nor what happens to your professional organization or whether you can continue affiliation with NEA."[137] Shifting to the offensive, he proudly pointed out that Virginia, North Carolina, Georgia, and Florida had elected Negroes to the Board of Directors, while other states, espousing civil rights ideals, had done nothing in that area:

> Do you know for example which states have the most Negro people? Well, New York has the greatest number of any state. Illinois runs a close second. Ohio, Pennslyvania, Michigan, and California— each of these states has about as many Negroes as Georgia, Alabama, Tennessee, or Florida. As you look around, does each of those states

have Negro delegates in proportion to the Negro population in their state? . . . Somewhere in the Bible is that famous admonition, "He that is without sin, let him cast the first stone."[138]

Immediately after Deer's concluding remarks, Dr. Wade Wilson, James Gilliam, and Mrs. Ruby Gainer, all of whom are Negroes, spoke for Tornillo's motion. But Ginger and Dickenson Guiler, chairman of the Ohio delegation, rallied the organizational forces against any changes, and it soon became apparent that many people opposed the amendment. Attempting to clarify his intentions, Tornillo assured them that the amendment implied no deadline for dual affiliate mergers. He carefully commended the Board's action, but he felt, however, the amendment made "clear to the nation and the world our intentions."[139] Deer continued to emphasize the deadline implications of the amendment. Finally debate was halted, and the delegates rejected the amendment by a voice vote.

Tornillo proposed two more amendments but, unfortunately got bogged down in parliamentary procedure. Ironically, Joseph Seigman and Mrs. Edna Griffin, both from Pennsylvania, spoke favorably for the amendment, but no one made a seconding motion; consequently, Tornillo was defeated again.

At this point, the New York delegation made an interesting admission. Prior to the debate on the Board's motion, it had agreed to back the Board even though many of the delegates supported Tornillo's position. Peter Goudis effectively expressed his quandary over this commitment when he accepted the resolution, but issued, with his acceptance, a warning:

I say let them prove it. I say give them their resolutions. I say I will be at the next convention. I want to hear that their sentiments as our leaders were correct and that mine, and perhaps yours, in wishing for something stronger were incorrect. And the proper way to desegregate, the easiest way to desegregate, the quickest way to desegregate, is through the resolution which they in their consultation, present to us. They have, in effect, gone out on a limb. They have told us, the body delegate, and recommend to us that this is the way to do it. I say let's accept it, and then let's see what their report tells us next year. . . . I ask you to tell them by supporting the motion that has been made by the Board, "We want you to show us as leaders, that you were correct, and we will await the final decision at the next convention." But that will be the time when we who want this done strongly will prevail.[140]

Shortly after this presentation, the delegates passed the Board of Directors' resolution.

On the following day, the Assembly debated the resolution on desegregation in the public schools, an almost parenthetical hassle over the Board's resolution. The Resolutions Committee proposed the same resolution passed in 1962, and immediately, Vernon McDaniel, a Negro from Texas, moved to amend it by adding item "g" in the first paragraph of the resolution as follows: "Extension of the principles of desegregation as it applies to the professional membership in organizations affiliated with the NEA."[141] He argued that a pattern was evolving that stressed open memberships, citing the plans of the Urban Secretaries, the move of the DCT toward single affiliates, the pending merger of the NEA-ATA, and the Assembly's endorsement of President Kennedy's proposed civil rights legislation. George Deer offered his usual opposition, while Wade Wilson, Mrs. Gainer, and Jesse Moses supported the amendment, with Ewald Turner, a former NEA president, concurring.[142] Joseph Parlett of Maryland summed up the need for the amendment's passage by saying: "We have a resolution in which the NEA is telling the schools of the country and other organizations to desegregate. An amendment has been proposed to add that we apply the same philosophy to ourselves. If we pass the resolution and not the amendment, we are going to look right silly."[143] The amended resolution passed with only Louisiana, Mississippi, and Georgia opposing it.

Reaction to the NEA Desegregation Resolution

During the 1963 convention, the Assembly presented a schizophrenic attitude toward civil rights. Approving the proposed federal civil rights program and accepting guidelines for voluntary desegregation of affiliates, the delegates defeated a moderate attempt to clarify the Board's motion. Then, they passed a slightly amended version of the desegregation resolution similar to Tornillo's amendment, which they had previously rejected. Through this haze of confusion, a significant fact remained. Regardless of the debate over dual affiliates, the Board's resolution did not actually threaten the dual affiliates' status, thus allowing the southern delegations to support the Board's plan, while opposing all others.

This indecisive action prompted national criticism. *Time* magazine, in an article upon teacher organizations, indicated that "unlike the NEA, the union has a good civil rights record."[144] *Newsweek* was more caustic as it accused the Association of "shilly-shallying on segregation within its own ranks."[145] The action at Detroit did not escape Carl Megel's sharp observations:

> The NEA has equivocated on civil rights continuously. Even at the 1963 convention, a resolution was presented to require integration of all their areas. This resolution was scuttled, as have been all the other resolutions. The NEA has not seen fit to take a strong, positive position in the area of integration, and they are still maintaining segregated locals in eleven states.[146]

The American Teachers Association, at its national convention, generally favored merger with the NEA. Dr. Lucius Pitts, president of the ATA, maintained that the Negro must play a more significant role in policy making, if the merger were to occur. He pointed out that no Negroes were on the Executive Committee, and only four Negroes were serving on the NEA Board of Directors.[147]

Posture of the "NEA Journal" during 1963

During 1963, the *NEA Journal* continued to broaden its scope concerning the urban and racial aspects of education. In January, the magazine carried a fifteen-page supplement on disadvantaged people in the United States. In the March edition, the editor featured an article called "Teaching About Civil Rights."[148] After the convention, the magazine printed the desegregation resolution.[149] In December, the first major articles about school desegregation occurred: two of them dealt with integration of the classroom,[150] while the other article outlined the successful merger of dual affiliates in Dade County, Florida.[151]

The magazine carried only four pictures of Negroes during 1963; one of these, however, was particularly interesting because it showed the new NEA interest on voluntary merger of dual affiliates. It was a picture of the Dade County salary committee, which was comprised of four teachers, two of whom were Negroes.[152]

Integration in the NEA from 1964 to 1967 | 6

In a democracy, the people have to want to do what must be done.   LYNDON B. JOHNSON

1964 marked the tenth anniversary of the historic Supreme Court decision *Brown* v. *The Board of Education.* School desegregation moved very slowly; some states had made practically no effort to integrate. Showing wide versatility in impeding the court decision, state legislatures passed 400 enactments aimed at preventing integration, with Louisiana alone accounting for 199 of them.[1] Clarendon County, South Carolina, one of the school districts directly involved in the 1954 decision, still had not desegregated.

School desegregation statistics showed that fifty-four percent of the black children in the border states and the District of Columbia attended integrated schools, but only two percent of the 2,900,000 black children in the eleven southern states had desegregated.[2] Louisiana had integrated but three schools,[3] while Mississippi had allowed only four schools to integrate.[4]

Staff desegregation became an issue during 1964. The United States Court of Appeals ruled that Duval County, Florida, had to stop assigning teachers on a racial basis. This was the first court ruling on faculty desegregation.[5] As the year progressed, Florida, Tennessee, and Virginia began some staff desegregation, but none occurred in Arkansas, Louisiana, Alabama, South Carolina, North Carolina, Mississippi, and Georgia.[6]

Because of the Supreme Court decision *Griffin* v. *The School Board of Prince Edward County,* the public schools in Prince Edward County reopened in September 1964. Significantly, the NEA filed an *amicus curiae* brief in the case. J. Rupert Picott deserved much credit for involving the NEA, for his organization, the Virginia Teachers Association, and local NAACP officials were able to persuade Thurgood Marshall to talk with northern NEA members, leading to the subsequent NEA action.[7] The brief stated, "The survival of democracy requires that every state maintain a system of free public education and safeguard the education of all. The public school is not expendable."[8] The words were not new, for the NEA had said them for years, but it marked the first time that the NEA officially advised a court in an effort to translate words into deeds.

The struggle to speed school integration received its biggest boost when President Johnson signed the Civil Rights Act of 1964. This was the broadest civil rights stance the government had taken since 1875. The main provisions of the law were:

(1) it outlawed racial discrimination in most hotels, restaurants, theaters, and similar places;

(2) it authorized the Attorney General to initiate suits or to intervene on behalf of an aggrieved person in school discrimination or other cases;

(3) it forbade racial discrimination by employers or unions;

(4) it permitted the halting of funds to federally aided programs in which discrimination was allowed to exist; and

(5) it prohibited registrars from applying different standards to white and Negro voting applicants.[9]

The law had large implications for all aspects of education, giving the Commissioner of Education the right to withhold federal funds from NDEA grants, school lunch and milk programs, and federally impacted areas if segregation continued. It required school districts to file desegregation plans with the commissioner's office. The law had some relevance to the NEA because of the clause forbidding discrimination by employers and unions. No trouble existed with the first point because the Association had been cited by the Urban League in 1954 for its hiring practices, but the second point presented a possible area of difficulty. During the struggle between the NEA and the AFT over the bargaining election in Milwaukee, Wisconsin, the NEA affiliate had to be recognized as a union, according to a Wisconsin law, before an election could be held.[10]

The conflict between the NEA and the AFT continued to rage

during 1964, spreading to many schools throughout the nation. During 1963-1964, twenty-five confrontations occurred, with the NEA winning eighteen.[11] The NEA won major elections in Milwaukee, Wisconsin; Rochester, New York; and Newark, New Jersey; significantly, the Association had less than twenty-six percent of total membership in all of those cities.[12] The Milwaukee election was bitterly contested, with Walter Reuther and William Carr making many appearances for their respective organizations. The NEA lost two key cities to its rival. The Detroit teachers supported the AFT affiliate by a plurality of 1,800 votes, while at Cleveland, Ohio, the teachers selected the union by a 2,701 to 2,026 margin.[13]

During the interim between the 1963 and the 1964 conventions, the NEA attempted to implement the Board of Directors' guidelines regarding the merger of dual affiliates and the merger of the NEA and ATA. Dr. Carr tried to hold a meeting with the executive secretaries of the dual affiliates but was unsuccessful because "too many were fully occupied in the fall months."[14] Finally, all but four of them met in May 1964, and "shared experiences and developed understandings concerning the problems and viewpoints of the associations involved."[15] In the meantime, James McCaskill, visiting the state and local affiliates, discussed the potential merger problems. Also, the Joint Committee of the NEA-ATA established a "sociological study of the steps necessary for a merger of the two associations."[16] Meanwhile, Carr met with the NEA Board of Directors in February 1964, and discussed "implementation of the motion adopted by the Representative Assembly in Detroit."[17]

While the Board of Directors expressed a willingness to talk about integration, the American Association of School Administrators seemed uninterested in the matter. Francis Keppel addressed the AASA meeting at Atlantic City, praising the civil rights movement because it "had shaken education out of its complacency."[18] The administrators ignored his speech. During the convention, ten general meetings, thirty expert sessions, and 120 section meetings were held; integration was not a major issue at any of these. When asked why it had not been discussed, the AASA president replied, "Most members were not facing problems of integration."[19]

Meanwhile, behind-the-scenes maneuvering occurred within the NEA ranks, causing some of the Association staff and leaders to become suspicious. Certain NEA members, unhappy with the Association stance on integration, had formed the National Committee of Educators for Human Rights whose basic purpose was to improve the Association's posture on civil rights. Pat Tornillo was a leader of this committee, and many "young, rising leaders" of the NEA also held NCEHR membership.[20] Referring to this committee, Mrs. Irvamae Applegate said, "The Tornillo group represents a new image of the NEA."[21] The significance of the NCEHR is that it marked the coalescing of the liberal NEA faction, which would eventually exert great influence through the Department of Classroom Teachers and the Representative Assembly, as both of these units would be at the forefront of NEA policy making by 1966.

The NCEHR held its first meeting at Seattle, Washington, during the 1964 NEA convention. Teachers from sixteen states were represented and some of the members were: Pat Tornillo, Joseph H. Whelpton, Miss Louise Alford, and Mrs. Ruby Gainer representing Florida; Stan McEachran, Wesley Ruff, and F. J. Johnson representing Washington; Raymond MacLaughlin, Kenneth Preston, Pat Basile, Morris Beider, and Boyd Bosma representing Michigan; Edward Elliot, Keith Goldhammer, Ewald Turner, and Harold Bock representing Oregon; Wade Wilson, Walter O'Brien, and Harvey Zorbaugh representing Pennsylvania; Henry Gray and Mrs. Maurelle Martin representing Arizona; Robert Richards, Joseph Parlett, and Mrs. Regina Parlett representing Maryland; J. Rupert Picott and Chet Lyons representing Virginia; S. J. Whisenhunt, Mrs. Lula Mary Beatty, and Mrs. Beulah Johnson representing Alabama; Hudson Barksdale and Walker Solomon representing South Carolina; H. E. Tate from Georgia; Charles Lyons from North Carolina; C. J. Duckworth from Mississippi; Vernon McDaniel from Texas; Frank Brainard from Minnesota; and Peter Goudis from New York. The committee also had writers from *Newsweek* and *Newsday* who advised them on the writing of the integration resolution.[22]

The 1964 NEA Convention

The NEA held its annual convention at Seattle, Washington, from June 28 to July 3, and over 6,000 delegates transacted the Association's business. Federal aid and segregation were the chief topics. Robert Wyatt devoted his entire presidential address to federal aid, while Francis Keppel's topic was "Segregation and the Schools." Opposing segregation, Keppel urged the teachers to join with the civil rights organizations to defeat racial intolerance. "There is a natural alliance between the cause of education and the cause of civil rights. We must preserve and foster it. Then we shall shape new dimensions of democracy for all of our children and for our children's children."[23]

A fight over the status of the dual affiliates began to take shape early in the convention. Urging the delegates to end dual affiliation, Miss June Shagaloff, a special assistant for the NAACP, charged the NEA with "equivocation and silence" upon this matter.[24] At a press conference, Carr and Wyatt tried to minimize the existence of the dual affiliates. Carr, referring to the pending merger of the NEA and ATA, said that some Negroes were afraid of not being heard in a larger organization. His statement had direct implications for the merger of dual affiliates because of similar Negro fears. Wyatt, admitting to the existence of the dual affiliates, expressed a feeling that the NEA was moving rapidly toward the elimination of racial barriers.[25]

That evening, Dr. Carr gave his annual address, "The Year of Decision." He reported on the Utah situation and examined the status between the NEA and the AFT. Much of his speech related to the Association's racial progress since 1963. Asserting that the states had made positive steps toward the merger of dual affiliates through voluntary efforts, he advised the Assembly against taking additional action: "I, therefore, strongly advise against any attempt of the NEA to coerce or threaten its affiliates. Such an attempt would retard or halt voluntary progress such as I have reported to you."[26] By recommending continuation of voluntary merger, Carr did not alter his basic position. Apparently, he based his decision on the fact that a few states had merged voluntarily since the creation of the dual affiliates in 1952.

The remaining states having dual affiliates were the hard core area. Less than 70,000 students had been integrated in that area since the 1954 court decision, with much of the desegregation occurring because of court action; therefore, some people had good reason to suspect voluntary efforts. It was becoming clear that Dr. Carr's position was going to be challenged.

The Department of Classroom Teachers offered the first test against the conservative NEA position. Many of the members reflected a basic unhappiness with the Administration's executive bodies because of the handling of the sanctions' fight in Utah. Others, representing urban associations, realized the AFT's advantage because of the union's nonsegregation policy. Significantly, much of this agitation was led by the NCEHR.[27]

The DCT made some progressive moves during the year. The members chose Mrs. Elizabeth Duncan Koontz, a black teacher, as president-elect. Her election had some obvious implications. First of all, she was a member of a "separate but equal" affiliate from North Carolina. Second, her election was meaningful when viewing NEA-AFT rivalry, as no Negro in the AFT hierarchy held as high an elected position as the DCT had bestowed upon Mrs. Koontz.

Also the DCT failed to heed Dr. Carr's advice on not pressuring the southern delegations to end dual affiliates. After a heated debate,[28] the delegates voted narrowly, 1,004 to 985, for the elimination of membership restrictions by July 1, 1965, and for integration of the state and local associations by July 1, 1966.[29] The alternative was expulsion from the NEA. The vote showed the increased effectiveness of the liberals within this organization, but even though the NCEHR prevailed in the DCT, the fight in the Assembly was going to be tougher because the organizational forces controlled much of the convention machinery.

The desegregation resolution reached the Assembly on July 3. Guy Jewell proposed the same resolution that passed in the 1963 convention, with one small exception that stated: "Make available the good offices of the NEA to state and local affiliates which request help in making joint plans for merger."[30] As usual, the Resolutions Committee backed the organizational stance. The fight began when Pat Tornillo moved to amend the resolution as follows:

> An important goal of education is the elimination of prejudice and bigotry from the public mind. As educators, we are dedicated to the principle of equal rights for all.
> In light of this principle, the Representative Assembly instructs the officers and directors of the National Education Association:
> 1.   To direct all local, district, and state associations affiliated

with the National Education Association to take immediate steps
to remove all restrictive membership requirements dealing with
race, creed or ethnic groups.

2. To take immediate action to develop plans to effect the
complete integration of all local and state affiliates whose memberships are now limited to educators of specifically designated
racial, religious, or ethnic groups.

Affiliates whose memberships reflect the above-mentioned restrictions shall be given until July 1, 1966, to revise their constitutions and bylaws, where necessary, to take whatever steps are required
to expedite the complete removal of all restrictive labels, and to present a plan to effect the complete integration of their associations.

Should an affiliated association fail to comply with these requirements by July 1, 1966, the Executive Committee shall have
discretionary powers to take necessary action.[31]

The position considerably softened the DCT's position, as Tornillo
pointed out the amendment's lack of an "integrate or else" clause:
"Restrictive labels shall have been removed, and a plan must be
developed and presented. . . . It does not say that dual organizations
must, in fact, be merged. It does say a plan must be presented by
July 1, 1966."[32] J. Rupert Picott and Boyd Bosma seconded the
motion, thus precipitating a sixty-eight minute debate.[33]

George Deer, who by this time had become the spokesman for the
South, elaborated on gradualism. Possessing a keen ability to probe
his opponent's weaknesses, he displayed his talents well by showing
that Negroes had been elected as NEA Board members from four
southern states, while those delegations advocating a stronger integration amendment failed to elect a proportional number of Negro
members to the Assembly: "Several of those states sponsoring this
amendment have more Negroes in their population than any of those
southeastern states. Many of them have two, three, and even four
members of the Board of Directors. . . . A casual glance over the
floor will show that these states have not even felt like electing Negro
teachers as delegates to the convention in any significant manner."[34]
Referring to the forced mergers as "shotgun weddings," he diametrically opposed the amendment because of the threatened deadlines
that carried "the threat of expulsion."[35] Deer's speech was significant
in that it represented a passing of an era. This was the last time that
a speech of this nature was employed by those opposing merger of

dual affiliates; henceforth, the South would rely upon its bureaucratic control of the white affiliates to impede merger efforts.

After three more Southerners echoed Deer's sentiments, representatives from throughout the nation supported Tornillo's amendment,
thus paving the way for an immediate acceptance of the amendment
by a voice vote. The 1964 Resolution on Desegregation in the Public
Schools read:

> The National Education Association views with deep concern the
> problems which accompany the evolving process of desegregation in
> the public schools in response to the changed legal status of the pub-
> lic schools initiated by the Supreme Court decisions on desegregation.
>
> The National Education Association pledges continued sup-
> port of the United States Supreme Court decision on school de-
> segregation. Because this process involves fundamental questions of
> human rights as well as central issues of professional status, it is
> fitting that the Association restate the principles that guide it in
> approaching these problems:
>
> a.   Support of democratic principles and of the free society
> which embodies them.
>
> b.   Respect for law as an inescapable condition for maintain-
> ing an orderly society.
>
> c.   Protection of individual rights as the first and highest duty
> of democratic governments.
>
> d.   Support and protection of orderly processes in protesting
> unfavorable laws.
>
> e.   Recognition of the dangers inherent in unrestrained and
> unlawful protests of judicial decisions.
>
> f.   Maintenance of free public education served by a free and
> dignified profession.
>
> g.   Desegregation of professional organizations affiliated with
> NEA, with dual associations jointly seeking an equitable solution.
>
> In the light of these principles, the Representative Assembly
> hereby requests the officers and directors of the Association to
> plan and initiate actions which will—
>
> a.   Assure the maintenance of free public education.
>
> b.   Promote goodwill, fairness, and respect for law.
>
> c.   Offer possibilities of reducing hostility.
>
> d.   Alleviate anxieties among teachers and officials who ad-
> minister the public schools.
>
> e.   Support local and state associations which seek to protect
> teachers whenever their professional rights and status are unfairly
> menaced.

f. Openly commend, for efforts to improve conditions, local and state officials of public school systems, directors and officers of local and state organizations, teachers and administrators of public schools, and private citizens.

g. Make available the good offices of NEA to state and local affiliates which request help in making joint plans for desegregation.

An important goal of education is the elimination of prejudice and bigotry from the public mind. As educators, we are dedicated to the principle of equal rights for all.

In light of these principles, the Representative Assembly instructs the officers and directors of the National Education Association—

a. To direct all local, district, and state associations affiliated with the National Education Association to take immediate steps to remove all restrictive membership requirements dealing with race, creed, or ethnic groups.

b. To take immediate action to develop plans to effect the complete integration of all local and state affiliates whose membership are now limited to educators of specifically designated racial, religious, or ethnic groups.

Affiliates whose memberships reflect the above-mentioned restrictions shall be given until July 1, 1966, to revise their constitutions and bylaws, where necessary, to take whatever steps are required to expedite the complete removal of all restrictive labels, and to present a plan to effect the complete integration of their associations.

Should an affiliated association fail to comply with these requirements by July 1, 1966, the Executive Committee shall have the discretionary powers to take necessary action.

The Association commends the communities which have made progress toward desegregation in such a manner as to assume their responsibility to maintain the public schools and their obligation to recognize the political and professional rights of teachers. It commends also the officers and directors of the National Education Association for their vigorous and effective support of state and local associations when the professional rights and status of teachers were unfairly menaced. Particularly it commends the alertness of the officers and directors in establishing a fund from which interest-free loans could be made to teachers whose salary payments were delayed because of problems involved in desegregation. The Association recognizes that Americans of goodwill in every state are seeking, within the areas possible for them, to support the integrity of public education and the principles to which the National Education Association is devoted. The nation is indebted to these loyal citizens who display in their lives the highest American ideals.[36]

Reaction to the NEA Desegregation Resolution

The NEA took a few more steps toward liberalizing its integration position by establishing specific guidelines and dates for the desegregation of it affiliates. The Assembly proposed no alternatives to the affiliates that failed to meet the requirements, but instead, they allowed the Executive Committee to have "discretionary powers to take necessary action."[37] The Assembly thus ignored Carr's pleas for no further action on dual affiliates.

Some state educational journals lauded the NEA's action. The *Ohio Schools* referred to the resolution as the NEA's "strongest stand in its history of civil rights," pointing out that the resolution's passage came within twenty-four hours after President Johnson had signed the Civil Rights Act of 1964.[38] The Wisconsin teachers were told that "the NEA hammered out a forceful position for the profession" regarding civil rights,[39] while another journal said that the NEA "took a no holds barred stand on civil rights."[40]

On the other hand, one observer, who preferred the DCT's tougher stand, called the NEA's position a "crouch."[41] *Newsweek* was lukewarm in its evaluation: "The enforcement of its deadline provisions had been turned over to a traditionally cautious NEA Executive Committee. . . . Many delegates seemed to feel that a weakened resolution was better than none at all."[42]

The South also reacted to the resolution. Frank Hughes, executive secretary of the Georgia Education Association, predicted that his group would become an independent organization.[43] Floyd Barnes, the Mississippi Education Association's executive secretary, reported that he was contacted by a Mississippi newspaper regarding the future of the NEA. He told the paper, "The question will be solved in Mississippi, not Seattle."[44] Significantly, the cover of the *Mississippi Educational Advance* contained a picture of the American flag at half mast, with newspaper clippings telling of federal support of school integration appearing in the picture's background.

In the wake of the 1964 convention, the AFT made merger overtures to the ATA, but the Negro organization turned to the NEA, agreeing to merge under these conditions:

(1) that the NEA increase the number of qualified Negroes on its staff at all levels

(2) that regional offices be set up in strategic areas and be

    staffed with integrated personnel to implement the merging of
    state associations

(3)   that present ATA headquarters in Atlanta be used as one of
      the regional offices to implement the proposed merger

(4)   that NEA agrees to accept all the ATA life membership as
      NEA life members

(5)   that ATA funds be set aside for specific ATA projects before
      the group assets are turned over to the NEA.[45]

Posture of the "NEA Journal" during 1964

In 1964, the magazine's index listed nine articles relating to integration. Many of these also were related to urban education, thus continuing the link between these two pressing educational problems. A significant article appeared on the closing of the Prince Edward County schools.[46] This was the first official *NEA Journal* statement regarding this southern technique to avoid integration. The article was simple but effective. Comparing the NEA Platform and Resolutions with the language of the Virginia Supreme Court, which upheld the school district's action, the editor found the decision to be diametrically opposed to the NEA's position regarding the maintenance of free public schools.

The number of Negro pictures appearing in the magazine increased to eleven. Quite diversified, they ranged from Adam Clayton Powell's photograph[47] to a full-page, colored picture showing a black elementary student.[48]

DEVELOPMENTS IN 1965

During 1965, the nation completed its first year under the new civil rights legislation, and the law's effect upon school desegregation become apparent. The total number of black students integrated into the District of Columbia and the border states' schools reached seventy percent. Having integrated eighty percent of their students, Delaware and West Virginia led the states in this region.[49] The southern states increased their integration efforts to six percent.[50] Texas, Tennessee, and Virginia's desegregation percentages ranged from ten to seventeen percent, while Louisiana, Alabama, and Mississippi had barely begun integration.[51] Meanwhile, the United States Office of Education accepted 880 school districts' plans for desegregation during the year.[52]

During the 1965-1966 school year, the war between the NEA and the AFT widened, as 203 bargaining elections were held with the NEA winning 176.[53] The NEA lost its biggest prize when the Philadelphia teachers selected the union. The Philadelphia Teachers Association, an NEA affiliate, had a greater membership percentage than the other large locals that the AFT had won; therefore, the defeat was a bitter one for the Association.

Confident of victory, the Philadelphia Teachers Association asked the school board for an early election, and both sides waged an intensive fight, with the AFT emphasizing the dual affiliates in order to embarrass the NEA. Stinnett claimed that the union's skilled propagandizing of the dual affiliates was a factor in the union's victory.[54] Almost ninety-eight percent of the eligible personnel voted, and the union won 5,403 to 4,671.[55] The causes of the defeat had serious implications as they were indicative of the NEA's basic policies in urban education:

(1)   total frustration of the Philadelphia teachers to substandard conditions and continuing decline of the city schools.

(2)   the growing trend of militancy among teachers and their revolt against administrator dominance.

(3)   the social revolution prevalent in the racial, ethnic, and religious struggles.[56]

The NEA also became involved in a battle with the Oklahoma state government in an effort to improve educational conditions in that state. The Oklahoma Education Association, an NEA affiliate, had been advocating educational reforms, requiring tax reforms and school consolidation. The state was reluctant to make the necessary moves, so, after a number of rebuffs, the OEA imposed sanctions in March 1965.[57] Shortly afterward, the NEA imposed national sanctions.[58]

Pressure mounted against the state government, as sanctions proved effective, and finally, the legislature voted to improve salaries, to allocate more money for textbooks, and to establish a more favorable tax structure. Kalkstein said, "Sanctions were most unquestionably the most telling blow dealt in the war."[59]

By the end of 1965, the NEA was showing increased signs of militancy, with sanctions being the most obvious manifestation. Using this tool twelve times since 1962, the NEA had found sanctions to be more effective than resolutions; consequently, sanctions, along with professional negotiations, became the chief Association weapons against the AFT.[60]

Still another factor in contributing to the NEA agressiveness was the influence of the young, male teacher. Sam Lambert pointed this out in an *NEA Journal* article.[61] He argued that today's teacher is better educated, more career oriented, and more aggressive than his older counterpart. Furthermore, Lambert indicated that this new breed of teacher demanded a more significant role in educational policy making. Relative to this point, Kalkstein attributed the leadership in the Oklahoma battle to this kind of teacher. Stanley Elam showed that the NEA, responding to change, was bringing to its staff aggressive people like Allan West, who helped direct the Utah sanctions' dispute. Significantly, West headed the Urban Project, which was at the vanguard of educational activities ranging from developing ghetto education projects to coping with the AFT.[62]

In addition to the increasing aggressiveness of the NEA, the AFT sometimes found itself hamstrung because of its labor affiliations. Two classic examples illustrated this weakness. During the Oklahoma battle, state officials suggested a sales tax as the means of easing the educational pressures, but the union opposed this move, thus losing any chance it had of gaining additional teacher support.[63] The same thing occurred in Indiana where the AFT instituted legal proceedings to block a proposed sales tax, ultimately costing the state nearly $40 million previously earmarked for educational expenses.[64]

This year also witnessed the passage of the Elementary and Secondary Education Act, allocating over $1 billion for public and private schools throughout the nation. The NEA had perennially advocated federal aid, but it could not regard this law as a complete victory because of the Association's opposition to private school aid. Critics of the Association regarded this law as indicative of the gradual erosion of the NEA's influence since the mid-1950s.[65]

The 1965 NEA Convention

The NEA held its annual convention in the heart of occupied territory—New York City. The *New York Times* reported two probable reasons for this: (a) to enable the teachers to attend the World's

Fair; and (b) to show the New York City teachers the progress of the Association.[66] The convention, held from June 27 to July 2, had an official delegate attendance of 7,222 people, the largest number of delegates ever to participate in an NEA convention.

The convention's highlight was President Lyndon B. Johnson's address. This was the first time since 1938 that the nation's president had personally addressed the NEA convention. Calling the delegates "fellow educators," he reminded them that he was "still on a leave of absence."[67] His speech was well received and punctuated by frequent applause, with the greatest ovation occurring when he mentioned civil rights for black teachers. He used this occasion as a means of announcing future educational plans pertaining to civil rights. President Johnson proposed a National Teacher Corps to fight poverty throughout the nation and also announced a fellowship program for teachers displaced by integration. He also indicated that the federal government would supply refresher courses to the unemployed teachers. Expressing concern about the dismissal of black teachers, he applauded the action that the NEA had taken.[68] After completing his address, he received a two-minute standing ovation from the teachers.

Although President Johnson's speech overshadowed all the other events at the convention, other facets of his appearance could not be overlooked. Indirectly, he gave the Association a great morale boost in its struggle against the AFT. In using the convention as a platform to tell the nation of the administration's educational plans, he also gave the NEA very favorable national attention.

Prior to the President's arrival, business had proceeded as usual. Dr. Carr presented his annual report, emphasizing four major areas: (a) the use of sanctions; (b) the rise of professional negotiations; (c) federal aid to education; and (d) the unity of the teaching profession. The last point dealt exclusively with NEA involvement in civil rights as he specifically listed the merger progress of the dual affiliates:

> In Alabama the two state affiliates have officially informed me that they are committed to presentation of a joint plan next year. . . . In Georgia the process of amending the constitution of the Georgia Education Association has begun. . . . In Mississippi, representatives of the two state associations have met to discuss the common prob-

lems and further meetings are planned. The North Carolina Education Association voted five to one to remove the word white
from its constitution. The South Carolina Education Association,
by a four to one vote, amended its constitution to delete the white
membership clause. The Tennessee Education Association's constitution contains no racial restrictions. . . . The Texas State Teachers
Association, by a very large majority, removed racial restrictions
from its governing documents.[69]

Carr then told of the ways in which the Association was aiding racial
progress. These ranged from NEA workshops and seminars dealing
with racial problems to the Board of Directors establishing a Committee of Human Rights of Educators as part of the Professional
Rights and Responsibilities Commission. The committee's chief purpose was to raise a fund of $1 million for the aid and protection of
teachers displaced by the integration strife.[70] Pursuing this point
further, Carr emphasized, "The Association cannot compromise on
this issue, for if any teacher can be dismissed without good cause, no
teacher is secure."[71] He completed his civil rights presentation by
announcing that the NEA and the ATA merger would occur in 1966.

Carr's address presented some significant aspects worthy of comment. Almost a third of his entire address pertained to civil rights,
thus indicating the role that civil rights had begun to play. Ironically,
much of the progress cited by Carr resulted from the 1964 integration
resolution that he opposed. Regardless of the actual progress made,
the dual affiliates remained. Voluntary desegregation did not appear
to be moving rapidly.

The status of the dual affiliates never stopped being a source of
agitation for the NEA leaders. On the opening day of the convention,
Mrs. Edinger and Dr. Carr defended the dual structure. Albert
Shanker, president of the UFT, had appeared on a local television
program and charged the NEA of having "thousands of teacher
organizations which are a hundred per cent segregated."[72] Mrs.
Edinger, while admitting the existence of dual organizations, said
that only four states, Louisiana, Georgia, Alabama, and Mississippi,
had racial restrictions. Carr echoed his previous feelings when he
intimated that many black teachers had reservations about the
merger of the dual affiliates.

The desegregation resolution reached the Assembly on July 2. As
usual the Resolutions Committee proposed the same resolution passed

in the previous convention. Mrs. Catherine Barrett of New York moved to amend the resolution by adding this statement in the resolution's fourth paragraph following the words "Representative Assembly": ". . . calls for a study to stress the need for creating and staffing a human relations commission as a channel through which members can be involved in resolving current problems relating to human relations. The finding of such a committee shall be reported to the next annual meeting of the NEA."[73] It was seconded by James Cullen from New York, and some discussion followed pertaining to a potential conflict between the amended resolution and the Human Relations Subcommittee of the Professional Rights and Responsibilities Commission.[74] Charles Deubel assured the delegates that no conflict existed; therefore, the delegates passed the amendment with no expressed opposition.

Robert Bogen of Arlington, Virginia, moved to amend the fifth paragraph of the resolution so that the words "jointly developed" occurred before the word "plan." Bogen's amendment was seconded by Ronald Paul of Washington, and the delegates voted their approval without any discussion.

The final amended version read:

> The National Education Association views with deep concern the problems which accompany the evolving process of desegregation in the public schools in response to the changed legal status of the public schools initiated by the Supreme Court decisions on desegregation.
>
> The National Education Association pledges continued support of the United States Supreme Court decision on school desegregation. Because this process involves fundamental questions of human rights as well as central issues of professional status, it is fitting that the Association restate the principles that guide it in approaching these problems:
>
> a. Support of democratic principles and of the free society which embodies them.
>
> b. Respect for law as an inescapable condition for maintaining an orderly society.
>
> c. Protection of individual rights as the first and highest duty of democratic governments.
>
> d. Support and protection of orderly processes in protesting unfavorable laws.
>
> e. Recognition of the dangers inherent in unrestricted and unlawful protests of judicial decisions.
>
> f. Maintenance of free public education served by a free and dignified profession.

g. Desegregation of professional organizations affiliated with NEA, with dual associations jointly seeking an equitable solution.

In the light of these principles, the Representative Assembly hereby requests the officers and directors of the Association to plan and initiate actions which will—

a. Assure the maintenance of free public education.

b. Promote goodwill, fairness, and respect for law.

c. Offer possibilities of reducing hostility.

d. Alleviate anxieties among teachers and officials who administer the public schools.

e. Support local and state associations which seek to protect teachers whenever their professional rights and status are unfairly menaced.

f. Openly commend, for efforts to improve conditions, local and state officials of public school systems, directors and officers of local and state organizations, teacher and administrators of public schools, and private citizens.

g. Make available the good offices of NEA to state and local affiliates which request help in making joint plans for complete integration and merger.

An important goal of education is the elimination of prejudice and bigotry from the public mind. As educators, we are dedicated to the principle of equal rights for all.

In light of these principles, the Representative Assembly calls for a study to investigate the need for creating and staffing a human relations commission as a channel through which members can become involved in resolving current problems relating to human relations. The findings of such a study shall be reported to the next annual meeting of the NEA. The Representative Assembly further instructs the officers and directors of the National Education Association—

a. To direct all local, district, and state associations affiliated with the National Education Association to take immediate steps to remove all restrictive membership requirements dealing with race, creed, or ethnic groups.

b. To take immediate action to develop plans to effect the complete integration of all local and state affiliates whose memberships are now limited to educators of specifically designated racial, religious, or ethnic groups.

Affiliates whose memberships reflect the above-mentioned restrictions shall be given until July 1, 1966, to revise their constitutions and bylaws, where necessary, to take whatever steps are required to expedite the complete removal of all restrictive labels, and to present a jointly developed plan to effect the complete integration and merger of their associations. Should an affiliated association fail to comply with these requirements by July 1, 1966, the Executive Committee shall have the discretionary powers to take necessary action.

The Association commends the communities which have made progress toward desegregation in such a manner as to assume their responsibility to maintain the public schools and their obligation to recognize the political and professional rights of teachers. It commends also the officers and directors of the National Education Association for their vigorous and effective support of state and local associations when the professional rights and status of teachers were unfairly menaced. Particularly it commends the alertness of the officers and directors in establishing a fund from which interest-free loans could be made to teachers whose salary payments were delayed because of problems involved in desegregation. The Association recognizes that Americans of goodwill in every state are seeking, within the areas possible for them, to support the integrity of public education and the principles to which the National Education Association is devoted. The nation is indebted to these loyal citizens who display in their lives the highest American ideals.[75]

Reaction to the NEA Desegregation Resolution

Civil rights at the 1965 convention was not the explosive issue it had been in previous conventions, but it continued to play a vital part throughout. Dr. Carr featured civil rights prominently in his address; the Board of Directors had established a Subcommittee on Human Rights and initiated a fund to raise a million dollars for displaced teachers (Million Dollar Defense Fund); the Representative Assembly reaffirmed its position to eliminate racial membership requirements; and the NEA and ATA moved toward merger.

The convention revealed an NEA still beset by a general feeling of uneasiness. The Assembly approved sanctions against Oklahoma and began talks about imposing sanctions against Florida. Although Fred Hechinger reported that the NEA desegregation resolution was "a vital act," he indicated that many members felt that the resolution was "too moderate."[76] These people believed that the NEA should talk less and act more, and this was best described by a delegate who said, "We can resolute all we want to, but what we need is action."[77] Dr. Marion Donaldson, chairman of the Committee on Citizenship, said, "The organization must stop being a sleeping giant."[78] Perhaps President Johnson captured the basic spirit for activism when he told the delegates, "The time for talking and dreaming and philosophizing and writing platforms is gone, and the time for doing things instead of talking about them, is here."[79]

The challenge for immediate action faced the NEA, for troubled times loomed ahead. The widening gap between the teacher and the administrator, a contributing factor in union victories, was exacerbated by the increasing militancy of the teachers. This required Association intercession on behalf of the teachers in disputes with the local boards or state authorities. The NEA also had to create a new image in order to cope realistically with the urban problems. Finally, the Association had to adopt a more aggressive civil rights position by eliminating dual affiliates and helping the displaced black teacher. These were huge problems that caused Fred Hechinger to react pessimistically, for he thought that the NEA was "still dominated by prissy school marmism."[80]

Posture of the "NEA Journal" during 1965

During 1965, the *NEA Journal* carried thirteen major articles dealing with the educational problems of the black people, with six pertaining to ghetto education. The Subcommittee on Human Rights, created by the NEA Board of Directors, was spotlighted in two articles. In one of these J. Rupert Picott outlined the NEA defense of seven black educators who lost their positions in Giles County, Virginia.[81] The NEA contested the dismissals, resulting in lengthy legal action that led to the reversal of the school board's decision.[82] This case was a prime example of the Million Dollar Defense Fund at work, as the NEA and the Virginia Teachers Association assumed all the costs for the seven teachers. Another article focused upon the Negro's attempt to secure higher education, while the remaining articles dealt with some aspect of the integration crisis.

The magazine also published eleven photographs of Negroes. The photograph on the October cover of the magazine included a black child. The same issue also displayed a picture of Richard Batchelder, the NEA president, talking with a black teacher.[83]

DEVELOPMENT IN 1966

Statistically, school desegregation showed a modest improvement during 1966. The South had integrated sixteen percent of its

black students, a significant increase from the past year. Mississippi, Louisiana, South Carolina, Alabama, and Georgia had integrated from three to ten percent of their Negro students; Arkansas, North Carolina, and Florida's integration efforts ranged from
fifteen to twenty-one percent; and Virginia, Tennessee, and Texas
led the region by integrating twenty-five to forty-seven percent of
their black students.[84] In fact, the South had nearly 35,000 more
black students attending integrated schools than the border states.
But even by combining the desegregated Negro students in both
regions, the total reached only 943,000, meaning that seventy-five
percent of the black students in that eighteen state area still attended segregated schools. These statistics gave added meaning to
Harold Howe's statement that "schools throughout the nation remain almost as segregated today as they were in 1954 when
the Supreme Court decided that racially segregated education
was illegal."[85]

Faculty desegregation reflected nearly the same average as student desegregation. Schools in the two regions had desegregated
about thirty percent of black teachers. The South had desegregated 41,000 black teachers, while the border states integrated 8,000
black faculty members.[86]

The NEA was busy in this particular field as it held conferences helping teachers exchange ideas on desegregation and making them aware of the federal guidelines on desegregation.[87] Also, an
NEA Task Force, a joint effort of the Association and the United
States Office of Education, studied staff desegregation in the border states and the South during 1965 and issued its report in 1966.
The report showed that 688 black teachers had lost their positions
for racial reasons.[88] Dr. Eddie Morris, a member of the study
team, reported that a few states were beginning to comply with the
1954 Supreme Court decision but "there is little student desegregation or even less faculty desegregation" in Alabama, Georgia,
Louisiana, Mississippi, South Carolina, and Virginia.[89]

Meanwhile, the American Teachers Association held its annual
convention at Miami Beach, Florida, just prior to the NEA convention. The ATA delegates gave final approval to merger with
the NEA.[90] The Negro officials indicated that the NEA would

open up a regional office at Dallas, Texas, which would be operated by an integrated staff. The NEA had already opened a similar office at Atlanta, Georgia, as part of the agreement leading to the merger.

The 1966 NEA Convention

Shortly after the conclusion of the ATA convention, the NEA moved into Miami Beach for its convention, held from June 26, to July 1, 1966. Turbulent weather greeted the delegates.[91] It was a harbinger, as they realized that the convention's prime issue would be the status of the dual affiliates. The Assembly heard addresses given by Larry O'Brien, United States Postmaster General, and John Gardner, secretary of Health, Education and Welfare, but the key speeches were presented by Dr. Carr and NEA president Richard Batchelder.

Dr. Carr, reaffirming his basic position that the NEA had always maintained open membership, reviewed the creation of the dual affiliates and stressed how the number of dual affiliates had been voluntarily reduced to eleven state organizations. Outlining the provisions of the 1964 desegregation resolution, he emphasized merger progress:

The Arkansas and Tennessee Education Association have no written membership barriers. . . . The Virginia Education Association . . . has voted to admit all members of its merged affiliates. . . . Constitutional amendments have eliminated former racial bars to membership in Alabama, Georgia, Mississippi, North Carolina, South Carolina, and Texas. . . . From North Carolina, on June 15, I received a joint report signed by the presidents and executive secretaries in the two state wide affiliates. This document traces the specific steps taken since 1960 to the present and the next steps ahead. . . . In Louisiana, a restrictive clause remains, but a resolution of the LTA convention authorizes a constitutional revision committee which will meet in November. A joint committee from the two affiliates is at work in Georgia. From South Carolina I have a joint report. . . . From Alabama comes the report. . . . that their joint committee on Resolution #12 will meet at least once in the next quarter to deal with such topics as guidelines for local affiliates during transition, dues, property, and constitution until its task is completed. . . . On July 1, the Florida Education Association, with 40,000 members including several hundred Negro members, and the

Florida State Teachers Association, with 10,000 members including some white members, will combine. . . . A resolution terminating the Texas State Association was approved by its executive committee on January 8, and will be submitted to its delegate assembly in about a month.[92]

Citing additional mergers of local affiliates, Carr continued his theme that the key to the abolition of dual affiliates was each state's voluntary efforts at desegregation.

Later, Richard Batchelder, addressing the Assembly on the convention's theme, "Free to Teach," gave a forceful speech with particular emphasis upon immediate implementation of the 1964 desegregation resolution. In doing so, Batchelder went beyond Carr's voluntary approach, as he indicated that the NEA could wait no longer for merger to occur:

The NEA Executive Committee will execute the mandate of the past two NEA Representative Assemblies. The July 1 deadline is Friday of this week. Your Executive Committee will meet on Saturday, July 2, to take the necessary steps so that no affiliate of the Association has any racial barrier to membership and that programs proceed to effect the unity of our local and state affiliates. The day of dualism is over; the day of unity is here. I will recommend on Saturday that the Executive Committee exercise its authority given to it by Article V, Section 3, by the Bylaws and proceed to implement these matters pursuant to the procedures already adopted.[93]

Batchelder thus delivered the strongest speech ever made by an NEA leader against segregated affiliates. Batchelder now began to move the Association away from Carr's voluntary approach to desegregation. Significantly, this marked the first public instance where the president and the executive secretary had a difference of opinion. Perhaps a major reason for this was Carr's retirement announcement, which encouraged the NEA president to assert himself more positively.

The Department of Classroom Teachers heeded Batchelder's speech when it voted overwhelmingly to expel any affiliate that did not either desegregate or develop desegregation plans by July 1, 1967. This constituted a victory for the National Committee of Educators for Human Rights, for, although the original DCT resolution had no compliance date, the NCEHR successfully amended the resolution.

When the Assembly debated the desegregation resolution, however, the delegates were confused regarding the argument over what constituted compliance with the resolution. They were sure of only two things: (a) Florida had carried out the Assembly's mandate; and (b) Louisiana had made practically no effort at desegregation. The status of the other states remained obscure. For example, some of the delegations thought that a letter or even a phone call to Association headquarters indicating any action whatsoever upon merger was sufficient to comply with the 1964 resolution.[94]

Mrs. Maxine Smith, chairman of the Resolutions Committee, proposed the 1966 desegregation resolution. Failing to clear up the confusion, the resolution did not even contain a specific date for merger. Thus, "a one hour emotion-charged debate" occurred in which Pat Tornillo, Morris Beider, and Robert Bogen played significant roles.[95] Beider moved to amend the resolution by inserting the following statements:

> The Representative Assembly mandates the NEA Executive Committee to take immediately the following steps:
> 1. The Executive Committee shall determine if there is a lack of adequate plans, jointly developed, to comply with all provisions of NEA Resolution No. 12 of 1965; it shall suspend or disaffiliate any affiliate as soon as it finds it to be in noncompliance because of a failure to act in good faith, but no later than September 30, 1966.
> 2. The Executive Committee shall report its findings and actions to the membership in the December issue of the *NEA Journal* and the *NEA Reporter*.
> 3. Merger of affiliates in accordance with adequate plans, jointly developed, must be completed by June 1, 1967, unless the jointly developed plans submitted by July 1, 1966, have been approved by the Executive Committee. Affiliation will be continued or authorized after June 1, 1967, only for associations which have been found by the NEA Executive Committee to have complied with NEA Resolution No. 12 of 1965 and 1966.[96]

Tornillo added his support by indicating that the delegates were tired of waiting for the states to act voluntarily:

I believe that this Delegate Assembly is tired of waiting and tired of the bad faith or the lack of good faith, whichever way you want to put it, that has taken place. It is time to take whatever action is necessary. And I believe if you read this amendment carefully, you will see that it is fair.

It is taking care of those states that have in good faith submitted jointly developed plans. There is no deadline for those states, but there is a final cut-off for all states that have not begun to move. That is June 1, 1967. It still leaves in the hands of the Executive Committee the power to suspend which would not disaffiliate a local, and still leaves it in the hands of the Executive Committee to work with those locals and reinstate them rather than disaffiliate them, if from now until June 1, 1967, they have shown in good faith that they are willing to move to a position that is right, not just for the National Education Association but for this country.[97]

Bogen spoke for the amendment because he felt that it clarified compliance guidelines and procedures.

At this point, a delegate asked Batchelder what he intended to recommend to the Executive Committee concerning the status of the Louisiana Teachers Association. Expressing a desire to speak as a delegate, Batchelder yielded the rostrum to Mrs. Applegate. Before he could respond, the delegates supporting the amendment shouted him down.[98] He returned to the rostrum, and within minutes the convention approved the amendment by a voice vote.[99]

After the passage of the amendment, Mrs. Mildred McCormick, vice-president of the Louisiana Teachers Association, explained her state's current position. Claiming that progress had been made even though "our mores are completely different," she emphasized that a committee had been formed that would examine the LTA's constitution regarding racial membership barriers.[100] The LTA could not take action on the committee's recommendations until the state convention in November, thus making it impossible for the LTA to comply with the current NEA integration resolution. With tears in her eyes, she expressed fear that the resolution would have great effect upon the Louisiana teachers: "Your decision here today will have a very great effect in what it is possible for us to do, either encouraging us to continue our efforts, or severing the umbilical cord that has fed us the NEA understanding and encouragement that so many of you have given us through the years."[101]

After Mrs. McCormick's concluding remarks, Felton Brown, another Louisiana delegate, attempted to rekindle old fears. He felt that if the Association imposed its deadline upon the LTA, 'it would drive many teachers in the Orleans Parish to affiliate themselves with the American Federation of Teachers."[102] The delegates applauded him for his statements.

Brown's words began to take effect, as a Minnesota delegate proposed to change the amendment making the deadline for compliance December 31, 1966, rather than September 30, 1966.[103] This would enable the LTA to remove its racial restrictions without necessitating suspension proceedings. Batchelder attempted to discourage the change:

> I think that we are going to get into difficulties. A specific date like this date is going to change other areas that you will have to think through and decide what to do. We are going to get into difficulties if after passing an amendment to do something, we then open ourselves to a general amendment again. This is really discussing a motion after we have already made a decision on it.[104]

The delegates, however, did not want to stop debate. Miss Beulah Osburn, a Kansas delegate, moved that the Assembly reconsider the amendment. Loud applause greeted this motion. Two California delegates opposed this action, but New Hampshire and Tennessee delegates seconded the motion. It appeared as if the delegates were having second thoughts about the deadline when Batchelder recognized in rapid succession Arthur Simons, Ezra Moore, Pat Light, and Robert Bogen. Simons opposed reconsideration; Moore asked for a clarification of a point; Light yielded to Bogen who checked the reverse tendencies of the Assembly:

> Speaking as an individual. I think that hearing the speakers from Louisiana may have created the wrong impression in the minds of some of the delegates who passed this amendment, because in Point 1 of the amendment there is a specific provision that would mean that the Louisiana teachers are not going to be concerned, if I understand their intent, about a September 30 to December 31 or any other deadline. 1 will read it carefully and explain what the intent is, and what I think the literal interpretation would have to be.
> This is speaking of the Executive Committee: It shall suspend or disaffiliate any affiliate as soon as it finds it to be in noncom-

pliance because of a failure to act in good faith. You can be in non-compliance by September 30, but not be suspended or disaffiliated provided you have acted in good faith. (Applause)

Mr. President, I believe that I understood the speakers from Louisiana to tell us that they have been acting in good faith. We have understood that they have been acting in good faith, and therefore, this was only to take care of any problem where good faith has not been exercised, because we don't feel that the National Education Association can continue to condone bad faith in any of our affiliates in this important matter.

And therefore, I speak against the motion to reconsider.[105]

At this point, Batchelder asked for a vote to reconsider the discussion on the amendment. The Assembly rejected it, causing George Wickman, a Californian, to move for an end to the entire debate. The delegates concurred. Batchelder presented the amended resolution for a final vote, and amid a cry of "no" from the audience, the delegates approved the amended resolution.

The amended resolution read:

> The National Education Association views with deep concern the problems which accompany the evolving process of desegregation in the public schools in response to the changed status of the public schools initiated by the United States Supreme Court decisions on desegregation and reinforced by the Civil Rights Act of 1964.
>
> The National Education Association pledges continued support of the Supreme Court decisions on school desegregation. Because this process involves fundamental questions of human rights as well as central issues of professional status, it is fitting that the Association restate the principles that guide it in approaching these problems:
>
> a. Support of democratic principles and of the free society which embodies them.
>
> b. Respect for law as an inescapable condition for maintaining an orderly society.
>
> c. Protection of individual rights as the first and highest duty of democratic governments.
>
> d. Support and protection of orderly processes in protesting unfavorable laws.
>
> e. Recognition of the dangers inherent in unrestrained and unlawful protests of judicial decisions.
>
> f. Maintenance of free public education served by a free and dignified profession.
>
> g. Unification of dual organizations affiliated with NEA, with both groups jointly seeking an equitable solution.
>
> An important goal of education is the elimination of prejudice

and bigotry from the public mind. As educators, we are dedicated to the principles of equal rights for all.

Among the unsolved problems arising out of the process of desegregation there are two which the Association can help most to meet. These are the problem of the human rights of educators and that of the dual associations.

The human rights of educators require defense by the Association and pose responsibilities for it. In situations where desegregation is taking place, an Association study has recently found that educators, particularly Negroes, are sometimes dismissed, intimidated, or otherwise unfairly treated. The Association condemns such violations of human and professional rights, commends the work of its Committee on Civil and Human Rights of Educators, and calls for an expanded effort by the Association to prevent and correct violations of those rights.

On the problem of dual associations, the Representative Assembly has in past years made clear its opposition to the organization of educators on a segregated basis. A deadline for presenting jointly developed plans for the unification of dual associations passed on July 1, 1966. Some associations have failed to meet the deadline. The assembly recognizes that failure to meet deadlines despite intense and sincere efforts should be treated differently from failure to meet deadlines because of ill will or lack of intent on the part of one or both groups.

The Representative Assembly mandates the NEA Executive Committee to take immediately the following steps:

1. The Executive Committee shall determine if there is a lack of adequate plans, jointly developed, to comply with all provisions of NEA Resolution 12 of 1965; it shall suspend or disaffiliate any affiliate as soon as it finds it to be in noncompliance because of a failure to act in good faith, but no later than September 30, 1966.

2. The Executive Committee shall report its findings and actions to the membership in the December issue of the *NEA Journal* and the *NEA Reporter*.

3. Merger of affiliates in accordance with adequate plans, jointly developed, must be completed by June 1, 1967, unless the jointly developed plans submitted by July 1, 1966, have been approved by the Executive Committee. Affiliation will be continued or authorized after June 1, 1967, only for associations which have been found by the NEA Executive Committee to have complied with NEA Resolution 12 of 1965 and 1966.[106]

Reaction to the NEA Desegregation Resolution

The *Michigan Education Journal* told its readers, "Negro teachers in the South—still fettered by racial bigotry and stalling tactics—have cause to applaud the actions of the 104th annual convention of the National Education Association."[107] The Florida delegation, which had merged during the convention, offered this advice to the remaining dual affiliated states, "We recommend our effort as a beginning for our sister states, and we pledge to this union our sacred trust that we will make it work."[108]

The Virginia and Georgia educational journals carried the desegregation resolution but offered no comments; however, the *Mississippi Educational Advance* indicated its opposition to the resolution, but C. A. Johnson, the executive secretary of the MEA, assured the teachers that the MEA was not going to bolt the NEA: "For our teachers to abdicate [from the NEA] would mean no voice from Mississippi to proposals with which we disagree—it would delight some to see us get out and I'm not at all interested in pleasing them. We have an obligation to represent our state the best way we can—for long as we can."[109]

Merger of the ATA with the NEA

Although the proposed merger of dual affiliates caused some major obstacles during the convention, the merger of the ATA with the NEA came about very smoothly because of the careful preparations of the two organizations. After the tentative approval of the merger, the Joint Committee worked at solving the organizational problems prior to the actual merger. In addition to staffing the regional offices in the South and the Southwest, the NEA agreed: (a) to accept all ATA life members as NEA life members; (b) to transfer all cash assets of the ATA into an NEA fund designed to defend civil rights of black teachers; and (c) to accept two ATA staff members as employees of NEA staff.[110]

All of the state delegations seconded Batchelder's merger motion, and the Assembly unanimously accepted the plan. On the evening of June 28, while the delegates sang the "Battle Hymn of the Republic," representatives of the two organizations signed the historic agreement.[111]

Even though ATA membership was 41,000, the merger failed to swell the NEA ranks, for at least ninety percent of the ATA members held NEA membership in the dual affiliates.[112] The merger was significant because it became another NEA milestone that placed additional pressure upon the South to end dual affiliates.

Although the Joint Committee of the NEA-ATA played a significant role in the successful merger, the committee never assumed a dominant role in the desegregation debates. Individual members, such as J. Rupert Picott, figured prominently in the debates, but he spoke either as an individual or for his state association rather than for the Joint Committee. After the Supreme Court decision of 1954, the committee seemed content to issue innocuous reports, consequently remaining in the NEA background.

This can best be illustrated by examination of some of the committee's reports presented to the NEA convention. Throughout the 1950s the committee emphasized the treatment of minorities in textbooks. One of the committee's chief activities was the circulation of an intergroup relations kit among educators.[113] After 1954, the committee continued efforts "toward the integration of members in minority groups in the program of the NEA."[114] In 1958, the committee promised "to promote the best it can the smooth transition from segregated to integrated schools."[115] At the Saint Louis convention, where the integration debate reached such bitter proportions, the committee's chief activity was sponsoring: "An open meeting that proved to be very popular with all the convention delegates—a discussion of the basic principles and current challenges in the field of human relations."[116] Even in 1963, the committee told the NEA Board of Directors that it endorsed the 1962 desegregation resolution. After 1963, the committee's work became more meaningful as merger plans progressed, but most of the work was done behind the scenes. Throughout 1954 to 1966, the committee frequently appeared to function as an unnoticed NEA appendage, generally reflecting an inherent conservatism.

The Integration Controversy's Effect upon Selection of an Executive Secretary

Prior to the beginning of the 1966 convention, Dr. Carr had indicated that he was going to retire after his present contract expired. The Board of Trustees immediately began to lay the groundwork for the selection of his successor, but the Assembly opposed this action even though the trustees possessed this constitutional prerogative. The Assembly's successful effort was described elsewhere in this paper; but, significantly, certain common links appeared between the integration battle and the move to curb the Board of Trustees' power, for these two disputes showed clearly the basic division within the NEA. The California and Florida delegations supported the amended desegregation resolution and also helped create a steering committee that limited the Board of Trustees' selection of an executive secretary. The results of the roll call vote for the establishment of the steering committee proved to be revealing. The liberal faction won 1,548 to 1,403, but in analyzing the individual state votes, it became apparent where the ten states maintaining dual affiliates stood on this matter.[117] These states voted overwhelmingly by a 406 to 90 margin to support the Board of Trustees without the steering committee's encumbrances.[118] This vote showed those states' satisfaction with the Board of Trustees's selection of the executive secretary, hence, their satisfaction, also, with Dr. Carr's performance as executive secretary.

Posture of the "NEA Journal" during 1966

The *NEA Journal* featured seven major articles on the racial situation during 1966. Three of them dealt with the education of the disadvantaged, while one emphasized the Million Dollar Defense Fund. The magazine covered the merger of the ATA with the NEA and spotlighted the 1966 desegregation resolution. The final article was an interview with Mrs. Irvamae Applegate, president of the NEA, concerning the implementation of the desegregation resolution. Although the magazine did not run as many articles on the racial situation as in immediately previous years, four were significant because they related directly to the NEA's attempt to come to grips with its internal racial problems.

During 1966, the magazine printed eleven photographs of Negroes. The October issue featured a cover picture of a black teacher appearing with two children, one white and the other Negro. Still another picture showed Vice-President Hubert Humphrey with a black teacher.[119] In the last two issues of the year, the magazine showed pictures of some of the leaders in Negro education, thus highlighting the theme of merger within the organization.

Status of NEA Membership in States
Maintaining Dual Affiliates

From 1962 to 1966, the NEA passed progressively stronger desegregation resolutions, but the threatened withdrawal of southern
states never materialized. Table 4 shows that the national membership of the NEA increased at an annual rate of 40,000 teachers;
however, the dual affiliate states' growth was proportionately
greater. In 1962, these states had 174,184 NEA members or
twenty-one percent of the Association's total membership, whereas
NEA membership in those states increased to 237,437 in 1966,
twenty-four percent of the total NEA membership. Every southern
state had a net increase of NEA members over this five-year span.

Table 4

Total NEA Membership from 1962 to 1966 with Individual
State Membership for that Same Period for States
Maintaining Dual Organizations*

Organization	1962	1963	1964	1965	1966
NEA	812,497	859,505	903,384	943,581	986,113
Alabama	18,918	19,307	20,277	19,120	21,273
Arkansas	9,300	9,747	9,818	10,048	10,352
Florida	20,567	22,803	24,362	26,041	27,797
Georgia	23,583	25,293	26,014	23,458	25,059
Louisiana	1,375	2,555	2,868	2,955	3,675
Mississippi	3,550	3,826	3,979	4,110	4,669
North Carolina	33,949	35,734	38,597	40,131	37,211
South Carolina	9,510	10,892	11,226	11,705	12,809
Tennessee	24,007	24,736	26,082	26,517	28,251
Texas	30,563	32,791	35,072	38,308	41,535
Virginia	19,462	21,394	21,927	23,650	24,806

NEA Handbook, 1962 to 1966.

Implementation of the Integration Resolution

With the completion of the 1966 convention, the NEA civil
rights struggle entered a new phase in which the Executive Committee had to implement the Representative Assembly's integration
mandate. Previously the Executive Committee had not been char-

acterized by its liberal tendencies, but since 1964 this body had
become somewhat more responsive to the Assembly's wishes.

The 1966–1967 Executive Committee was composed of Mrs.
Irvamae Applegate, president; Braulio Alonso, president-elect;
Richard Batchelder, past president; Lyman Ginger, treasurer; F. L.
Schlagle, chairman of the Board of Trustees; Mrs. Hazel Bain;
Alfred Cordova; Mrs. Thelma Davis; George Fisher; G. Baker
Thompson; and Miss Mabel McKelvey.[120] Examination of the Committee's composition revealed that it was about evenly split between
the liberal and the conservative NEA factions. Batchelder and
Alonso emerged as the new image of the NEA. Mrs. Applegate
was sympathetic toward integration, while Cordova had previously
spoken for a stronger Association stance during an Assembly
debate. The conservative element was clearly evident as Ginger
and Miss McKelvey had always taken a cautious integration approach, while Thompson and Schlagle were associated with the
organizational forces. Although Mrs. Davis was past president
of the DCT, she was from Georgia, a dual affiliate state. Fisher
and Mrs. Bain had not taken a public stand upon the integration dispute.

The Executive Committee met the day after the 1966 convention adjourned, in order to implement the desegregation resolution.
Batchelder moved that the NEA temporarily suspend the Louisiana
Teachers Association until that organization could show cause why
it should not be expelled from the NEA. Miss McKelvey seconded
the motion, and all of the members concurred.[121] The Executive
Committee sent copies of the suspension proceedings to all of the
states maintaining dual affiliates.

On October 3, 1966, Mrs. Applegate, Alonso, and Thompson
met with LTA officials at New Orleans for a hearing upon the
LTA suspension. The hearing disclosed that the LTA governing
body had placed on its November ballot a constitutional revision
calling for the elimination of membership restrictions. G. Baker
Thompson said "that a spirit of goodwill and cooperation prevailed" at this "show cause" meeting;[122] consequently, shortly after
the hearing, the Executive Committee agreed to the following
motion made by Braulio Alonso:

(1) That the Executive Committee place in abeyance the temporary suspension of the Louisiana Teachers Association affected by the resolution adopted July 2, 1966, until the next annual meeting of the Louisiana Teachers Association to be held November 20–23, 1966, and thereafter as long as said Association continues to demonstrate its good faith in relation to Resolution 66–12 of the NEA Representative Assembly of 1966;

(2) That services and recognition rendered to the Louisiana Teachers Association should be authorized by the NEA president and executive secretary so long as the suspension is held in abeyance; and

(3) That if in the event the constitution of the Louisiana Teachers Association is not amended at its annual meeting on November 20–23, 1966, to eliminate the restriction of the Louisiana Teachers Association of its membership to white persons, the Louisiana Teachers Association shall be disaffiiliated from the NEA on November 28, 1966, without the necessity of further action by the Executive Committee.[123]

The Executive Committee's action seemed questionable because this decision exposed the Committee to justifiable criticism from people advocating a strong NEA position, for the Committee's decision to reinstate the LTA pending its annual convention was the same move that the Assembly had rejected at the 1966 convention. Reportedly, the Executive Committee came under heavy internal criticism because of this action.[124]

The Louisiana Teachers Association held its annual state convention November 20–23, knowing that the ranks of dual affiliates had dwindled and that it had to drop its racial restrictions or face permanent expulsion from the NEA. Individual teacher feeling ran high against the NEA, and M. E. Wright, president of the LTA, expressed his association's position well when he told the delegates:

I regret and resent, as I am sure many of the LTA members do, action taken without any real regard for conditions or problems in our state. I only wish that some who strike noble postures, utter pious expressions, and take action affecting others rather than themselves, had to live with consequences of their actions and experience the things that I have experienced in the recent months amid the remains of what was a fine public school system . . . We must put aside our bitterness if we can, and make decisions based upon a coldly intellectual assessment of facts and the logical effects of our actions upon the future of our profession. This matter will be thoroughly debated at our 1966 convention. May our own good reasons lead us to a sound conclusion.[125]

The delegates chose the NEA over local pressures by voting 579 to 183 to drop racial membership restrictions from the LTA constitution.[126] Mrs. Applegate commented upon this action: "The Louisiana teachers, by their decision, have demonstrated their faith in the American ideal of providing equal opportunity for all of its citizens. I am confident that LTA will continue to demonstrate its good faith and join with its seven sister states in the South in moving toward full compliance with NEA policy."[127]

Meanwhile, the dual associations in Virginia agreed to merge. The Virginia Teachers Association voted 217 to 7 for the merger, while the white affiliate, the Virginia Education Association, concurred by a 1,229 to 250 margin.[128] The black affiliate in Texas had already agreed to disband. During this same period of time, South Carolina and Tennessee moved closer to mergers that would be consummated before the beginning of the 1967 NEA convention.

Clearly the stronger civil rights expression of the Assembly and the unprecedented suspension of the LTA were factors in the flurry of state merger activities between the 1966 and 1967 NEA conventions. All states had eliminated racial membership restrictions, but the Assembly's mandate called for merger of dual affiliates; consequently, the Executive Committee's role in 1967 would be to continue applying pressure and giving guidance to the remaining states so that all teachers could belong to an organization granting full, equal, and fair representation for all members.

DEVELOPMENTS IN 1967

On the national level, 1967 was a year of extremes in regard to civil rights. Some Negroes reached positions undreamed of a decade ago, while simultaneously a conservative trend appeared that threatened to retard racial progress. President Johnson appointed Thurgood Marshall to the United States Supreme Court, the highest position ever accorded to a Negro. Elsewhere, two Negroes were elected mayors of major cities in the country.

While a few Negroes were moving ahead at unprecedented levels of achievements, many more black people were falling dangerously behind, hopelessly enmeshed in their ghetto environment; consequently, during 1967, "the summer of discontent" exploded in a violent, almost blind fury, as major riots racked over twenty cities throughout the United States. Suffering the most devastating riot in the nation's history, Detroit had over forty people killed, while property damages soared to $250,000,000.[129] Lootings, bombings, and angry demonstrations spread rapidly. Newark and New Haven suffered similarly, and civil unrest erupted into violence at Chicago, Los Angeles, and Milwaukee.

The violent turmoil in the black community caused many people, laymen and authorities alike, to reexamine contemporary society in an effort to understand these upheavals, which, frighteningly enough, appeared to be perennial. They found that the causes were not new but that these riots were symptomatic of the basic ghetto ills, festering for many years.[130] Daniel Moynihan had identified causes of unrest as early as 1965. Claiming that the struggle had gone beyond civil rights, he argued that the Negroes wanted to gain equality on the same terms as the other people in the society. Moynihan, however, predicted that this would be difficult to achieve since "the racist virus in the American bloodstream affects us," and gloomily pointed out that the Negro life was actually worsening in terms of income, standard of living, and school atendance.[131] The McCone Commission, organized to study the Watts Riot, substantiated Moynihan's beliefs, identifying lack of job skills, unemployment, poverty, and illiteracy as elements of a cycle leading to more violence.[132]

These basic ills of Negro urban life had not changed by 1967; instead, they had become more aggravated. The cities wrestled with ghetto education without relieving de facto segregation; ghetto housing was even more substandard and overcrowded; and unemployment in the ghetto averaged from five to twelve percent higher than the national average.[133]

Even more alarming than the pessimistic ghetto statistics, which indicated the magnitude of the problems, was the reappearance of a virulent form of white racism, giving rise to the fear that many white people just did not care about the Negro. A Harris survey in 1967 showed that more white people accepted a stereotyped view of Negroes, i.e., Negroes are lazy, keep untidy homes, have loose morals, thus reflecting an anti Negro prejudice and revealing a marked reversal of the survey trends taken from 1963 to 1966 on the same matters.[134]

It seems evident that the riots were a major contributing factor to the rebirth of white racism, as many white people were confused and frightened by the violence. Even the traditional two-party system appeared to be threatened by a third party candidate who appealed to the basic, cultural fears of many Americans.

As much as a few Americans desired it, time could not be stopped nor could it be rolled back to another era where the solutions to problems were elementary. The Supreme Court decision of 1954 created a momentum of change that was sustained by many elements in the nation, thus accounting for the additional revamping of many of the nation's institutions. The NEA is a case in point. The Association was slow in the initial involvements of civil rights, but as the internal and external pressures mounted, it gradually took the necessary steps, sometimes hesitatingly, that led to the improvement of equal opportunity within its ranks. Evidence of this is the resolution that established the guidelines for desegregation of the southern state associations and the subsequent role of the Executive Committee that attempted to implement it.

Executive Committee's Implementation of Desegregation Resolution in 1967

Meeting with NEA field representatives and legal counsel, the Executive Committee planned for further implementation of the Assembly's integration mandate, and at its meeting in February, the Committee approved the following resolution:

Resolved: It is the belief of the Executive Committee that the purpose of resolution 66-12 is to bring about the merger of dual associations in each state.

(1) State associations which will not be merged by June 1, 1967, must submit to the Executive Committee by May 1, jointly developed and jointly approved plans for producing merger. These

plans should include at least the following topics with a schedule of target dates for action: (a) name of the association; (b) committees and commissions; (c) staff; (d) assets and liabilities; (e) local affiliates; (f) representatives; and (g) officers.

(2) The Executive Committee will meet May 21, 1967, to evaluate the plans described in the preceding paragraph.

(3) If the plans described in paragraph one are not approved, by the Executive Committee, a decision will be made regarding the status of the state affiliate.

Prior to June 1, 1967, if a merger has not been consummated or a merger plan satisfactory to the Executive Committee has not been jointly approved, then the Executive Committee will institute disaffiliation proceedings.[135]

After this time, the Committee met at least every month reviewing merger plans and making recommendations to the states involved. In the interim, it became apparent a merger was not a simple task, for many problems arose such as transfer of property, assumption of debts, proper staff balance, protection of minority rights, and selection of an executive secretary; consequently, it was not until June that the Committee found the six dual affiliated states to be in compliance with the intent of the desegregation resolution.

This did not mean that the merger difficulties had ended; on the contrary, they really had just begun, for the Executive Committee had approved only each state's intent to comply with the resolution. The real hard negotiations were just beginning; therefore, all of the basic problems regarding the creation of a new association from two established organizations had to be solved prior to a successful merger. Since these mergers required an equal partnership between the white and the black teachers, the Executive Committee was realistic enough to agree to the 1969 target dates.

The 1967 NEA Convention

The annual NEA convention was held at Minneapolis, Minnesota, from July 2 to July 7, 1967. Almost 6,000 delegates heard the Vice-President of the United States, Hubert H. Humphrey, deliver the major address to the convention. The convention was significant for another reason, as the delegates witnessed the transfer of the NEA executive power from Dr. Carr, who resigned his position a year before his contract expired, to Dr. Sam Lambert, the new NEA executive secretary.

Dr. Carr's final report to the Assembly proved revealing. Presenting a progress report of his administration, he stressed four major areas that affected the NEA: (a) education and civil rights; (b) the role of the federal government; (c) the quality of education; and (d) the militant teacher. Initially he made a very interesting admission, "Civil rights, in one respect or another, have profoundly concerned every NEA meeting."[136] He reemphasized two major principles: "the National Education Association should avoid and repudiate every least evidence of racial discrimination" and "the unity of the teaching profession should be preserved."[137] Once again denying that the Association practiced discrimination, he cited such NEA contributions to civil rights as: insisting on integrated housing for delegates; hiring practices for the NEA staff; fighting for desegregation of students and faculties; urging the elimination of dual affiliates; creating a defense fund for teachers displaced by civil rights disputes; and defending teachers in courts of law.[138] Then he expressed his satisfaction in giving to his successor a unified national organization: "It is a great deal of satisfaction at this moment to be able to say that the education associations in every state are affiliates of the National Education Association. . . . I hope to be able to hand over to my successor the responsibility for a national organization which remains one organization."[139]

He closed his civil rights presentation by interpreting his civil rights policies: "The Association is today able to exert that influence on a nationwide basis only because in the past it has moved with restraint and patience. Some, perhaps many, have felt that the Association policy in civil rights should be more radical and rapid. In my view, however, the achievement of the widest possible consensus has been, and is, the price of continued effectiveness."[140]

Mrs. Applegate continued the civil rights theme as she devoted two-thirds of her presidential address to racial progress of the NEA. She gave the Assembly a complete briefing on merger of dual affiliates and cited the many ways in which the NEA was working in this area:

Through conferences, workshops, publications, programs, units of the NEA have worked on problems stemming from integration of schools and school faculties. A recent example is a project of the Student NEA, part of the National Commission of Teacher Education and Professional Standards. In 1966, it launched a series of ten conferences in cooperation with Emory University, to help Negro and white students explore together their roles in making integration work. Other examples are Negro History Week and work with textbook publishers to guarantee inclusion of minorities in textbooks. During the coming academic year, the departments and divisions of the NEA have planned approximately seventeen integrated conferences, seminars, clinics, and workshops in the Southeastern states, and this is but one small part of our program.[141]

The desegregation resolution came up for adoption on the last day of the convention, and the chairman of the Resolutions Committee, Fred Clark, asked for its acceptance. E. B. Palmer, chairman of the National Committee of Educators for Human Rights, spoke for the resolution. He felt that the Assembly could do nothing further toward the resolution's implementation because of the Executive Committee's approval of the merger plans. He issued a warning that the delegates could "do much should an impasse occur," thus reasserting delegate pressure upon the states to affect merger by their target date of 1969.[142] In closing, he told the delegates: "This resolution is the means by which all races can achieve full participating civil and professional status. I urge this august body of delegates to adopt Resolution 67–12 as submitted by the Board of Directors."[143]

The resolution passed by a voice vote, and in effect, continued the Executive Committee's role in implementing merger of the dual associations, but Palmer emphatically reminded everyone that the Assembly would act if the terms of the resolution were not fulfilled.

The 1967 NEA resolution on desegregation read:

Individual worth derives from quality as a person, not from origin in race, creed, or class. The strength of America rests upon the utilization of the human resources of all.

Individual personality is enhanced and the national interest furthered by educational opportunity which involves children formally and informally, in diverse cultures.

Education must seek to eliminate prejudice and bigotry from

the public mind, support democratic principles and the free society which embodies them, and uphold respect for law, protection of individual rights, and use of democratic processes to effect change.

a. *Civil Rights.* The Association calls upon Americans to eliminate by statute and practice barriers of race, national origin, religion, sex, and economic status which prevent some citizens from exercising rights that are enjoyed by others, including liberties defined in common law and the Constitution and statutes of the United States. All individuals must have access to public education, to the voting booth, and to all services provided at public expense.

b. *School Desegregation and Integration.* The Association endorses the decision of the United States Supreme Court in Brown vs. Board of Education and urges compliance with subsequent federal laws and regulations in this area. The Association recommends that policies and guideline statements for school desegregation should be in keeping with the intent and provisions of the Civil Rights Act of 1964 and should be uniformly applicable throughout the nation's schools. Schools educating children in formerly segregated systems, those serving children of migrant workers, and those where the family language is other than English should receive sufficient funds, equipment, materials, and staff to carry out programs leading to quality education. It directs its state and local affiliates to seek in all communities adherence to the spirit and the letter of the law.

c. *Personnel Practices in Education.* The Association believes that the important criteria for evaluating educators for employment, retention, or promotion are professional competence, successful experience, and ethical practice. The Association calls upon all local affiliates to secure and enforce personnel policies and practices which embody this belief. It urges all American school boards to adopt such policies and practices. It calls for activities that will assist all educators to have access to employment opportunities such as NEA* SEARCH and the DuShane Fund for Teacher Rights.

d. *Housing for Educators.* The Association believes that all educators should be free to reside in the communities of their choice and calls upon all local affiliates to lead in breaking down barriers which limit this freedom.

e. *Minorities in Textbooks.* The Association believes that educational materials—textbooks, reference materials, audio-visual materials, and supplementary reading in all subjects—should portray our cultural diversity and the achievements of minority groups and calls upon all state and local affiliates to focus the professional judgement of their members upon this imperative.

f. *Merger of State and Local Affiliates.* The Association believes every educator has the right to participate fully in the professional association of his choice in any community or state. This right shall not be denied by constitution or practice on racial grounds. The Association notes that all previously segregated associations now affiliated have either merged or are merging according to requirements of the Executive Committee. It commends these associations. It recognizes that much remains to be done to bring legalism to life. It directs the officers and staff to continue to provide leadership and assistance and charges the Executive Committee to complete the task and intent outlined by Resolution 66–12.

g. *Protection of Minorities in Association.* The Association calls upon all affiliates to provide avenues for participation by all members. Members of minority groups should have positions on committees, opportunity to attain leadership, and the right to represent their local and state associations. Each affiliate should adopt policies and/or establish constitutional procedures and structures through which minority groups can express and resolve grievances arising from association practices. The officers and staff of the NEA should develop procedures for mediation whenever necessary.

h. *Implementation.* Responsibility for implementation rests with the Executive Committee. It shall direct the Executive Secretary to develop programs of implementation, those which innovate and those which correlate existing activities. The Executive Secretary shall assign staff responsibilities as needed and shall involve in these efforts all agencies of the Association, its affiliates, and other public and private agencies. Implementation of this resolution shall be a major charge upon every officer and staff member of the Association.

In any region, state, or school system in the United States where educators of more than one race are employed, no unit of the Association shall allocate Association funds for or arrange or engage in any activity, program, meeting, or conference in which the participation of members of minority groups is in any manner impeded.[144]

During the convention, the delegates made another significant move when they elected Mrs. Elizabeth Duncan Koontz, NEA president for 1968. Respected highly for her leadership capacities, Mrs. Koontz represented the new image of the NEA, i.e., the teachers' right to assume a greater responsibility for their profession. When asked whether she was elected because of her race, she replied, "I think it is incidental that I am a Negro. I would not have accepted the nomination had I thought it was because of my race."[145] Peter Janssen, however, regarded her election as "choosing a popular Ne-

gro for student council president, while the effective organizational
power rests somewhere else."[146] There is much truth to his observa-
tion, as the executive secretary possesses great power via his longer
term, greater salary, and vast appointive powers; however, it should
also be remembered that the Assembly had rebuffed the executive
secretary a few times since 1963, thus causing recent NEA presidents
to assume a somewhat more confident leadership role. Therefore,
this writer accepts *Newsweek's* interpretation that Mrs. Koontz's election ". . . will help the NEA overcome its reputation of representing
white, rural school teachers and give it a fresh face in its battle for
teachers' loyalties with the rapidly growing, militant, and urban
oriented American Federation of Teachers."[147]

Posture of the "NEA Journal" during 1967

During 1967, the *NEA Journal* presented the largest number and
the widest range of articles dealing with Negro education and its con-
comitant areas in the magazine's history. These articles did more than
reveal the Association's commitment to civil rights: they improved
the reader's knowledge in this vital aspect of American education.
The magazine examined the reactions to federal guidelines for desegregation and reviewed the significance of the Coleman Report.
It continued the emphasis upon education for the disadvantaged
child, looking at some of the educational innovations in that area.
Three excellent articles appeared on Negro higher education, while
another article called for sensitivity training in the classroom.

During the same period of time, the magazine published eighteen
pictures of Negroes that presented a broad spectrum of Negro participation in education. The September issue featured a cover picture
of Sam Lambert, appearing with a Negro and a white teacher. The
remaining pictures ranged from black students at Howard University
to integrated classrooms and from Negro college president to a black
elementary teacher.

From 1960 to 1967, the NEA underwent a transformation characterized by its aggressive civil rights stance. Two related factors
affected much of the Association's position: rivalry with the American Federation of Teachers and the revitalization of the NEA urban
affiliates. The union attacked the NEA at its most vulnerable area—

the urban affiliates—and exploited the Association's Achillean racial stance, thus placing the NEA on the defensive position throughout much of this period.

After endorsing the Supreme Court position in 1961, and creating the Urban Project in the following year, the Representative Assembly, led by aggressive, urban-oriented teachers, moved against the dual affiliates in 1964. Keeping constant pressure against the involved states, the Assembly successfully steered the Association to a position where five states had merged by 1967, while the remaining states agreed to merge by 1969.

Symbolically, Mrs. Koontz's election as NEA president was a racial milestone, for it could have never happened prior to 1964. Perhaps more significantly, her election was a victory for many NEA members who recognized the need for reform, fought for the necessary changes, and ultimately, changed the directional course of the NEA.

The New Era | 7

The wave of the future is coming and there is no fighting it.
ANNE MORROW LINDBERGH

The NEA continued further liberalization of its civil rights posture at the annual convention held at Dallas, Texas, in 1968. While adopting the same integration resolution passed at the 1967 convention, the Assembly installed Mrs. Koontz as the NEA president; endorsed the creation of a Human Rights Center; extracted apologies from Dallas officials with regard to a racial incident; appropriated money for the DuShane Fund for Teachers Rights; and made additional membership changes within the Executive Committee.

In her presidential address, Mrs. Koontz said that the profession "has a date with reality." Listing a nine point program for this achievement, she stressed the problems relating to the racial situation:

> We find thousands of teachers working under severe tensions of dismissals, unfair treatment, and subtle and overt intimidation because they have no job security—too many have continuing contracts which protect the community but do little for the teacher. These conditions must go. We must remove every imposed restriction which interferes with the full exercise of professional, civic, and human rights of educators everywhere.[1]

The Representative Assembly accepted the recommendations of an NEA task force for the creation of the Human Relations Center. Braulio Alonso hailed it as, "The most significant and exciting organizational change in the NEA for more than a decade."[2] The center's main purposes were to "Help plan, develop, and promote activities related to the protection and advancement of civil and human rights of educators and students."[3] Significantly, Samuel B. Ethridge, previously associated with the PR&R Commission, was appointed to head the center. This appointment placed Ethridge upon the twelve member NEA Cabinet, the first Negro ever to have gained such a position.

The Assembly became involved in a racial incident when Mooki Vitus Molapo, an NEA guest, was denied service in a Dallas tavern because of his race. While Alonso announced plans to enter suit against the tavern owner and the city of Dallas, the delegates threatened to adjourn the convention early. Dallas officials averted this drastic retaliatory action when the president of the Chamber of Commerce and the Dallas mayor apologized in behalf of the city. Continuing pressure from the Assembly delegates for affirmative NEA action, however, led to a symbolic march to the John F. Kennedy Memorial.

The delegates augmented the DuShane Fund by appropriating money directly from the NEA budget.[4] Prior to 1968, the fund depended entirely upon voluntary contributions from individual NEA members who were interested in fair and equitable treatment for teachers. Established in 1949, the fund has been responsible for some major court decisions regarding teachers who had lost their jobs because of racial reasons.

The convention also witnessed additional changes in the Executive Committee, thus reflecting the Assembly's influence upon this executive arm of the NEA. When Lyman Ginger did not seek reelection, delegates elected Nelson Kreuze, a coordinator of federal projects from Battle Creek, Michigan, as NEA treasurer. The delegates elected Wade Wilson to the other remaining position. Significantly, nine members of the committee were teachers, two were black, and Wilson was one of the charter members of the National Committee of Educators for Human Rights. The Executive Committee therefore exhibited a considerable philosophical difference from its previous composition.

Since 1966, the NEA has achieved considerable integration within its leadership and staff. Mrs. Koontz has been active in Association work for over a decade, and, along with black membership on the Executive Committee, six Negroes belong to the NEA Board of Directors. In addition to Ethridge's cabinet position, many black educators now hold committee assignments in the organizational structure. Finally, it must be pointed out that Negroes comprise a third of the entire NEA staff.[5]

These facts assume even more significance when examining the rivalry between the NEA and the AFT, as they are manifestations of the NEA's seizure of the offensive in its fight with the union. The offensive can be attributed to the Association's recent philosophical changes and the AFT's tactics during the 1968 teachers' strike in New York City.

At one time, many differences existed between the two organizations: (1) the NEA's lack of appeal to urban teachers; (2) the NEA's insistence upon inclusive membership; (3) the NEA's scorn for the AFT's emphasis upon collective bargaining and the strike as tools in disputes; (4) the AFT's aggressive civil rights policy; and (5) the AFT's affiliation with organized labor. Ironically, only the last distinction remains effective in 1970, while all of the others have been altered drastically.

The first case in point is NEA membership. The NEA is a huge organization with nearly 1,200,000 members who belong to 8,500 local affiliates. For the past decade, the NEA has been growing at an annual rate of 40,000 members; therefore, in the past four years, the NEA has acquired new members totalling more than the entire AFT membership. Significantly, almost half of the AFT's membership is located in three states, New York, Illinois, and Michigan, thus indicating the union's difficulty in expanding its base through other areas of the country. On the other hand, the NEA is gaining gradual acceptance in many urban areas. In 1968, the NEA had 253,000 members in the urban areas of the nation, an increase of 110,000 in seven years.[6]

A second point concerns the changing relationship between the teacher and the administrator, a result of increased teacher militancy. In most disputes, the chief school administrator is part of management; consequently, most of the lesser administrators also assume the school board's philosophy. For the record, the NEA still maintains its umbrella membership requirements, but certain threatening modifications are beginning to appear as a result of NEA militancy. The AASA has become disenchanted with the NEA and voted to become an associated organization with the National Education Association.

This is the loosest connection a department can have with the NEA; the subsequent step would be separation. If the AASA were to leave the NEA, it would seem logical that the Secondary School Principals and the Elementary School Principals, each maintaining department status in the NEA, would be affected by this move. Relative to this point, the chief school administrators left the Michigan Education Association and joined an organization with the Michigan School Boards Association and the Michigan School Officials Association. Shortly afterward, the elementary and secondary principals withdrew their membership from the MEA.[7]

While the AFT still emphasizes collective bargaining and strikes as its weapons in securing its demands, the NEA has recently added tougher weapons to its arsenal, euphemistically calling them professional negotiations and sanctions. The NEA employs these tools to achieve ends identical with those sought by the union: more money, better working conditions, and a greater share in policy making. If these weapons fail, NEA affiliates have not shown a total reluctance to strike, as illustrated by the Florida dispute in 1968.

The most interesting position, however, has been that of the AFT in relationship to its past civil rights posture. The United Federation of Teachers, a 55,000 member affiliate of the AFT, became involved in a thirty-three day strike in New York City that practically destroyed its liberal racial image, for the strike pitted the union against the black community, who wanted more control over the local schools.[8] The Ocean Hill-Brownsville board, an eight-school experimental unit where local people control curriculum, budget, and staff, suspended ten white teachers, thus triggering a conflict that culminated in the teacher walkout. The strike was acrimonious with neither side showing much restraint and was further complicated by overtones of racial hostility, appearing between the black community and the Jews, who dominate the union.[9]

The strike ended in an uneasy compromise with most of the major issues remaining unsolved; the consensus, however, seems to be that the UFT lost much more than it gained. Stephen Zeluck, president of the New Rochelle Federation of Teachers, referred to the settlement as a "Pyrrhic victory": "For in 'winning' the UFT will be blamed by the black movement for the death of community control. In 'winning' the UFT will have contributed heavily to the white-black polarization taking place in the country, and all that it portends."[10]

Significantly, during the height of the strike in New York City, the AFT's president, David Selden, asked the NEA Executive Committee to consider merger discussions with the union. The committee rejected the request, and Mrs. Koontz cited three reasons for the rejection: (1) serious internal problems within the union; (2) the poor financial condition of the union; and (3) the member disenchantment within the AFT.[11]

The NEA, however, could not afford to stand back and watch the AFT writhe indecisively over its internal problems, for the Association faced an internal crisis of similar magnitude. Members focused their attention upon the parent organization as it attempted to affect meaningful merger, while simultaneously moving to ensure proper black representation in all of the southern states.

The NEA's entry into the civil rights arena was fraught with many organizational perils and pitfalls due primarily to inexperience. Initially, most members regarded integration as a simple matter of the dual affiliate mergers, whereas they completely overlooked or woefully misunderstood the social, psychological, and cultural aspects of integration; consequently, many unforeseen problems developed when five states integrated their state associations between 1966 and 1967.

A careful study of the *NEA Handbook* revealed some significant facts of the comparison of the newly merged organizational structures of Florida, Virginia, Tennessee, Texas, and South Carolina with the dual organizational framework in these states prior to merger. The analysis showed that in all cases the white affiliate remained dominant. For example, the merged association retained the name of the white affiliate; the white educational journal was continued and its editor remained the same; and only a few instances existed where a black staff member was transferred to the newly merged unit. The executive secretary of the Palmetto Education Association, W. E. Solomon, became the assistant executive secretary and director of special projects of the South Carolina Education Association.

This raised some interesting points that provided further insight into the actual merger status in these five states. First, no black educator became executive secretary of the merged associations. Second,

J. Rupert Picott, executive secretary of the Virginia Teachers Association, joined the NEA staff shortly after the merger, and Mrs. Rosena Willis, director of field service for the VTA also moved to the NEA staff. It is quite revealing that no suitable positions could be found for these people on the newly merged Virginia Education Association's staff. Finally, two of the "new" executive secretaries, Robert Williams of Virginia and Edward Henderson of Florida, had been outspoken critics of the dual affiliate mergers.

The NEA also committed a tactical error in the South Carolina merger that has yet to be rectified. In its idealistic haste to achieve integration, the NEA attempted to bargain in "good faith", failing to consider the local politics involved in the South Carolina schools. As a result, the school superintendents pressured the black teachers and principals to accept a merger plan favorable to the white organization. The white affiliate even hinted at the possibility of a black president for the merged affiliate.

After the merger, Mrs. Ellen T. Watson, a former president of the black affiliate, became vice-president of the South Carolina Education Association but advanced no further. Solomon wanted to transfer $25,000 of the Palmetto Education Association's money into a defense fund for black teachers displaced by school integration. Eventually, the merged organization voted $1,000 to the project. Meanwhile, the SCEA moved to eliminate all vestiges of the PEA. The merged association took over the PEA's bank account, sold the PEA building, and took away Solomon's expense account.

Still another problem arose that had serious implications for all black affiliates. In some states where integration occurred, school districts closed black schools, thus affecting the transfer, demotion, or displacement of black educators. South Carolina practiced this procedure, and particularly the black principals suffered. Prior to the merger, the PEA protected them to some degree, and if necessary the black affiliate could appeal to the NEA for aid. Under the merger, however, the white organization had complete control; consequently, the black principals failed to receive a fair hearing. The lack of representation was a factor in the remaining black affiliates' reluctance to merge until they could be guaranteed fair representation.

The merger in Texas was no less astounding, and once again

it appeared as if the state organization had outflanked the NEA. At the NEA convention in 1964, only a few Texas delegates voted for the liberal desegregation resolution, thus indicating the general attitude toward affiliate merger. By 1966, however, the Texas State Teachers Association eliminated its racial membership restrictions, technically accepting the desegregation resolution. At the same time, the black affiliate voted to disband; consequently, only one educational organization remained; however, the black affiliate did not share its assets with the remaining organization. Instead a trust fund for black teachers was established, and Vernon McDaniel, executive secretary of the black affiliate, became executor of the fund.

Mrs. Applegate, chairman of the Compliance Committee, alluded to the merger problems while giving her report at the Dallas convention. She reported that the "paper work" for the merger had been completed in Florida, Virginia, South Carolina, Tennessee, and Texas. Then she reiterated, "I said, as far as the paper-work goes," thus indicating that meaningful merger had not occurred even though dual affiliates had been eliminated during 1966 and 1967.[12] She also said that Arkansas, Alabama, Mississippi, Georgia, Louisiana, and North Carolina were "still working on the paper work."[13]

Mrs. Applegate's presentation was very guarded and frequently cloaked in vague generalities. Apparently she felt that too much specific information would endanger the negotiations, but she attempted to provide some insight into the extreme difficulties involved in the merger talks.

> In the state to which I am referring, we moved along very, very slowly, by starts and stops. We got the name agreed to, we got committees named, or at least identified, we agreed that the staff of both associations would be retained, and so on. And then we started to figure out representation. And that is where we got hung up.
>
> Your president, your president-elect, your past president, and two NEA staff members met with this group in order to attempt to resolve the impasse. We offered professional mediation services. We met until quite late one night and agreed that maybe this was the way to get around this hurdle.
>
> The subcommittees then went back to their own groups, and

the next morning when we met in joint committee again, this offer of mediation was rejected. The groups hoped that they could continue perhaps to work some things out before we got to this stage.[14]

Then she briefly discussed the crux of the merger problem:

> But now, we are to the point where our big problem comes, and that is representation. That is the problem which we all must face. As we look at the state associations and the states where we are talking about merger—we see that we have two growing concerns, two successful corporations, which are really more alike than they are different.
>
> And what we must resolve is to establish a balance of power between these two growing concerns, a system of checks and balances, so that the members of each association can be assured that their needs are met, that they can participate and be represented.[15]

Closing on an optimistic note, Mrs. Applegate predicted that her Compliance Committee would eventually dissolve because of the complete implementation of the desegregation resolution: ". . . we will be able to discontinue the Compliance Committee and throw out Resolution 12. And I really am very optimistic. I think it is going to happen so soon that I will still be around and with enough energy, enough youthful energy, to leap with joy."[16]

The report was accepted by the delegates, but her deliberate vagueness caused some delegate unrest, as a Michigan delegate asked whether the compliance date could be moved up to 1968. Alonso pointed out that the date had been established by the Representative Assembly and that the Compliance Committee is "operating under that date."[17] He also pointed out that the compliance date was but one year away. The issue was pressed no further.

This question raised an interesting point. The desegregation resolution called for full implementation by 1969 or else the recalcitrant states would be disaffiliated. The Assembly had directed the Executive Committee to affect dual affiliate merger and the Compliance Committee functioned through the Executive Committee. Since the mergers consummated between 1966 and 1967 left a great deal to be desired, the activists in the Assembly had legitimate reason for concern; however, their fears were allayed in October 1968, when it became evident that the Executive Committee was beginning to follow the election returns.

The Executive Committee established a criteria for the evaluation of the merger plans and compliance with the Assembly's desegregation resolution. The purpose was clear: to avoid the mistakes made in the earlier mergers. The major points of the plan were: (1) to create a new educational association from the two old ones; (2) to call for two-thirds votes on certain key issues and to maintain equal representation on important commissions and committees, thus providing protection of minority group membership; (3) to give local educational associations one year to merge after the state associations have integrated; (4) to guarantee that the executive secretary not assigned to head the new organization be assigned a position of importance with a salary commensurate to the person who is second in command; (5) to provide for a neutral third party to aid in the merger movement if agreement was not reached by December 1, 1968; and (6) to call for binding arbitration if agreement was not reached by December 15, 1968.

The Association relented upon the last point. Early in 1969, it stipulated that a factfinder would be employed at NEA's expense in an effort to solve the merger impasse before the 1969 convention convened at Philadelphia, Pennsylvania. The rational behind this move was obvious. Since the affiliates in question faced immediate suspension, resentment and distrust arose in these states toward the NEA; therefore, the employment of the factfinder softened somewhat the dominant role played by the Association and allowed the states a bit more time to arrive at an acceptable agreement. Thus by applying steady pressure but yet always keeping the merger discussions open, the Executive Committee hoped to resolve the difficulties. In doing so, the NEA recognized the complexities of the issues because the merger difficulties varied from state to state.

For example, the greatest problem existed in Louisiana where a wide gulf lay between the two affiliates. Traditionally, in most southern states, some avenues of communication existed between segregated affiliates because the black organization generally depended upon its white counterpart for support relative to the legislative process. This was not the case, however, in Louisiana. Relations between the two associations had deteriorated to such a point that each unit went its separate way, appealing to the extremist views in each affiliate. Consequently, when the NEA factfinder recommended a guarantee for forty percent black representation in each group, a black president in the fifth year of the merger, equal representation on all of the important committees and commissions, and an antidiscrimination clause in the merged unit's constitution, both factions rejected the proposal. Merger in the foreseeable future appears dim because of the polarization of the white conservatives and the militant black educators.

The merger situation looks almost as bleak in Mississippi. The white affiliate, the Mississippi Education Association, failed to support the factfinder's recommendations for a co-presidency between 1970 to 1976, proportional membership in the house of delegates, and a two-third's vote requirement for passage of any measure in the house of delegates; consequently, the MEA delegates overwhelmingly defeated the merger proposal, even though the Mississippi Teachers Association, the black affiliate, accepted the plan. Referring to the merger struggle as a "checker game", Charles A. Johnson, executive secretary of the MEA, said, "The delegates have voted and I'm ready to make the MEA as good an organization as it can be, with or without the NEA."[18]

The major obstacles to the merger are the membership provisions guaranteed to the black educators and the necessary two-third's vote upon all measures in the house of delegates. Both provisions are interrelated in that the latter accords virtual veto power to the black members of the association, while the former guarantees their proportional membership. Ironically, the MEA complained most vigorously about the proportional membership clause because of this stipulation's direct opposition to the one man–one vote concept. National officials, however, still express hope that a merger will occur, but realistically, the impasse can be solved only if the MEA leaders openly support the factfinder's decision.

The merger situation in North Carolina remained muddled prior to the 1969 NEA convention. Racial tensions had always existed, but the merger problems were complicated by other factors. The North Carolina Teachers Association, the black affiliate, owned 4,000 acres of beachfront property, the Hammocks, and a credit union, ownership of which it would not surrender. On the other hand, the members of the white affiliate, the North Carolina Education Association, are covered by a liability insurance program and new members can not benefit from the policy unless the present members vote extension of the insurance. This has not occurred.

The NEA factfinder recommended the following points for merger: (1) an eight year period where the black educators would be guaranteed complete protection; (2) a black president for the second and fifth year of the merger; (3) the present executive secretary of the NCEA to receive the same position in the merged organization; and (4) the Hammocks and the NCTA credit union not a part of the merger. The NCTA rejected the proposals because it wanted the guarantee period set at eleven years, a black president elected every three years over the eleven year period of guarantee, and its present executive secretary considered for the similar position in the merged unit. The white affiliate generally opposed the plan because of its contradiction to the one man–one vote concept.[19]

Then in a bizarre twist, the NCEA accepted the merger plans. Apparently, a motivating factor was the continuation of the "checker game" with the NEA. The Executive Committee had already suspended the white affiliate from Mississippi for rejecting the merger plan, thus establishing a precedent; therefore, the Executive Committee had no alternative but to suspend the NCTA for its action. This was drastic action but the NEA continued the merger talks, and finally after a two day session between the two state organizations in August 1969, the affiliates reached agreement upon a tentative merger. The allocation of delegates to the Representative Assembly was changed, whereas the NEA factfinder's report remained the same.[20]

One of the big hangups in the Alabama talks was over the selection of a name for the new association. The black affiliate wanted a new name, while the Alabama Education Association argued for the continuation of its present title. The AEA regarded tradition highly since its original charter was granted in the 1850s. The Alabama State Teachers Association countered by pointing out that the name must be different since change is relevant to merger. Buttressing this position, one black leader explained, "After all, we were slaves a hundred and ten years ago." Eventually they reached a compromise by retaining the Alabama Education Association's name but placing underneath the letterhead the following: formerly the Alabama State Teachers Association and the Alabama Education Association. The agreement also guaranteed a black president to head the merged unit in 1971–1972 and 1973–1974.[21] Black educators gained proportional representation, and proper safeguards were designed to protect minority rights. All staff members of the two organizations were retained without loss of pay and chairmanships of the key organizational committees and commissions would be rotated on an established schedule.

Approval came May 16, 1969, three years and twenty-five meetings after initial talks had begun. The ASTA ratified the plan by a near unanimous vote, while the AEA accepted the plan by a two to one margin. Perhaps an article in the *Alabama State Teachers Association Journal* captured the prevailing mood of most educators concerning the merger:

> Admittedly, the plan is not completely satisfactory to either segment of the joint committee or to either of the respective memberships. . . . But in the final analysis, the joint committee agreed that, all factors being generally considered, this is the best plan they could devise for the formation of a unified professional organization in the state that will best serve the interests of all the teachers in the state.[22]

The Georgia Education Association and the Georgia Teachers and Education Association also agreed to the merger prior to the NEA established deadline, but not without some bitterness expressed by the delegates concerning the merger provision that the new organization, the Georgia Association of Educators, would guarantee a black president every third year for nine years.[23] One man said, "It will be just like Russia, you can vote but someone tells you who to vote for."[24] Dr. Frank Shumke, president of the GEA, the white affiliate, answered this criticism by pointing out that black candidates must make up the entire presidential slate every three years; he stressed, however, that all people could vote in the election.[25] Unlike the white affiliates in Louisiana and Mississippi, the GEA endorsed the merger terms and urged their members to ratify unification.

Arkansas accepted the merger terms on the first day of the NEA convention at Philadelphia. The terms followed the criteria developed by the Executive Committee. Forrest Rozzell, the executive secretary of the white affiliate, acquired the same post in the new organization, while T. E. Patterson, the executive secretary of the black organization, became the assistant executive secretary of human relations, a vital position in the merged organization. Patterson's staff was retained and black representation was fixed at the proportional rate of membership.

In the meantime, the National Education Association met its desegregation problem head on at the organization's 107th annual convention held at Philadelphia, Pennsylvania. On the opening day of the 1969 convention, the delegates refused to seat the white affiliate representatives from Louisiana and Mississippi and the black affiliates from North Carolina and Louisiana.[26] Commenting upon the elimination of most dual affiliates, Sam Lambert said, "I'm rather proud that we have been able to bring about a merger of voluntary organizations."[27] Expressing optimism for the resolution of the difficulties in the unmerged states, he told a press conference, "Our biggest hangup is that it's [merging] not entirely a race issue. Some [education associations] have savings, real estate, trust funds, separate officers. These are corporate problems."[28]

Many NEA members immediately challenged his statement concerning the merger not being a race matter, but open dispute with the executive secretary is not uncommon anymore. Significantly, the integration gains have been made without the dissolution of the NEA, as some southern states' veiled hints of bolting the Association never materialized. It is true that the NEA suffered membership losses in the affected states, but the civil rights progress made by the organization more than offset the membership reduction, allowing the NEA to become a model for other national organizations plagued by desegregation problems.

The American Bar Association, The American Medical Association, and many labor unions have recently come under fire for their alleged racial practices, especially at the state and local levels of organization. All of these groups could benefit from the NEA experience, for what other national integrated organization can boast of having had a black president or having black people upon its national executive committee? Can the AMA foresee a day when a black doctor will head a southern state chapter of the AMA? For that matter, are black doctors guaranteed their basic professional rights in southern medical societies? Are all labor unions opening up their membership to black workers? Relative to the educational profession, the NEA can answer these questions affirmatively.

The NEA integration battle is not over, however, because the state affiliates still outside the pale must merge in order to assure black educators their basic rights. Much credit accrues to the Executive Committee, for this organization, through the Compliance Committee, has played a paramount role in the mergers in Alabama, Georgia, and Arkansas, where the rights of the minority have been protected. Here, the NEA has established the machinery for the continuation of minority rights, presenting its members with a two-fold challenge: to maintain a constant vigilance that the civil rights progress made in these states not be reversed and to effect more equitable rights for the minority members in those states that merged prior to 1968.

After the NEA accomplishes internal integration, it can devote complete attention to the other pressing issues relevant to the racial crisis. For example, the Association must increase its already significant efforts for the protection of teachers displaced because of school integration. The NEA must focus upon the crisis in the urban schools throughout the nation. Devoting almost exclusive attention toward urban education may require still another major directional change for the NEA—merger with the American Federation of Teachers—so that all of the profession's energy will extend into this potentially explosive area.

Notes

Introduction

1. National Education Association, *Equal Opportunity for All* (Washington, D.C.: NEA Urban Services, 1967), p. 3.

Chapter 1

1. National Education Association, *NEA Handbook for Local, State, and National Associations* (Washington, D.C.: National Education Association, 1968), p. 18. (Hereafter referred to as *NEA Handbook* and the year of publication.)
2. Edgar B. Wesley, *NEA: The First Hundred Years* (New York: Harper and Brothers, 1957), pp. 328–329.
3. National Education Association, *The National Education Association of the United States Addresses and Proceedings, 1910* (Washington, D.C.: NEA Association, 1910), p. 34. (Hereafter referred to as *NEA Proceedings*, followed by year of publication.)
4. Wesley, *NEA: The First Hundred Years*, p. 329.
5. Mildred Sandison Fenner, *NEA History* (Washington, D.C.: National Education Association, 1945), p. 41.
6. "Sorry Spectacle at Boston," *Educational Review*, XL June–December, 1910:319–320.
7. Ibid., p. 321.
8. *NEA Proceedings, 1910*, p. 33.
9. Ibid., p. 34.   10. Ibid., pp. 34–35.
11. John R. Kirk, "Discussion: NEA Convention at Chicago," *Educational Review*, XLIV (June–December, 1912):311–314.
12. *NEA Proceedings, 1912*, pp. 32–42.
13. Ibid.   14. Ibid., p. 37.
15. "The Old Order Changeth," *Educational Review*, XLIV (June–December, 1912):321.
16. "Sorry Spectacle at Boston," *Educational Review*, XL (June–December, 1910):319–320.

17. Charles H. Judd, "Editorial Notes," *Elementary School Teacher,* XII (September, 1911–June, 1912) : 494–495.
18. National Education Association, *Yearbook and List of Active Members of the NEA* (Ann Arbor: National Education Association, 1915), p. 47.
19. Ibid.
20. National Education Association, *Yearbook and List of Active Members of the NEA* (Washington, D.C.: The Association, 1917), pp. 46–47.
21. *NEA Bulletin,* VI, no. 5 (April, 1918) : p. 23.
22. National Education Association, *Yearbook and List of Active Members of the NEA* (Washington, D.C.: The Association, 1918), pp. 43–44.
23. *NEA Bulletin,* VIII, No. 1 (September, 1919) : 17.
24. *NEA Bulletin,* VIII, No. 2 (October, 1919) : 7–8.
25. *NEA Bulletin,* VIII, No. 3 (November, 1919) : 22.
26. *NEA Bulletin,* VIII, No. 4, (December, 1919) : 23.
27. "The Reorganized National Education Association," *School Review,* XXVIII (September, 1920) : 481.
28. Ibid., p. 482.
29. "The Salt Lake Meeting," *Educational Review* LX (June–December, 1920), 170–172.
30. Ibid., p. 169.   31. Wesley, *NEA: The First Hundred Years,* p. 332.
32. Ibid., p. 348.   33. *NEA Handbook, 1968,* p. 49.
34. Ibid., p. 152.   35. Ibid., p. 137.
36. Ibid., p. 153.   37. Ibid., p. 60.   38. Ibid., p. 153.
39. Ibid., p. 152.   40. Ibid., p. 154.   41. Ibid.
42. Ibid., p. 63.   43. Ibid., p. 43.   44. Ibid., p. 44.
45. Ibid.   46. Ibid., p. 27.
47. *NEA Proceedings, 1967,* p. 363.
48. *NEA Handbook, 1968,* p. 44.   49. Ibid., p. 27.
50. *NEA Proceedings, 1967,* pp. 507–509.
51. Myron Lieberman, *Education as a Profession* (Englewood Cliffs, New Jersey: Prentice Hall, Inc., 1956), p. 265.
52. *NEA Reporter,* VII (July 19, 1968).
53. Erwin Stevenson Selle, Organization and Activities of the National Education Association. (New York: Columbia University, 1932), pp. 39–41.
54. Lieberman, *Education as a Profession,* p. 268.
55. Letter from Lyle W. Ashby, May 22, 1968.
56. Wesley, *NEA: The First Hundred Years,* p. 333.
57. Letter from Henry Stoudt, May 8, 1968.
58. *Newsweek,* July 17, 1967, p. 54.
59. *NEA Handbook, 1968,* p. 27.
60. *NEA Reporter, VII* (July 19, 1968).
61. Wesley, *NEA: The First Hundred Years,* p. 327.
62. Interview with Jane Walker, June 17, 1968.
63. *NEA Proceedings, 1966,* pp. 150, 253–256.
64. NEA Proceedings, 1967, p. 365.   65. Ibid., p. 364.
66. Stanley E. Elam, "What's Ahead for the NEA?" *Phi Delta Kappan,* XLVIII (April, 1967) : 388.
67. *NEA Proceedings, 1966,* pp. 221–224.
68. *NEA Proceedings 1967,* p. 504.

69. Letter from Herschel C. Heritage, May 9, 1968.
70. *NEA Handbook, 1968*, p. 45.   71. Ibid., p. 46.
72. National Education Association, "Powers and Duties of NEA Official Bodies," mimeographed (Washington, D.C.: NEA, 1961), pp. 12–13.
73. Ibid., pp. 14–15.   74. Ibid., p. 11.
75. Wesley, *NEA: The First Hundred Years*, p. 386.
76. Fenner, *NEA History*, p. 59.
77. Letter from Henry Stoudt, May 8, 1968.
78. Fenner, *NEA History*, p. 60.
79. The number has been reduced to ten, as a result of the United States Congress granting approval for changes in the NEA Charter.
80. *NEA Proceedings, 1967*, pp. 307–360.
81. The position of chairman of the Board of Trustees is no longer needed, since the Board of Trustees was eliminated as a result of changes in the NEA Charter.
82. *NEA Handbook, 1968*, p. 49.
83. National Education Association, "Powers and Duties of NEA Official Bodies," p. 13.
84. Ibid., p. 15.
85. Wesley, *NEA: The First Hundred Years*, p. 386.
86. Letter from Thelma Davis, member of the Executive Committee, June 2, 1968.
87. Interview with Jane Walker, June 17, 1968.
88. Letter from Thelma Davis, June 2, 1968.

Chapter 2

1. The NAACP reported that nearly 2,400 Negroes were lynched during 1889 to 1918.
2. Virgil Clift, "History of Racial Segregation in American Education," *School and Society*, LXXXVIII (May 7, 1960): 224.
3. Roger Butterfield, "Hard Reality of Freedom," *Life* Magazine, November 29, 1968, p. 65.
4. Stephen Wright, "The Negro College in America," *Harvard Educational Review*, XXX (Summer 1960): 287.
5. Roger Butterfield, "The Mobilization of Black Strength," *Life* Magazine, December 6, 1968, p. 93–94.
6. Kelly Miller, "Forty Years of Negro Education," *Educational Review*, XXXVI (June–December, 1908): 495.
7. "Further Discrimination Against Negro Schools," *Outlook*, December 15, 1900, pp. 912–913.
8. "The Negro Common Schools," *Outlook*, July 12, 1902, pp. 676–677.
9. John Hope Franklin, "Negro in America," *Encyclopaedia Britannica*, XVI: 196.
10. James Dillard, "The Negro in Rural Education and Country Life," *NEA Proceedings, 1921*, p. 582.
11. Ibid.

12. "Rural Schools for Negroes," *School and Society,* XXI (June 6, 1925): 677.
13. Althea Washington, "Supervision in Public Rural Schools for Negroes," *The Journal of Negro Education,* I (Summer, 1932): 235.
14. *NEA Proceedings, 1885,* p. 532; *NEA Proceedings, 1918,* pp. 555–556.
15. *NEA Proceedings, 1898,* pp. 330–335; *NEA Proceedings, 1900,* p. 489.
16. *NEA Proceedings, 1908,* p. 91.
17. *NEA Proceedings, 1894,* pp. 185–186.
18. *NEA Proceedings, 1890,* pp. 254–285.
19. Ibid., pp. 254–256.
20. *NEA Proceedings 1889,* pp. 202–209.
21. *NEA Proceedings, 1900,* pp. 482–84; *NEA Proceedings, 1916,* pp. 106–111.
22. *NEA Proceedings, 1886,* p. 229.
23. *NEA Proceedings, 1890,* pp. 497–505.
24. *NEA Proceedings, 1900,* p. 490.
25. *NEA Proceedings, 1889,* pp. 548–553; 587–597.
26. *NEA Proceedings, 1884,* p. 128.
27. Ibid.   28. Ibid., p. 129.
29. *NEA Proceedings, 1896,* p. 215.
30. Ibid., p. 216.
31. Notice the emphasis upon the hand, the head, and the heart.
32. *NEA Proceedings, 1896,* p. 216.   33. Ibid., p. 217.
34. *NEA Proceedings, 1904,* p. 130.   35. Ibid.
36. Ibid., p. 131.   37. *NEA Proceedings, 1904,* p. 134.
38. *NEA Proceedings, 1908,* pp. 87–93.

Chapter 3

1. Mordecai W. Johnson, "Negro Opportunity and National Morale," *NEA Journal,* XXX (September, 1941): 167.
2. "Statistics of Negro Elementary and Secondary Education," *School and Society,* XXX (April 13, 1929): 481.
3. J. Clarice Brooks, "Student Personnel," *The Journal of Negro Education,* I (Summer, 1932), 259–265.
4. Charles H. Thompson, "The Education of the Negro in the United States," *School and Society,* XLII (November 9, 1935): 626.
5. Felton Clark, "Recent Legislation in Louisiana and Negro Education," *School and Society,* XLI (March 2, 1935): 295.
6. Johnson, "Negro Opportunity and National Morale," pp. 167–168.
7. Stephen Wright, "The Negro Colleges in America," *Harvard Educational Review,* XXX (Summer, 1960): 287.
8. John A. Morsell, "Schools, Courts, and the Negro's Future," *Harvard Educational Review,* XXX (Summer, 1960): 186.
9. Virgil Clift, "History of Racial Segregation in American Education," *School and Society,* LXXXVIII (May 7, 1960): 225–226.
10. Thurgood Marshall, "An Evaluation of Recent Attempts to achieve Racial Integration through Resort to the Courts," *The Journal of Negro Education,* XXI (Summer, 1952): 319.

11. R. I. Brigham, "The Price of Segregation," *Survey Graphic,* XXXV (May, 1946) : 156–157.
12. Wright, "The Negro Colleges in America," pp. 289–290.
13. Morsell, "Schools, Courts, and the Negro's Future," p. 186.
14. Virginius Dabney, "Southern Crisis: Desegregation Decision," *Saturday Evening Post,* November 8, 1952, p. 101.
15. Ibid.
16. "The Supreme Court: The Segregation Issue," *Time,* December 22, 1952, p. 13.
17. George Jones, *The American Teachers Association Note Book* (Montgomery, Alabama: American Teachers Association, 1963), p. 3.
18. *NEA Proceedings, 1928,* p. 30.   19. Ibid., p. 54–55.
20. Research Division, National Education Association, "Summary of Activities of the Joint Committee of NEA-ATA," mimeographed, (Washington, D.C.: National Education Association, 1942), pp. 2–3.
21. George Jones concurred with the writer on this hypothesis because the number of Negro delegates to the Representative Assembly has always been difficult to assess. Based on some scattered statements gleaned from various NEA publications, this writer would guess that only a few Negroes attended the NEA conventions prior to 1943 as official delegates. Perhaps some incidents did occur because of segregated facilities, but there were not enough Negro representatives to force delegate action; therefore, it is more practical to justify this action on a patriotic basis.
22. *NEA Proceedings, 1943,* p. 189.
23. Ibid., 191.   24. Ibid., p. 190.   25. Ibid., pp. 190–191.
26. Ibid., p. 191.   27. Ibid., p. 192.   28. Ibid.
29. Ibid., 30.   Ibid., p. 193.
31. *NEA Proceedings, 1949,* p. 195.   32. Ibid., p. 198.
33. Ibid., p. 119.   34. Ibid., p. 127.   35. Ibid., p. 137.
36. Ibid., p. 138.   37. Ibid.   38. Ibid., p. 187.
39. Ibid., p. 201.   40. *NEA Proceedings, 1950,* p. 107.
41. Ibid.   42. Ibid., pp. 108–109.   43. Ibid., p. 112.
44. Walter Ridley, "Joint Action Toward Unity," *NEA Journal,* XLI (November 1952) : 512.
45. *NEA Proceedings, 1950,* p. 115.
46. *NEA Proceedings, 1951,* p. 208.   47. Ibid., p. 298.
48. Ridley, "Joint Action Toward Unity," p. 511.
49. This position was merely honorary, and another Negro, J. Rupert Picott, was elected a vice-president in 1954.
50. *NEA Proceedings, 1952,* p. 214.

Chapter 4

1. *Time,* May 24, 1954, p. 21.
2. *New York Times,* May 18, 1954.
3. *Nation's Schools,* LIV (July, 1954) : 25.   4. Ibid., p. 29.
5. *New York Times,* May 18, 1954.
6. *Time,* May 24, 1954.

7. Charles H. Thompson, "Between Court Decision and Court Decree," *The Journal of Negro Education*, XXIII (Fall, 1954) : 401–403.
8. *New York Times,* May 18, 1954.   9. Ibid.
10. Mary E. Owen, "Impressions from the NEA Summer Meeting," *The Instructor,* LXIV (September, 1954) : 11.
11. *NEA Proceedings, 1954*, pp. 22–23.
12. Ibid., p. 23.   13. Ibid., p. 141.
14. *NEA Proceedings, 1954*, p. 123.
15. Ibid., p. 124.   16. Ibid., p. 122.   17. Ibid.
18. *New York Times,* July 4, 1954.
19. •*NEA Proceedings, 1954*, pp. 124–125.
20. *NEA Handbook, 1954.*
21. *New York Times,* July 4, 1954.
22. *NEA Journal,* XLIII (September, 1954) : 330, 355–356.
23. Ibid., pp. 349–350.
24. *NEA Proceedings, 1954*, p. 213.
25. J. Rupert Picott, "Desegregation of Public Education in Virginia: One Year Afterward," *The Journal of Negro Education,* XXIV (Fall, 1955) : 369–370.
26. Herbert Doddy, "Desegregation and Employment of Negro Teachers," *The Journal of Negro Education,* XXIV (Fall, 1955) : 406–407.
27. Ibid., p. 407.   28. Ibid., p. 408.
29. C. H. Parrish, "Desegregation in Public Education: A Critical Summary," *The Journal of Negro Education,* XXIV (Summer, 1955) : 385.
30. Myron Lieberman, "Segregation's Challenge to the NEA," *School and Society,* LXXXI (May 28, 1955) : 167–168.
31. Ibid., p. 167.   32. *NEA Proceedings, 1955*, p. 58.
33. John H. Starie, "The New Ark's a Moverin," *NEA Journal,* XLIV (September, 1955) : 361.
34. *NEA Proceedings, 1955*, pp. 24–49.   35. Ibid., p. 46.
36. Ibid., p. 138.   37. Ibid., p. 139.   38. Ibid., p. 140.
39. Ibid., p. 141.   40. Ibid., p. 142.   41. Ibid.
42. *NEA Journal,* XLIV (May, 1955) : 259–260.
43. *NEA Journal,* XLIV (September, 1955) : 324.
44. *NEA Journal,* XLIV (October, 1955) : 388.
45. *Newsweek,* September 19, 1955, pp. 35–36.
46. William A. Bender, "Status of Educational Desegregation in Mississippi," *The Journal of Negro Education,* XXV (Summer 1956) : 285.
47. J. Rupert Picott, "Status of Educational Desegregation in Virginia," *The Journal of Negro Education,* XXV (Summer 1956) : 345.
48. Preston Valien, "Status of Educational Desegregation," *The Journal of Negro Education,* XXV (Summer 1956) : 365–368.
49. W. E. Solomon, "Educational Desegregation in South Carolina," *The Journal of Negro Education,* XXV (Summer, 1956) : 321–323.
50. *NEA Proceedings, 1956*, p. 5.   51. Ibid., p. 33.
52. *New York Times,* July 2, 1956.
53. Ibid.   54. Ibid.
55. Mildred E. Whitcomb, "Roses and Resolutions at Portland," *Nation's Schools, LVIII* (August, 1956) : 92.

56. *New York Times,* July 3, 1956.
57. *New York Times,* July 4, 1956.
58. *NEA Proceedings, 1956,* p. 138.
59. *New York Times,* July 8, 1956.
60. "NEA Sidesteps the Real Issue," *America,* July 21, 1956, p. 374.
61. James L. McCaskill, "How the Kelley Bill Was Lost and Why," *NEA Journal, LXV* (September, 1956) : 363-366.
62. Ibid., p. 363.   63. Ibid., p. 366.
64. *NEA Journal,* XLV (January, 1956) : 3.
65. *NEA Journal,* XLV (February, 1956) : 67.
66. *NEA Journal,* XLV (September, 1956) : 331.
67. *New York Times,* April 5, 1957.
68. *New York Times,* April 10, 1957.
69. *School and Society,* LXXXIV (May 11, 1957) ; *Progressive Education,* XXXIV (June, 1957).
70. "Centennial of the NEA," *School and Society,* LXXXV (May 11, 1957) : 169.
71. Lloyd P. Jorgenson, "Social and Economic Orientation of the National Education Association, *"Progressive Education,* XXXIV (July, 1957) : 100.
72. William G. Carr, "NEA Service to American Education," *School and Society,* LXXXV (May 11, 1957) : 160–163.
73. Ibid., p. 161.   74. Ibid., p. 162.
75. Jorgenson, "Social and Economic Orientation," p. 101.
76. Myron Lieberman, "Civil Rights and the NEA," *School and Society,* LXXXV (May 11, 1957) : 166–168.
77. "News and Trends," *NEA Journal,* XLVI (February, 1957) : 67.
78. Charles H. Thompson, "Editorial Comments," *The Journal of Negro Education,* XXVI (Winter, 1957) : 2.
79. Ibid.   80. *NEA Proceedings, 1957,* p. 57.
81. *New York Times,* July 3, 1957.
82. Arthur H. Rice, "NEA Starts Second Century," *Nation's Schools,* LX (August, 1957) : 50.
83. *New York Times,* July 6, 1957.
84. Rice, "NEA Starts Second Century," p. 50.
85. *NEA Proceedings, 1957,* pp. 194–195.
86. Ibid., p. 194.   87. Ibid.
88. Rice, "NEA Starts Second Century," p. 50.
89. *NEA Proceedings, 1957,* p. 195.
90. Ibid.   91. Ibid., pp. 195–196.
92. *New York Times,* July 1, 1958.
93. *New York Times,* July 4, 1958.
94. *NEA Proceedings, 1958,* p. 182.
95. Ibid., pp. 184–185.   96. Ibid., p. 185.
97. Ibid.   98. Ibid., pp. 185–186.
99. *New York Times,* July 5, 1958.
100. Mildred Whitcomb, "Teachers Celebrate the Fourth," *Nation's Schools,* LXII (August, 1958) : 32.
101. *New York Times,* July 5, 1958.
102. *NEA Proceedings 1958,* p. 187.

103. Ibid., p. 201.   104.   Ibid.
105. *New York Times,* July 5, 1958.
106. *Newsweek,* July 14, 1958, p. 80.
107. "Protestantism Speaks on Justice and Integration," *Christian Century,* February 5, 1958, pp. 164–166.
108. Charles Thompson, "Editorial," *The Journal of Negro Education,* XXVIII (Winter, 1959) : 2.
109. Administrative Board of the National Catholic Welfare Conference, "Discrimination and Christian Conscience," *The Journal of Negro Education,* XXVIII (Winter, 1959) : 68.
110. Marvin Wall, "Events in Southern Education Since 1954," *Harvard Educational Review,* XXX (Summer, 1960) : 211.
111. "Resolutions," *School Administrator,* XVI (March, 1959) : 8.
112. *NEA Proceedings, 1959,* p. 225.
113. Ibid., p. 234.   114.   Ibid., p. 244.   115.   Ibid., p. 266.
116. *NEA Proceedings, 1960,* p. 190.
117. *Newsweek,* July 13, 1959, p. 54.
118. Arthur H. Rice, "NEA Debates Segregation," *Nation's Schools,* LXIV (August, 1959) : 60.
119. *NEA Proceedings 1959,* p. 42.
120. Ibid., p. 43.   121.   Ibid.   122.   Ibid., p. 44.
123. Ibid., p. 45.   124.   Rice, "NEA Debates Segregation," p. 61.
125. Ibid., p. 62.   126.   Ibid.   127.   Ibid.
128. *New York Times,* July 2, 1959.   129.   Ibid.
130. *NEA Proceedings, 1959,* p. 186.   131.   Ibid.
132. Ibid., p. 178.   133.   Ibid.
134. Ibid., pp. 186–187.   135.   Ibid., p. 187.
136. One southern delegate told George Jones, "You had better watch out because you have to go back and *live* in Alabama."
137. Ibid.   138.   Ibid., p. 193.
139. Ibid., p. 195.   140.   Ibid.
141. Comments from the floor were limited to only five minutes but Mr. Rozzell was granted permission from the Assembly to complete his presentation.
142. *NEA Proceedings, 1959,* p. 198.
143. Ibid.   144.   Ibid., p. 200.   145.   Ibid., p. 201.
146. Ibid.   147.   Ibid., p. 204.   148.   Ibid., p. 205.
149. *New York Times,* July 4, 1959.
150. Rice, "NEA Debates Segregation," p. 68.
151. William W. Brickman, "NEA and School Racial Segregation," *School and Society,* LXXXVII (September 26, 1959) : 364.
152. *New York Times,* August 19, 1959.
153. John Dane, "NEA Counsel," *Progressive Education,* XXXIV (July 1957) : 97.
154. *NEA Journal,* XLIV (November, 1955) : 524.
155. *NEA Journal,* XLV (September, 1956) : 366.
156. *NEA Journal,* XLVI (November, 1957) : 511.
157. *NEA Journal,* XLVIII (February, 1959) : 11.
158. *NEA Journal,* XLVIII (May, 1959) : 38.
159. *NEA Journal,* XLVIII (October, 1959) : 12.

Chapter 5

1. Jim Leeson, "Desegregation," *Southern Education Report,* I (January–February, 1966) : 28–29.
2. Eunice S. Newton and Earle West, "The Progress of the Negro in Elementary and Secondary Education," *The Journal of Negro Education,* XXXII (Fall, 1963) : 472–473.
3. "News and Trends," *NEA Journal,* XLIX (May, 1960) : 4.
4. Herman Talmadge, "Exclusive State Control Over State Education," *School and Society,* LXXXVIII (May 7, 1960) : 243–246.
5. Martin Oppenheimer, "The Student Movement: Year I." *The Journal of Negro Education,* XXXIII (Fall, 1964) : 398–399.
6. *NEA Proceedings, 1960,* p. 221.
7. Ibid.   8. Ibid., p. 233.   9. Ibid., p. 242.
10. Ibid., p. 15.   11. Ibid., pp. 54–62.
12. *Newsweek,* July 11, 1960, p. 83.
13. Ibid.   14. *New York Times,* June 27, 1960.
15. Carl Megel, president of the AFT, said that this action cost the AFT a loss of 7,000 members from 1956 to 1963; T. M. Stinnett disagreed with those figures, claiming that membership loss was close to 3,000 people. But regardless of whose statistics a person accepts, the losses were heavy because the AFT's membership in 1958 was only 58,000.
16. The eleven states were North Carolina, South Carolina, Florida, Arkansas, Georgia, Tennessee, Texas, Mississippi, Alabama, Louisiana, and Virginia. These states had 174,000 NEA members or nearly twenty-five percent of the total Association membership.
17. *New York Times,* June 27, 1960..   18. Ibid.
19. Arthur Rice, "NEA Budges on Integration, Ponders Salary Negotiations," *Nation's Schools,* LVI (August, 1960) : 98.
20. Ginger and Stout were members of the Executive Committee, and Buford was a member of the Board of Trustees.
21. *NEA Proceedings, 1960,* p. 169.   22. Ibid., p. 170.
23. Ibid., p. 182.   24. Ibid., pp. 171–172.   25. Ibid., pp. 172–173.
26. Ibid., p. 173.   27. Ibid., pp. 173–175.   28. Ibid., p. 176.
29. Ibid., pp. 176–178.   30. Ibid., p. 179.   31. Ibid.
32. It is important to note that before the situation was beclouded by parliamentary maneuvering, the 1960 convention expressed its desire for a "strong" resolution by a plurality of 153 votes.
33. Ibid., p. 183.   34. Ibid.   35. Ibid.
36. Ibid., p. 184.   37. Ibid.   38. Ibid., p. 185.
39. Ibid., pp. 185–191.   40. Ibid., p. 191.
41. This study was approved by the Board on June 25, 1960. It consisted of an annotated bibliography, without editorial comment, of thirty-one doctoral dissertations, thirty-three research and professional studies, and fifty-one descriptive reports.
42. *NEA Proceedings, 1961,* p. 265.
43. "Quality Education: The Goal of the NEA," *Georgia Education Journal, XXVII* (September, 1960) : 16.
44. *New York Times,* July 3, 1960.
45. *Pittsburgh Courier,* July 9, 1960.

46. *New York Times,* August 20, 1960.   47. Ibid.
48. Ibid.
49. "AFT Sets Its Goals," *Scholastic Teacher,* LXXVII (September 21, 1960):2T.
50. M. Elizabeth Matthews, "Edna Griffin — Big City Teacher," *NEA Journal,* XLIX (October, 1960):51–52.
51. Jean D. Grambs, "Understanding Group Relations," *NEA Journal,* XLIX (December, 1960):43–44.
52. Matthews, "Edna Griffin — Big City Teacher," p. 51.
53. "Negro Progress in 1961," *Ebony,* XVII (January, 1962):21–23.
54. Mr. Duncan is the brother of Mrs. Elizabeth Duncan Koontz, who became the first Negro president of the NEA in 1968.
55. Leeson, "Desegregation."
56. "News and Trends," *NEA Journal,* L. (October, 1961):3.
57. Nancy Arnez, "A Thoughtful Look at Plcaement Policies in a New Era," *The Journal of Negro Education,* XXXIV (Winter, 1966):48.
58. Ibid., p. 50.
59. "Negro Progress in 1961," *Ebony,* XVII (January, 1962):21–23.
60. "News and Trends," *NEA Journal,* L (January, 1961):4.
61. *NEA Proceedings, 1961,* p. 27.
62. Interview with George Jones, NEA staff director of Urban Education, December 10, 1968.
63. *NEA Proceedings, 1961,* p. 278.
64. Ibid., pp. 221–227.   65. Ibid., p. 166.   66. Ibid., p. 187.
67. Ibid., pp. 193–194.   68. Ibid., p. 196.   69. Ibid., p. 198.
70. Ibid., p. 201.   71. Ibid., p. 206.   72. Ibid., p. 207.
73. Ibid.   74. Ibid., pp. 207–208.   75. Ibid., pp. 209–210.
76. *NEA Handbook, 1961,* pp. 60–61.
77. Arthur Rice, "NEA Takes a Stronger Stand on Segregation," *Nation's Schools, LXVIII* (August, 1961):86.
78. *Pittsburgh Courier,* July 15, 1961.
79. George Deer, "NEA Convention Report," *Louisiana Schools,* XXII (September, 1961):43.
80. *New York Times,* August 26, 1961.
81. "News and Trends," *NEA Journal,* L (January, 1961):3.
82. "News and Trends," *NEA Journal,* L (September, 1961):3.
83. "News and Trends," *NEA Journal,* L (November, 1961):3.
84. Leeson, "Desegregation."
85. "News and Trends," *NEA Journal,* LI (December, 1962):4.
86. "News and Trends," *NEA Journal,* LI (November, 1962):4.
87. *NEA Handbook, 1961,* p. 317.
88. T. M. Stinnett, *Turmoil in Teaching* (New York: Macmillan, 1968), p. 45.
89. Myron Lieberman, "The Teachers Choose a Union," *The Nation,* December 2, 1961, p. 444.
90. Fred Smith, "The Teacher Union vs. The Professional Organization," *School and Society,* XC (December 15, 1962):440.
91. *New York Times,* December 11, 1961.
92. *New York Times,* December 17, 1961.
93. "News and Trends," *NEA Journal,* LI (January, 1962):4.

94. "News and Trends," *NEA Journal,* LI (March, 1962) : 5.
95. Ibid.
96. *New York Times,* February 12, 1962.
97. Stinnett, *Turmoil in Teaching,* p. 48.
98. *NEA Handbook, 1962,* p. 92.
99. *NEA Proceedings, 1962,* p. 20.
100. Ibid., pp. 20–21.   101. Ibid., p. 51.   102. Ibid.
103. *Newsweek,* July 16, 1962, pp. 50–51.
104. Stinnett, *Turmoil in Teaching,* p. 4.
105. *NEA Proceedings, 1962,* pp. 397–398.
106. Ibid., pp. 171–173.   107. Ibid., p. 95.
108. *NEA Journal* LI (February, 1962) : 13.
109. Stinnett, *Turmoil in Teaching,* p. 69.
110. Leeson, "Desegregation."
111. "News and Trends," *NEA Journal,* LII (November, 1963) : 5.
112. "News and Trends," *NEA Journal,* LII (April, 1963) : 5.
113. "Scholastic Teacher Interview: Carl J. Megel," *Scholastic Teacher,* LXXXIII (October 4, 1963) : 25T.
114. "News and Trends," *NEA Journal,* LII (September, 1963) : 4–5.
115. *NEA Proceedings, 1964,* p. 290.
116. *New York Times,* July 1, 1963.   117. Ibid., p. 29.
118. *NEA Proceedings, 1963,* p. 17.   119. Ibid., p. 29.
120. Ibid., pp. 42–43.   121. Ibid., p. 32.   122. Ibid., p. 62.
123. *NEA Proceedings, 1964,* p. 284.
124. Ibid., p. 247.   125. Ibid.
126. *NEA Proceedings, 1963,* p. 21.
127. *New York Times,* July 6, 1963.
128. *Newsweek,* July 15, 1963, p. 52.
129. *NEA Proceedings, 1963,* pp. 204–206.   130. Ibid., p. 460.
131. Ibid., p. 210.   132. Ibid., p. 215.   133. Ibid., p. 106.
134. Ibid., p. 108.   135. Ibid., pp. 105–106.   136. Ibid., p. 163.
137. Ibid., p. 164.   138. Ibid.   139. Ibid., p. 169.
140. Ibid., p. 173. This speech was exceedingly unpopular with many delegates because of the challenging tone directed toward the Board; therefore, Goudis' civil rights activities would be confined to behind-the-scenes events for the next few years.
141. Ibid., p. 233.
142. He was the first past president to support civil rights from the floor of the Assembly, and it is interesting how quickly he drifted into organizational obscurity.
143. *NEA Proceedings, 1963,* p. 236.
144. *Time,* August 16, 1963, p. 45.
145. *Newsweek,* July 15, 1963, p. 53.
146. "Scholastic Teacher Interview: Carl J. Megel," *Scholastic Teacher,* LXXXIII (October 4, 1963) : 25T.
147. *New York Times,* August 4, 1963.
148. William J. Brennan, Jr., "Teaching About Civil Rights," *NEA Journal,* LII (March, 1963) : 43.
149. "The Voice of the Nation's Teachers," *NEA Journal,* LII, (September, 1963) : 25–26.

150. W. A. Bass, "In Nashville Schools," and John W. Leetson, "In Atlanta Schools," *NEA Journal,* LII (December, 1963) : 46–50.
151. Pat Tornillo, "In Dade County, Florida," *NEA Journal,* LII (December, 1963) : 51–52.
152. Ibid., p. 52.

Chapter 6

1. Erwin Kroll, "Ten Years of Deliberate Speed," *American Education,* I (December, 1964–January, 1965) : 2.
2. Jim Leeson, "Desegregation," p. 29.
3. Kroll, "Ten Years of Deliberate Speed."
4. Earle West and Walter Daniel, "Programs in the South," *The Journal of Negro Education,* XXXIV (Summer, 1965) : 311.
5. "News and Trends," *NEA Journal,* LIII (April, 1964) : 5.
6. "News and Trends," *NEA Journal,* LIII (May, 1964) : 4.
7. Interview with George Jones, December 10, 1968.
8. "News and Trends," *NEA Journal,* LIII (May, 1964) : 4.
9. *New York Times,* July 5, 1964.
10. Stanley Elam, "Union or Guild; Organizing the Teachers," *The Nation,* June 29, 1964, p. 652.
11. T. M. Stinnett, *Turmoil in Teaching,* p. 72.
12. *NEA Handbook, 1965,* pp. 355–356.
13. Stinnett, *Turmoil in Teaching.*
14. *NEA Proceedings, 1964,* p. 290.
15. Ibid., p. 20.   16. Ibid., p. 19.   17. Ibid.
18. *New York Times,* February 23, 1964.   19. Ibid.
20. *Newsweek,* July 11, 1966, p. 82.   21. Ibid.
22. Interview with Boyd Bosma, NEA Coordinator of Civil Liberties, December 10, 1968.
23. *NEA Proceedings, 1964,* p. 40
24. *New York Times,* July 29, 1964.   25. Ibid.
26. *NEA Proceedings, 1964,* p. 20.
27. *New York Times,* July 4, 1964.
28. A black teacher from Alabama, instrumental in getting seven Negro teachers from Alabama to vote for the NCEHR's position, had her life threatened and was harassed when she went back to Alabama to teach.
29. "Civil Rights Dominate NEA Convention," *Scholastic Teacher,* LXXXV (September 16, 1964) : 2T.
30. *NEA Proceedings, 1964,* p. 179.
31. Ibid.   32. Ibid., p. 180.
33. Interview with Boyd Bosma, December 10, 1968.
34. *NEA Proceedings, 1968,* p. 184.
35. Ibid.   36. Ibid., pp. 444–445.   37. Ibid.
38. "Turning Point," *Ohio Schools,* XLII (September, 1964) : 58.
39. "NEA Convention Highlights," *Wisconsin Journal of Education,* XCVII (September, 1964) : 24.
40. Tim Johnson, "Integration: The Big Issue at the NEA Convention," *Montana Education,* XLI (September, 1964) : 29.

41. Arthur Rice, "NEA Softens Integrate or Else Mandate," *Nation's Schools, LXXIV* (August, 1964) : 20.
42. *Newsweek,* July 13, 1964, p. 54.
43. "Civil Rights Dominate NEA Convention," *Scholastic Teacher,* LXXXV (September 16, 1964) : 2T.
44. "NEA Adopts Integration Ruling," *Mississippi Educational Advance,* XXXII (October, 1964) : 22.
45. "ATA Will Merge If . . .," *Scholastic Teacher,* LXXXV (September 23, 1964) : 6T.
46. "A Fundamental Principle Involved . . .," *NEA Journal,* LIII (January, 1964) : 16.
47. *NEA Journal,* LIII (April, 1964) : 43.
48. *NEA Journal,* LIII (May, 1964) : 13.
49. Leeson, "Desegregation," p. 31.   50. Ibid., p. 29.
51. Ibid., p. 31.
52. "News and Trends," *NEA Journal,* LIV (September, 1965) : 4.
53. Letter from Mrs. Irma Kramer, Assistant to the Deputy Executive Secretary of the NEA, November 19, 1968.
54. Stinnett, *Turmoil in Teaching,* p. 77.
55. "The PTA Continues Work Despite Union Win," *PSEA Reporter,* XXXIII (February 8, 1965) : 25.
56. Ibid.
57. Shawn Kalkstein, "Oklahoma's Education War: The Lesson It Can Teach a Nation," *Look,* January 25, 1966, pp. 82–84.
58. It is interesting to note how rapidly the Executive Committee responded in the Oklahoma battle in comparison to the Committee's extreme hesitancy in issuing sanctions against Utah.
59. Kalkstein, "Oklahoma's Education War," p. 85.
60. Barbara Carter, "The Teachers Give Oklahoma a Lesson," *The Reporter,* XXXIII (September 9, 1965) : 34.
61. Sam Lambert, "Angry Young Men in Teaching," *NEA Journal,* LII (February, 1963) : 17.
62. Elam, "Union or Guild; Organizing the Teachers."
63. Carter, "The Teachers Give Oklahoma a Lesson," p. 35.
64. Elam, "Union or Guild; Organizing the Teachers."
65. Peter Janssen, "NEA: The Reluctant Dragon," *Saturday Review,* June 17, 1967, pp. 72–73.
66. *New York Times,* June 27, 1965.
67. *NEA Proceedings, 1965,* p. 10.
68. The president gave his speech at the completion of the convention; therefore, he was referring to the action taken by the convention during the convention.
69. *NEA Proceedings, 1965,* pp. 22–23.
70. The NEA started this fund with much fanfare and raised money via donations from individual members, local affiliates, and state affiliates. This required quite a bit of time before a significant amount of money was raised; thus, critics claimed the fund would have had an immediate effect had it been funded directly from the NEA budget.
71. *NEA Proceedings, 1965,* p. 24.
72. *New York Times,* June 28, 1965.
73. *NEA Proceedings, 1965,* p. 159.

74. The reason for this fear was a rumor persisting that if the committee were established, some of the budget money scheduled for the PR&R Commission would be diverted to this new committee.

75. *NEA Proceedings, 1965,* pp. 413–415.

76. *New York Times,* July 4, 1965.

77. Ibid.   78. Ibid.

79. *NEA Proceedings, 1965,* p. 11.

80. *New York Times,* July 4, 1965.

81. J. Rupert Picott, "Displacement of Experienced Teachers without Due Process," *NEA Journal,* LIV (December, 1965) : 41.

82. *NEA Proceedings, 1966,* pp. 276–277.

83. *NEA Journal,* LIV (October, 1965) : 42.

84. Jim Leeson, "Guidelines and a New Count," *Southern Education Report,* II (January–February, 1967) : 31–32.

85. "Progress Report for 1966," *Ebony,* XXII (January, 1967) : 36.

86. Jim Leeson, "The Pace Quickens," *Southern Education Report,* II (April, 1967) : 37.

87. "News and Trends," *NEA Journal,* LV (April, 1966) : 3.

88. *NEA Reporter,* V (January 21, 1966).

89. *New York Times,* July 1, 1966.

90. *New York Times,* June 25, 1966.

91. "NEA Convention: Where the Action was," *Scholastic Teacher,* LXXXIX (September 16, 1966) : 1T.

92. *NEA Proceedings, 1966,* pp. 16–17.   93. Ibid., pp. 12–13.

94. *New York Times,* July 2, 1966.   95. Ibid.

96. *NEA Proceedings, 1966,* p. 190.   97. Ibid., p. 191.

98. His presidential address left no doubt what his actions would be, but some people felt that by specifically expressing his intentions he might trigger a countermove by the conservative element of the members aimed at killing the amendment, thus the advocates of the amendment would not allow him to speak.

99. *NEA Proceedings, 1966,* p. 192.

100. Ibid., pp. 194–195.   101. Ibid., pp. 195–196.

102. This threatened disaffection of NEA delegates to a New Orleans AFT affiliate would indeed have been ironic, for they would have been seeking membership in a predominantly black organization.

103. Ibid., pp. 196–197.

104. This had been done before. After two liberal amendments had been passed to the integration resolution at the 1960 convention, a substitute motion was passed, thus eliminating the liberal amendments.

105. Ibid., p. 199.   106. Ibid., pp. 471–472.

107. "New Delegates Push Civil Rights," *Michigan Education Journal,* XLIV (September, 1966) : 35.

108. Francine Richard, "The NEA Week That Was," *Illinois Education,* LV (September, 1966) : 17.

109. "Rains Came at Miami: But MEA Stays in NEA for a Good Reason," *Mississippi Educational Advance,* XXXIV (October, 1966) : 29.

110. *NEA Proceedings, 1966,* pp. 81, and 406.   111. Ibid., pp. 81–84.

112. *New York Times,* July 7, 1966.

113. *NEA Proceedings, 1958,* pp. 340–341.

114. *NEA Proceedings, 1955,* p. 301.
115. *NEA Proceedings, 1958,* p. 341.
116. *NEA Proceedings, 1960,* p. 349.
117. *NEA Proceedings, 1966,* p. 258.   118.   Ibid., pp. 254–256.
119. *NEA Journal,* LV (January, 1966) : 62.
120. *NEA Proceedings, 1967,* p. 510.
121. Ibid., p. 315.   122.   Ibid., p. 318.   123.   Ibid.
124. Interview with Boyd Bosma, December 10, 1968.
125. M. E. Wright, "The President's Message," *Louisiana Schools,* XXVII (November, 1966) : 41–42.
126. *NEA Reporter,* VI (January 16, 1967) : 1.
127. Ibid.   128.   *New York Times,* November 4, 1966.
129. "An American Tragedy: 1967 Detroit," *Newsweek,* August 7, 1967, p. 18.
130. National Advisory Commission on Civil Disorders, *Report of the National Advisory Commission on Civil Disorders* (New York: *New York Times* Company, 1968).
131. Leon Friedman, ed., "The Moynihan Report — The Negro Family: The Case for National Action," *The Civil Rights Reader* (New York: Walker and Company, 1967), p. 277.
132. Anne Henehan, "On-the-Spot in Watts," *Senior Scholastic Magazine,* LXXXIX (January 20, 1967) : 9–10.
133. *New York Times,* July 28, 1967.
134. *Newsweek,* August 21, 1967, p. 19.
135. *NEA Proceedings, 1967,* pp. 338–339.
136. Ibid., p. 18.   137.   Ibid., p. 19.
138. Ibid.   139.   Ibid.   140.   Ibid.
141. Ibid., p. 13.   142.   Ibid., p. 195.   143.   Ibid.
144. *NEA Handbook, 1967,* pp. 75–76.
145. "Elizabeth D. Koontz, President Elect: 1968 National Education Association," *Negro Historical Bulletin,* XXX (December, 1967) : 4.
146. Janssen, "NEA: The Reluctant Dragon," p. 72.
147. *Newsweek,* July 17, 1967, p. 54.

Chapter 7

1. *NEA Proceedings 1968,* p. 40.
2. "Teacher Power and the NEA," *CTA Journal,* LIII (October, 1968) : 9.
3. *NEA Reporter,* VII (July 18, 1968) : 1.
4. *NEA Handbook,* 1968, p. 390.
5. Letter from Mrs. Irma Kramer, November 19, 1968.
6. *NEA Handbook, 1968,* p. 392.
7. Myron Lieberman, "Implications of the Coming NEA-AFT Merger," *Phi Delta Kappan,* L (November, 1968) : 140.
8. Martin Mayer, "The Full and Sometimes Very Surprising Story of Ocean Hill, the Teachers Union Strike of 1968," *New York Times Magazine,* February 2, 1969, pp. 18–23.

9.   *Washington Post,* December 2, 1968.
10. Stephen Zeluck, "The UFT Strike: Will It Destroy the AFT?" *Phi Delta Kappan,* L (January, 1969) : 254.
11. *NEA Reporter,* VII (October 25, 1968) : 1.
12. *NEA Proceedings, 1968,* p. 131.
13. Ibid.   14. Ibid., p. 134.
15. Ibid.   16. Ibid., p. 135.   17. Ibid., p. 136.
18. Charles A. Johnson, "Editorial Comments," *Mississippi Educational Advance,* LX (May, 1969) : 9.
19. *North Carolina Education, "The Question of NCEA-NCTA Merger,"* XXXV (March, 1969) : 49–55.
20. Upon agreement of the tentative merger, NEA lifted the NCTA's suspension. Talks continued between the NCTA and the NCEA during the last half of 1969. At the NCTA convention held in December 1969, the NCTA delegates voted 555 to 22 to accept the NEA factfinder's recommendations; therefore, merger of the two groups will occur sometime in 1970.
21. *Florence (Alabama) Times,* May 18, 1969.
22. *Alabama State Teachers Association Journal,* "Ratification Vote on Merger Slated by ASTA-AEA," X May, 1969) : 22.
23. *Augusta Chronicle,* March 19, 1969.
24. *Atlanta Journal,* April 24, 1969.
25. *Atlanta Constitution,* April 24, 1969.
26. The LEA, the black affiliate from Louisiana, was restored to full membership status when it announced, December 30, 1969, that it had accepted the NEA factfinder's report concerning merger with the white affiliate, the LTA. The white affiliates of Louisiana and Mississippi, the LTA and the MEA, have been given until March 21, 1970, to show cause why they should not permanently be disaffiliated from the NEA.
27. National Education Association, "Communicator '69," p. 1.
28. Ibid.

Index

DATE DUE

MAR 4 '88			

DEMCO 38-297